Training Games for Career Development

James J. Kirk, Ed.D.

Lynne D. Kirk

with drawings by
Matthew J. Kirk
and **Brandon A. Kirk**

D1401551

McGraw-Hill, Inc.
New York San Francisco Washington, D.C. Auckland Bogotá
Caracas Lisbon London Madrid Mexico City Milan
Montreal New Delhi San Juan Singapore
Sydney Tokyo Toronto

Library of Congress Cataloging-in-Publication Data

Kirk, James J.
    Training games for career development / James J. Kirk, Lynne D.
Kirk : with drawings by Matthew J. Kirk & Brandon A. Kirk.
        p.   cm.
   Includes index.
   ISBN 0-07-034790-5 (pbk.)
   1. Career development—Handbooks, manuals, etc.   2. Employees,
Training of—Handbooks, manuals, etc.   3. Personnel management—
Handbooks, manuals, etc.   I. Kirk, Lynne D.   II. Kirk, Matthew J.
III. Kirk, Brandon A.   IV. Title.
HF5549.5.C35K57   1995
658.3′124—dc20   95-3943
                                                 CIP

1 2 3 4 5 6 7 8 9 0   SEM/SEM   9 0 0 9 8 7 6 5

ISBN 0-07-034790-5

The sponsoring editor for this book was James H. Bessent, Jr., the editing supervisor was Fred Dahl,
and the production supervisor was Suzanne Rapcavage. It was set in Futura by Inkwell Publishing
Services.

Printed and bound by Quebecor/Semline.

CONTENTS

PREFACE

If you have a passion for career development, love teaching career concepts to others, or just enjoy making learning fun, *Training Games for Career Development* is written for you. The book is designed to be used as a supplemental instructional resource by individuals who teach courses and conduct training workshops on a variety of career-related matters. Teachers, trainers, counselors, and consultants who work with groups on career-related matters will find its games a valuable addition to their professional libraries. Along with almost 60 games, the volume contains background information on numerous career subjects and a six-step game selection model to help users locate the game best suited to achieve their instructional objectives. The games themselves—which deal with a wide range of career topics, including career motivation, development, dynamics, climate, promotion, and management—can also be deployed to actually teach and reinforce career-related concepts.

Steps have been taken to make *Training Games for Career Development* user-friendly. A table of contents (pp. iii-iv) lists all the games and the pages on which they appear. The General Games Reference Table (pp. vii–viii) lists games alphabetically under major subject headings and codes according to their recommended instructional uses. Sources where readers can secure additional information on the subject matter are also provided at the beginning of each game.

The authors recommend that you use the career-building games in this volume in combination with other instructional strategies. For example, the games can be used in conjunction with lectures, small group discussions, or audiovisual presentations. The authors also recommend that games be used at various stages of the instructional process (for instance, as "ice breakers" at the initial coming together of a new group of learners, while introducing or helping participants become aware of new ideas, when teaching new concepts, during the reinforcement of previously taught material, or when assessing what participants know about specific career-related subjects). The recommended usage codings (the stages of instruction at which the authors suggest a game be played) are designed to help facilitators quickly identify games suited to their instructional purposes. Depending on the context in which a particular game is played, it can be used at more than one stage of the instructional process.

James J. Kirk
Lynne D. Kirk

Chapter One
THE GAME PLAN

SUBJECT MATTER BREAKDOWN OF GAMES

All the games contained in the book relate to some aspect of career building and/or work. They are listed in the General Games Reference Table under the following topics:

Career Motivation. Career Motivation/Resilience games help participants to become or remain interested in developing themselves careerwise.

Career Development. Career Development games assist players in gaining a better understanding of several well-known theories on occupational choice and development over the individual's life span.

Career Dynamics. Games in this grouping focus on various aspects of selected occupational fields.

Career Climate. These games familiarize players with companies who are among the leaders in their respective industries and the American workforce in general.

Career Promotion. Career Promotion games are linked to the skills involved in identifying and securing new career opportunities.

Career Management. Along with career politics, the contents of the Career Management games pertain to both well-known individual and organization career-building interventions.

GAME CODES

Besides being listed in the Games Reference Table under the six subject matter categories, games are coded as openers, expanders, teachables, reinforcers, and assessors. The codes pertain to various stages of the instructional process. A brief description of each classification follows:

Openers. Openers are appropriate when a group of learners has been assembled for the very first time or whenever many of the participants do not know each other. Such games are nonthreatening and last for less than 15 minutes. They typically call for the sharing of information about one another or require small groups of participants to combine their collective knowledge to accomplish specified tasks. The aim is to begin building group rapport and cohesion. *The Happy Hierarchy, Secretary's Dream Job,* and *My Notable Network* are some of the openers contained in this book.

Expanders. Sometimes the purpose of instruction is to introduce participants to new ideas that will later be covered in more detail. On other occasions the sole intent is to merely heighten individuals' current awareness levels regarding certain issues or happenings. In such instances, games that expand players' consciousness are appropriate. *Enhancement Scramble, Political Horse Cents,* and *Corporate Dig* are examples of expander games.

Teachables. After certain material has been introduced, a facilitator may want to explore certain ideas in depth. There may be a need for participants to be more than "casually aware" of certain events or notions. Games can be used to provide players a rudimentary knowledge of selected career content. *Matching Orientations, Super-O,* and *Resumé Race* are examples of such games. Whenever teachables appear in the book, they are accompanied by a brief background section covering the subject matter content of the game.

Reinforcers. Effective instruction or facilitation requires that previously taught concepts be reinforced. Games can be effectively used to review and/or reinforce previously taught material. The objective is to enhance players' long-term retention and application of what has been learned. Examples of reinforcer games include *RIASEC Bingo, Mentor Mania,* and *Anchor Act Ups.*

Assessors. Before you deliver a segment of instruction, it is often helpful to know what learners already know about the topic to be covered. This helps the instructor determine what to include and what to omit from the training. Furthermore, after the subject matter has been presented, it is important to know what concepts participants understand and can apply. This information enables facilitators to accurately evaluate the effectiveness of their instructional methods. Games can be a viable alternative to traditional forms of pre- and posttesting. Examples of assessors include *Heads Up 2000, Innies and Outies,* and *Baldertrash.*

HOW TO SELECT AN APPROPRIATE GAME

To use the games in *Training Games for Career Development* to supplement the instruction of career-related concepts, it is recommended that facilitators follow these simple steps:

Step 1. Write down a brief list of learning objectives for your program. In doing so, ask yourself, "What should participants be able to do after the instruction is completed that they were unable to do before the facilitation began?" If you have already prepared a list of objectives, review them carefully. Make certain that they are very clear concerning what participants should be able to do at the end of the training. An example of a clearly written objective is, "Participants will be able to identify which of Donald Super's career development stages they are currently in."

Step 2. Make a list of the information and/or concepts that participants will need to know to perform the behaviors associated with each career-related learning objective. With respect to the preceding learning objective ("Participants will be able to identify which of Donald Super's career development stages they are currently in"), learners would have to possess a working knowledge of Donald Super's career development theory.

Step 3. Use the General Games Reference Table and the Contents to locate games covering the information you want participants to learn (i.e., concepts identified in step 2). Turn to and read the general information on each game. Make a list of the games that are of greatest interest to you. The only game in the book that directly deals with the content of our sample is the game *Super O.*

Step 4. Decide at which point along the instructional continuum you will incorporate a game (i.e., during the initial gathering of a group of participants, upon the introduction of a new concept, while teaching a new concept, when reinforcing previously covered information, or during the pre- or postassessment of learners' knowledge of the topic). For example, let's suppose that a facilitator wants to present Donald Super's career development theory during a 40-minute lecture and then use a game to reinforce what was covered in the lecture.

Step 5. Refer to the General Games Reference Table for looking up the games identified in step 3. See which of the games are recommended for the stage of the instructional process you plan to use a game. Place a checkmark (✓) beside these items on your list of potential games. A glance at the General Games Reference Table indicates that the game *Super O* is recommended as a reinforcer. If no games are recommended for the instructional stage in which you would like to use one, consider using a game at a different time during the instruction, or consider how an existing game might be modified to achieve your instructional objectives.

Step 6. Carefully read and examine each of the games checked during step 5. In making your choice, think about the size of your group, their educational level, their employment backgrounds, and how well they know one another. Take into account the materials, room facilities, personal assistance, and time required to play the game. Finally, give some consideration to the skills you and any assistants will need to successfully facilitate the game. Figure 1.1 shows the key questions facilitators must answer when selecting an instructional game. Select one of the checked (✓) games from your list.

FACILITATION GUIDELINES

Facilitators can do several things to assure the successful deployment of an instructional game. When it seems appropriate, facilitators should do all or some of the following.

Before the game facilitators can:

✓ Have learning objectives clearly in mind.

✓ Make certain that a game directly relates to the stated learning objectives.

✓ Become familiar with all aspects of the game.

✓ Make certain that the facilities and resources needed to properly play the game are available.

✓ Prepare all game materials. Make extra copies for a few practice rounds or to replace lost items.

✓ If possible, test drive the game using a group of players similar to the would-be participants.

✓ Make any necessary revisions in the game.

✓ Plan the activities that will prepare participants for the game.

Figure 1.1. Game selection questions.

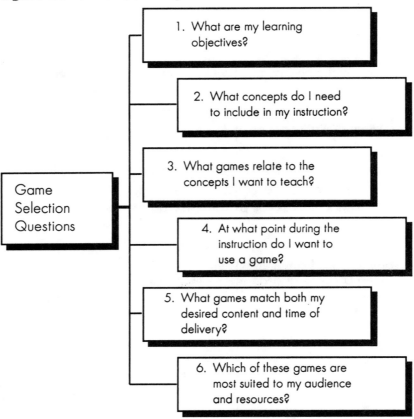

✓ Plan what will be done immediately after the game (i.e., during the debriefing period).

✓ Establish a warm and supportive learning climate.

✓ Engage in pregame learning activities.

During the game facilitators can:

✓ Explain the learning objective(s), rules, and procedures at the beginning of the game.

✓ With more complex games (i.e., games involving structured role plays), give more detailed instructions once materials have been passed out, specific roles have been assigned, and players have been assembled in their respective groups.

✓ Fill participants in on what they can expect to meet with during the game, especially events that may cause confusion or frustration. Explain that they may make errors, that they will not be penalized for making mistakes, and that these are merely part of the learning process.

✓ Take time to clearly state participants' roles in the game. Go over the type of assistance they will be given and the type of assistance they will not be given.

✓ Be caring and supportive. Assure players that they are capable of meeting the challenges at hand and that they should concentrate on learning and having fun.

✓ If an individual does not wish to participate in the game, invite her/him to help in facilitating the activity. For example, nonplaying participants can pass out gaming materials, keep score, and/or record their observations of what happened during the game.

✓ Expect the unexpected. Don't panic when things go differently than what was imagined. Modifications in the rules and procedures may have to be made during the game. However, these revisions must be kept to a minimum and not dramatically lessen any person's or team's chances of winning.

✓ Avoid interfering or getting involved in the actual playing of the game. Resist the temptation to give hints or clues. Do not protect people from the legitimate actions of other players or the natural consequences of their own behaviors.

✓ Avoid interrupting the game for an extended time.

✓ Take notes on what happened during the game. These observations may be discussed during the debriefing period. These notes can also help the facilitator make needed revisions in the game before its next deployment.

After the game facilitators may:

✓ Impress upon participants that the debriefing segment is very important in terms of the overall learning process.

✓ Invite participants to share insights they gained from playing the game.

✓ Ask participants to list some of the ways they intend to apply what they learned during the game.

✓ Have participants tell about some of the frustrations they encountered during the game and discuss whether these experiences contributed to or thwarted their overall learning.

✓ Read aloud some of the observations you recorded during the game. See if participants have similar impressions of what transpired.

✓ If the game was a gaming-simulation, discuss how closely it mimics real life. Solicit suggestions for making the game more true to life.

✓ Ask for other specific ideas for improving the game.

✓ Have participants evaluate the overall effectiveness of the game as an instructional strategy (i.e., determine the degree to which the game resulted in the group's accomplishing its stated learning objectives).

✓ Ask participants to compare the effectiveness of the game to other learning strategies (e.g., lecture, video tape, on-site visits), which might have been used to accomplish the same learning.

✓ Ask participants if they would look favorably upon the opportunity to play a similar game in the near future. Have them explain their answers.

THE NATURE OF GAMES

In this volume, the term "game" refers to activities requiring participants to perform tasks, play assigned roles, follow ground rules, and/or strive to reach a designated goal. In American society, games are often competitive social events that result in some players being "winners" and others "losers." Checkers, *Monopoly*, and baseball are examples of well-established American games.

People find games enjoyable for a number of reasons. The challenge they present often gets the heart racing, blood rushing, and adrenaline flowing. The result is a natural high. Since the outcomes of games are usually in doubt, they have a tendency to captivate peoples' attention. A psychological need for closure makes humans want to know how things are going to turn out (i.e., who will become the winners). In competitive games, the possibility of receiving a reward or special recognition for winning serves to heighten players' motivation to win. Finally, because most games are played in the company of other individuals, they also help satisfy the human need for social interaction.

Many educators and trainers consider games an effective instructional strategy. Depending on their design, games can be used to develop creativity, hone problem-solving skills, foster long-term retention of subject matter, and motivate reluctant learners to learn. They have been successfully deployed to enhance participants' communications and negotiations skills. More recently gaming has been used as a tool for building group cohesion and morale among members of self-directed work teams.

Games are often confused with simulations. A key distinction between the two is that *simulations* attempt to realistically mimic a slice of real life. They often attempt to mirror or model key features of a system, process, environment, or past event. For instance, simulations can be devised to replicate a company's production processes, career ladder system, or its new employee selection process. They can also be designed to represent crucial elements of a Theory X or Theory Y business climate. They can even be made to recreate a past event such as a company merger or downsizing. Games that incorporate representations of real life along with some of the features of games are sometimes referred to as *gaming-simulations*. *Monopoly*, *Clue*, and *Careers* are examples of gaming-simulations.

While gaming-simulations hold most of the instructional advantages of games, they have several added advantages. Chief among these advantages is that simulations permit learners to experience the interplay between various elements of a complex system. For example, a simulation that mimics the U.S. economy can permit players to assume the role of economic planners, making economic policies and decisions and experiencing their effects on unemployment, inflation, gross national product, and the environment. Another advantage of gaming-simulations is that they can provide a safe means of training people to perform life-threatening tasks. Simulations that mimic flight, the diagnosis and treatment of patients' illnesses, the resolution of hostage situations, and the removal of toxic chemicals from old storage facilities are of this type. They allow learners to practice certain job tasks without endangering their lives or the lives of others. A third advantage of gaming-simulations is their cost-effectiveness. For example, a student learning to fly an F16 can crash several times in a flight simulator without costing the taxpayers a dime. Similar crashes of actual planes would cost the nation millions of dollars and the lives of countless pilots.

THE NAMES OF THE GAME

Like many areas of education and training, gaming has many related terms and concepts. Listed below are several words associated with games. Their definitions are provided here to help novice facilitators become familiar with gaming jargon.

Card games. These games use cards as their primary medium. Examples include *Bridge, Rummy,* and *Rook.* The cards themselves are usually pieces of heavy laminated paper or cardboard of uniform sizes. They can contain symbolic representations of real life phenomena such as earthquakes and stock market crashes. They can have questions or directions written on them, which players are obliged to either answer or follow. Depending on the nature of the game and the information printed on the cards, they may be sorted, compiled, or arranged. A key advantage of cards is that they can be used either as a game's sole medium or in conjunction with other mediums (such as a game board). Turn to the game *Satisfaction 21* in Chap. 2 for an example of a simple card game.

Board games. As the name implies, these games are played around a large piece of cardboard. *Checkers* and *Monopoly* are favorite American board games. Colorful spaces and icons strategically located on a board can be made to represent almost anything (such as departments of an organization, steps in a job search, categories of selected information). Images on a board can visually depict concrete objects (such as different businesses in town) as well as abstract concepts (like career development stages). A major advantage of board games is that players usually come to the games with some understanding of how to play them. Perhaps their most limiting feature is that one board can normally accommodate only seven or eight players. See the game *Leads* in Chap. 6 for an example of a board game.

Puzzles. Sometimes referred to as "brain-teasers," puzzles represent problems in search of solutions. Crosswords and acrostics are popular puzzle formats. However, puzzles can come in other forms such as murder mysteries (like *How to Host a Murder*) and three-dimensional objects (*Rubik's Cube*). Puzzles are good for helping participants sharpen their analytical and problem-solving skills. However, care should be taken to select puzzles that are not too difficult for their intended audience. Otherwise, participants might become frustrated and lose interest in playing the game. Turn to the game *HRD Acrossout* in Chap. 4 for an example of a puzzle.

Mad libs. Simply put, mad libs are short stories with missing words. The missing words might be nouns, verbs, adverbs, adjectives, or any other parts of speech. The game is normally played in pairs. One member, who is in possession of the story, asks the other member of the pair to supply the missing words. After one partner's words have been inserted into the short story by the other partner, it is read aloud. The result is often an unusual and humorous anecdote. Mad libs are easy to write and make excellent openers for training sessions. They are a fun way of helping participants get acquainted. The ensuing laughter creates a relaxed learning environment. For an example of a mad lib, turn to the game *Secretary's Dream Job* in Chap. 3.

Role plays. Role plays call for participants to take on the identities of other persons. When children play house, taking on the role of Mommy and Daddy, they are engaging in role play. They are playing or acting out the part of another character. They are saying what they believe their parents would say in similar circumstances. They are taking the actions they believe their mommies and daddies would take.

Role plays can either be free wielding, as in the childhood game of house, or highly structured, as in *How to Host a Murder.* In free wielding role plays, participants are given very limited information about their stereotypic characters and the situations they are to act out. In more structured role plays, such as those in gaming-simulations, the persons playing the roles are provided more detailed information in the form of a scenario and character background cards. In addition, more specific directions are given for the participant to follow. See the game *Interviews à la Internationale* for an example of role plays in Chap. 6.

Case studies. Like mad libs, case studies are short stories. However, case studies are usually longer than mad libs and contain no missing words. They can be either real or imagined and include characters, places, organizations, the passing of time, and eventful happenings. When used in games, case studies often involve asking players to respond to the "correctness" or "appropriateness" of a character's actions. Case studies are frequently used as "story puzzles" (i.e., they present a problem requiring analysis and generation of solutions). Another use of case studies is as scenarios presented at the beginning of a gaming-simulation. When used in this manner, they provide players a contextual backdrop for the simulation. Skillfully written case studies can engrave an intensely lifelike image on the minds of participants—an image replete with the intricacies of real life situations and relationships. While it is difficult to write good case studies, they remain an excellent tool for teaching problem-solving and value clarification skills.

Computer games. The computer chip and the electronic revolution have ushered in the era of computer games, which, as the term implies, use the computer as their medium. Some of the early computer games were merely electronic versions of standard card, board, and table games. Computer versions of *Solitaire, Chess,* and *Ping Pong* have been around for several years. More recently, games like *Where in the World Is Carmen Sandiego, Sim City,* and *The Oregon Trail* have become best sellers. Because of the computer memory needed to store their sounds and three-dimensional graphics, newer games like *Flight Navigator* come on CD ROM instead of on floppy disks.

Computer games are becoming increasingly prevalent in training and education. Medical schools are using them to teach interns how to make diagnoses. Business schools are employing them to teach students how to make management decisions.

The major advantages of these games are that they help develop high-level problem-solving and decision-making skills and that they are interactive, allowing students to receive immediate feedback on the outcomes of their decisions. A potential disadvantage is their relatively high cost compared to other mediums.

Physical challenges. In addition to thinking, physical challenges require players to engage in activities using their physical agility and strength. Most sports comprise some form of physical challenge. Also in this category are the military games engaged in by armed forces, simulated moon walks carried on by NASA astronauts, and ropes courses used by many corporations to build group cohesion among the members of self-directed work teams. Physical challenges can be highly effective tools for teaching and/or assessing the various psychomotor skills of participants. A potential disadvantage is the risk of personal injury.

Exercises. An exercise can be any task or set of tasks participants are asked to perform, either individually or as a group. Exercises can include, but are not limited to, activities that involve self-assessment, organization assessment, creative problem solving, decision making, and short- or long-range planning. They are often used to process or apply previously taught information. Most exercises can be made competitive, thus causing them to take on gamelike characteristics. For an example of an exercise, see the game *Lovers and Fighters* in Chap. 3.

Tests. Whether a learning activity is considered a test or an exercise often depends on the purpose of the activity. Any activity—a puzzle, answering questions during a board game, or an in-basket exercise—can serve as a test. A test can be the primary activity around which a game is organized (as in *Jeopardy* or *Trivial Pursuit*). Test questions have correct and incorrect answers. Correct answers may be rewarded with the giving of play money, privileges, points, or special tokens. For an example of a test, turn to the game *Jobpardy* in Chap. 6.

Facilitate. As used in this book, "facilitate" refers to applying the principles of adult learning and gaming to instruction. The facilitator establishes a supportive learning climate, involves participants in designing and implementing learning activities, acts as a resource person for the group, and performs a variety of instructional tasks. The relationship between the instructor/facilitator and participants is characterized by collaboration, shared responsibilities, and mutual respect.

Debrief. A major responsibility of the facilitator is to debrief participants after a game has been played. *Debriefing* refers to the processing of information and insights gained during a game. The facilitator asks participants, either in small groups or as one large group, to respond to a series of questions regarding what they experienced during the game.

Frame. The term "frame" may cause some to think of the frame of a house (the beams, studs, and rafters to which everything else is attached). The term "frame" takes on a similar meaning in gaming. It is the basic structure of a game. For example, the basic structure of *Bingo* includes a board containing five columns and five rows, the random drawing of pieces that correspond to items printed on the board's 25 cells, and a goal of being the first person to identify five of the items drawn as appearing in a straight line along their playing board. One game's structure can be used as a model for creating other games. The game *Bingo* served as a frame for the creation of *RIASEC Bingo* in Chap. 3.

Virtual reality. At the cutting edge of electronic wizardry lies virtual reality. It joins human physical senses and movements to computer-generated images. The result is an artificial, three-dimensional, interactive environment that a player can barely distinguish from the real thing. Flight simulators that enable a pilot to see, feel, and hear exactly what she/he would see, feel, and hear in an actual cockpit employ virtual reality concepts and technologies.

Chapter Two
CAREER MOTIVATION/RESILIENCE GAMES

World-class organizations rely on highly motivated workers. They understand that the best business plans in the world cannot be brought to fruition without the total commitment of dedicated workers. Supervisors are trained to maintain high employee morale through better communications, greater employee need fullfillment, and improved coping skills.

All of the games in Chap. 2 are intended to help participants to become or remain interested in developing themselves careerwise. Three of the games (*Chapter 11, Feedback Fumbles #1,* and *Feedback Fumbles #2*) help participants to communicate more openly about their careers and job performance. Because today's workers look to their employing organizations and their careers for the satisfaction of a variety of needs, not just their financial needs, several games (such as *The Happy Hierarchy, Satisfaction 21, All-American Leg Roll,* and *Plateaued Playoffs*) assist supervisors in better understanding and meeting the needs of their subordinates.

The new demands being placed on companies and employees require workers to hone their coping skills. The games *Hocus Focus* and *Pathways Puzzle* concentrate on improving participants' goal-setting skills. *Balancing Act* and *Stressbusters* aid players in dealing with the challenges of balancing home and work lives and managing stress. The game *Empowerment Puzzle* identifies ways in which employees can be made to be both more productive and fulfilled.

ALL-AMERICAN LEG ROLL

TOPIC Self-Esteem

LEARNING OBJECTIVE Participants will be able to bestow sincere compliments on other players, thereby building their self-esteem.

NUMBER OF PARTICIPANTS Any number

PLAYING TIME 10-15 minutes depending on the number of players

REFERENCE None

REQUIRED MATERIALS A coin and two facing chairs

TO PLAY

1. Introduce players to the concept of self-esteem. Discuss the important role positive self-esteem plays in career success.

2. Explain to participants that there are many ways of building their own self-esteem and the self-esteem of others. One of these ways is to provide others positive feedback in the form of sincere compliments.

3. Advise players that they are about to engage in a little friendly contest of compliment giving.

4. Have players pair up with someone in the room they know fairly well.

5. Direct one person in each of the pairs to move to one side of the room and the other to move to the other side of the room.

6. Inform players that they are going to be asked to come to the middle of the room, be seated in facing chairs (approximately six feet apart), beat on their laps as if they were playing a drum roll, and hurl verbal compliments at their opponent. The person who shouts the most compliments within a 10-second time frame becomes the winner of the *All-American Drum Roll*. Only compliments that are shouted while the person is drumming her/his lap count.

7. Have a set of opponents come forward and be seated in the middle of the room.

8. Flip a coin to determine who will go first.

9. Give the first contestant 10 seconds to hurl compliments at her/his opponent while doing drum rolls. Record the number of compliments shouted.

10. Provide the opponent 10 seconds to hurl compliments back while doing drum rolls. Record the number of compliments shouted.

11. Declare the person who managed to get the most compliments in during the 10 seconds the winner and a "great esteem builder."

12. Repeat steps 7-11 until all players have had a chance at compliment hurling.

13. Debrief players. Ask players to explain how they felt when compliments were being hurled at them. Discuss other ways players can help one another build their self-esteem.

BALANCING ACT

TOPIC
Balancing One's Work and Personal Life

LEARNING OBJECTIVE
Participants will be able to identify the things that help and those that prevent people from achieving a balance between their work and personal lives.

NUMBER OF PARTICIPANTS
10-40 players

PLAYING TIME
15-30 minutes depending on the number of players

REFERENCES
Barnett, R. (1992, February). The myth of the miserable working woman. *Working Women,* pp. 62-88.

Cassidy, A. (1991, June). Salute to a real family man. *Working Women,* pp. 32-36.

Hales, D. (1992, March). Managing the dreaded dinner hour. *Working Women,* pp. 28-32.

Hickey, M. (1993, July). The case for commuting. *Working Women,* pp. 22-26.

Nash, J. (1992, June). Work strategies: find more time! *Working Women,* pp. 34-38.

Perry, S. and Dawson, J. (1992, November). Tune in to your primetime. *Working Women,* pp. 62-70.

Schmidt, V. and Scott, N. (1987, August 8). Work and family life: a delicate balance. *Personnel Administration,* pp. 40-46.

Tarkan, L. (1991, December). Stress relief: The '90s perk. *Working Women,* pp. 76-78.

REQUIRED MATERIALS
Balancing Maker Slips, Balancing Breaker Slips, and a coin

TO PLAY

1. Introduce players to the concept of work/life balance.
2. Go over the learning objective for the game.
3. Ask for two individuals from the audience to volunteer as team captains.
4. Have the two captains come forward. Explain that they are going to choose people from the audience to be on their teams.
5. Place a sufficient number of Balancing Maker Slips and Balancing Breaker Slips into a small paper bag for each member of the group to receive one slip of paper each. Make certain that the number of Balancing Maker and Balancing Breaker Slips are approximately equal in number.
6. Tell players that the bag you are about to circulate contains small slips of paper. Some of the slips contain *balancing makers,* which help people balance their work and personal lives. Advise them that other slips of paper comprise *balancing breakers,* which often make it very difficult to balance one's work and personal life.

7. Have each participant in the group draw one slip of paper from the bag. Tell participants that they can read their slips of paper but they are to keep the content to themselves for the time being.

8. Inform the captains that the goal of the game is for them to select a team from the audience that is "balanced" (i.e., a team with an equal number of players holding Balancing Makers Slips and Balancing Breaker Slips.

9. Ask the captains to flip a coin to determine who gets to select the first team member from the group.

10. Direct the captain who wins the toss to select a member of the group to come forward and be on her/his team.

11. Have the chosen team member read the contents of her/his slip of paper.

12. Record whether the member's slip is a balancing maker or balancing breaker.

13. Ask the other captain to select a member of the group to come forward and be on her/his team.

14. Have the chosen team member read the contents of her/his slip of paper.

15. Record whether the member's slip is a balancing maker or balancing breaker.

16. Repeat steps 10 to 15 until all members of the audience have been chosen.

17. Tally up the number of balancing makers and balancing breakers on each team.

18. Declare the team with the closest to equal number of balancing makers and balancing breakers winners and the "most balanced."

19. Debrief players. Discuss the struggle players are having achieving greater balance between their work and personal lives. Ask them to list some of the more successful actions they have undertaken to achieve greater balance in their lives.

BALANCING MAKERS AND BALANCING BREAKER SLIPS

To make a set of Balancing Maker and Balancing Breaker Slips, photocopy and cut out the following items.

BALANCING MAKERS

You balance work and personal life by maintaining a strong sense of humor.

You balance work and personal life by meditating.

You balance work and personal life by the use of a message answering machine.

You balance work and personal life by regular exercise.

You balance work and personal life by eating properly.

You balance work and personal life by limiting your intake of alcohol and caffeine.

You balance work and personal life by taking refuge in family and friends.

You balance work and personal life by delegating responsibilities to others.

You balance work and personal life by standing up to your boss and family members.

You balance work and personal life by attending family counseling.

You balance work and personal life through career counseling.

You balance work and personal life by taking advantage of your company's employee assistance programs.

You balance work and personal life through your company's flex-time program.

You balance work and personal life by taking advantage of your company's job-sharing program.

You balance work and personal life by taking advantage of your company's maternity and paternity benefits.

You balance work and personal life by taking advantage of your company's on-site child care.

You balance work and personal life by taking advantage of your company's sick leave for children's illness program.

You balance work and personal life by attending self-improvement courses.

You balance work and personal life by attending social activities.

You balance work and personal life by taking advantage of your company's work-at-home program.

You balance work and personal life by taking time during the work day to call your spouse.

You balance work and personal life by avoiding the practice of setting impossible standards.

You balance work and personal life by avoiding spending too much time fretting over unnecessary details.

You balance work and personal life by looking at the big picture before jumping into something.

You balance work and personal life by planning ahead.

You balance work and personal life by not procrastinating.

You balance work and personal life by minimizing interruptions.

You balance work and personal life by not wasting time on the phone.

You balance work and personal life by taking and scheduling time for family members.

You balance work and personal life by scheduling time for yourself.

You balance work and personal life by postponing your lunch until 1 P.M. (this extends the most productive hours of the day because most people reach their performance peak around noon).

You balance work and personal life by doing your most mentally challenging tasks in late morning when you are most mentally alert.

You balance work and personal life by doing simple manual repetitive tasks in midafternoon when your mental alertness drops.

You balance work and personal life by taking the same day off as your spouse and doing things together.

You balance work and personal life by doing things that relieve stress.

You balance work and personal life by weeding people out of your life who have negative attitudes about things that you have positive attitudes about.

You balance work and personal life by joining a support group.

You balance work and personal life by stopping to reflect on the things you enjoy in life.

You balance work and personal life by avoiding rush hour traffic.

BALANCING BREAKERS

You have the balance in your work and personal life broken when your boss asks you to work overtime to finish a report.

You have the balance in your work and personal life broken when your boss asks you to take an emergency business trip.

You have the balance in your work and personal life broken when the computer network breakdown at work puts you behind schedule.

You have the balance in your work and personal life broken when the secretary at work quits and it takes a month to hire a competent replacement.

You have the balance in your work and personal life broken when a colleague goes into the hospital for an operation and you are asked to handle his key accounts.

You have the balance in your work and personal life broken when a parent becomes gravely ill.

You have the balance in your work and personal life broken when someone crashes into your car, causing it to be in the repair shop for two weeks.

You have the balance in your work and personal life broken when you have to travel to another state and pick up your child who has come down with mono at college.

You have the balance in your work and personal life broken when your company sends you out of town to attend a two-week training program.

You have the balance in your work and personal life broken when an old friend who you haven't seen in ten years stops in for an unexpected three-day visit.

You have the balance in your work and personal life broken when your company switches over to a strange new accounting system.

You have the balance in your work and personal life broken when your company decides to change software companies.

You have the balance in your work and personal life broken when your spouse, who has applied for a new position in her/his company, must go out of town to participate in a two-day assessment center activity.

You have the balance in your work and personal life broken when a major snowstorm closes down the school system and you must arrange for child care for an entire week.

You have the balance in your work and personal life broken when the furnace goes out at home.

You have the balance in your work and personal life broken when the pastor at church asks you to host a missionary family for a month.

You have the balance in your work and personal life broken when the legislature passes a new law requiring your company to keep a host of new records of its business practices.

You have the balance in your work and personal life broken when you are called for jury duty.

You have the balance in your work and personal life broken when a neighbor asks you to take care of her/his children while the parent recoups from a bout with pneumonia.

You have the balance in your work and personal life broken when you must take a half a work day to defend last year's personal income tax return.

You have the balance in your work and personal life broken when major road construction increases your commuting time by 30 minutes to and from work.

You have the balance in your work and personal life broken when your professional organization bestows upon you a national award and you must take three days to travel to New York to receive it.

You have the balance in your work and personal life broken when a computer virus attacks the sole copy of your annual report.

You have the balance in your work and personal life broken when your company downsizes and gives you 20 percent of the workload previously done by a laid-off employee.

You have the balance in your work and personal life broken when you are asked to mentor a new employee.

You have the balance in your work and personal life broken when the auditors from your company's accounting firm request that you meet with them in the evening during the next two weeks.

You have the balance in your work and personal life broken when a friend at church asks you to teach her/his Sunday School class while she/he goes on vacation.

You have the balance in your work and personal life broken when the church board asks you to direct its major fall fund-raising activity.

You have the balance in your work and personal life broken when you get a pain in your side and have to go to the hospital to have your appendix removed.

You have the balance in your work and personal life broken when you must accompany your child's eighth-grade class on a day-long field trip.

You have the balance in your work and personal life broken when a friend who is running for the city council asks you to spend a couple of Saturdays a month passing out campaign literature.

You have the balance in your work and personal life broken when you are held up at work on a major project because another department is running three weeks behind schedule with their part of the work.

You have the balance in your work and personal life broken when at the last minute you discover a major error you made on a project that is due this Friday.

You have the balance in your work and personal life broken when your immediate supervisor is fired and you are asked to cover for her/him until the company can find a suitable replacement.

You have the balance in your work and personal life broken when your house catches fire.

You have the balance in your work and personal life broken when your spouse comes down with the flu.

You have the balance in your work and personal life broken when you jam a finger in the car door and are unable to use a keyboard for three days.

You have the balance in your work and personal life broken when you're elected to the city council.

You have the balance in your work and personal life broken when you sprain your ankle jogging and have to use a crutch for five days.

You have the balance in your work and personal life broken when you must appear in court for a traffic violation.

CHAPTER 11

TOPIC   Disclosing Career Information

LEARNING OBJECTIVE   Participants will be able to share their feelings about their careers and employing organizations.

NUMBER OF PARTICIPANTS   6-15

PLAYING TIME   15-30 minutes depending on the number of players

REFERENCE   None

REQUIRED MATERIALS   A medium-sized box (12 by 12 by 15 inches) and Court Orders sheet

TO PLAY

1. Introduce players to the concepts of self-disclosure and confidentiality. Emphasize the importance of each in career development workshops and training sessions.

2. Explain that they are going to pretend that the company they work for has declared bankruptcy. As a result, all employees have received a summons to appear in court. When they show up at the courthouse, they are ordered by the judge to forfeit a personal item of value. Fortunately, the court agrees to return the items provided an employee cooperates and supplies the requested career information.

3. Select two persons from the group to be court officials. One individual is to be the judge and a second person the bailiff.

4. Ask the judge to come to the front of the room and sit on a chair facing the group.

5. Ask the bailiff to come to the front of the room. Hand her/him a medium-sized box.

6. Direct the bailiff to pass through the group with the box and collect a personal item of value from each person (such as a belt, handkerchief, shoe, earring, ring, watch).

7. Ask the bailiff to stand behind the judge with the box containing the personal items.

8. Hand the judge a list of Court Orders.

9. Explain that, when the bailiff takes an item of value from the box and holds it above the judge's head (without the judge seeing it), the owner of the item must approach the bench (i.e., come and stand in front of the judge). The judge will then read the individual a court order demanding her/him to disclose some information. If the person does as ordered, the judge will direct the bailiff to return the item of value. If the person does not disclose the requested information, she/he will be held in contempt of court and sentenced to spend 30 days in the county jail.

10. Ask the judge to call the court to order and begin the proceedings as described in step 9.

11. At the end of the game, make sure that all personal items have been returned to their rightful owners.

12. Debrief players. Discuss why self-disclosure is important when asking for and receiving help with one's career. Ask players to identify the types of information they are most uncomfortable disclosing.

13. Reemphasize the importance of confidentiality. Remind players that what was disclosed in the room must remain in the room.

COURT ORDERS

1. In 100 words or less tell the court about your secret fantasy job.

2. Pretend that your boss is standing directly to your right. Tell her/him what you honestly think about your last performance review.

3. Share with the court what you really did the last time you played hooky from work.

4. An article praising you will soon appear in the company newspaper. Tell the court exactly how the headline of the story will read.

5. You just saved the company $5000. Explain to the court how you managed this saving.

6. Last week at work you made your worst blunder ever. Come clean and tell the court how you messed up.

7. You feel the need to vent some frustrations. Sing a few bars of "Take This Job and Shove It" to the court.

8. You have just written a book about your career. It has appeared on the *New York Times* bestseller list for 12 weeks. Tell the court some of your secrets of career success contained in the book.

9. You believe in reincarnation. It is your desire to come back in your next life as a member of a different profession. Tell the court the name of the profession.

10. You have the ability to discern the future by reading a person's palm. Predict an upcoming event in my [the judge's] career by reading my palm. Disclose this prediction to the court.

11. Last Friday you placed a piece of paper in the company's suggestion box. Tell the court what was written on the paper.

12. As a cost-saving measure, the company is considering doing away with your job. Explain to the court why this would be a terrible mistake.

13. You regularly conduct training workshops for managers on Total Quality Management. Give one piece of advice you give managers/team leaders in almost every workshop.

14. You have just received a call from Gossip Central. Tell the court the contents of this most juicy piece of gossip.

15. At the company's annual Christmas party you had several glasses of wine and felt the need to make a toast to the top brass. Tell the court what you said in your toast.

16. Your old work group has been reconstituted and made into a self-directing work team. Tell the court the name your team has given itself and why.

EMPOWERMENT PUZZLE

TOPIC   Worker Empowerment

**LEARNING
OBJECTIVE**   Participants will be able to list several ways to empower workers.

**NUMBER OF
PARTICIPANTS**   Any number

PLAYING TIME   7–12 minutes

REFERENCE   Scott, Cynthia D., and Jaffe, Dennis T. (1991). *Empowerment: Building a committed work-place.* Los Altos, CA: Crisp Publications, Inc.

Tracy, D. (1992). *Ten steps to empowerment: A common-sense guide to managing people.* New York: Quill.

**REQUIRED
MATERIALS**   Pencils and Empowerment Puzzle

TO PLAY
1. Introduce players to the concept of employee empowerment.
2. Go over the learning objective for the game.
3. Explain to players that they are going to be given 10 ways to empower their subordinates or colleagues at work. The only problem is that the empowerment strategies have been in some way distorted or mixed up.
4. Pass out a pencil and an Empowerment Puzzle, face down, to each participant.
5. Have players turn their puzzles over.
6. Go over the directions at the top of the page. Inform players that in the spaces below the puzzle box numbered 1–10, they are to write down as many of the empowerment interventions as they can make out. Advise them that they will only have three minutes to come up with their answers.
7. Have players begin decoding the puzzle.
8. Three minutes later, call "time."
9. Provide players the correct answers as they check their own puzzle sheets for accuracy.
10. Declare the person(s) with the most correct answers the winner(s).
11. Debrief players. Have players identify ways their organizations have attempted to empower workers. Discuss other ways workers might be more empowered.

21

Many organizations are expecting much more of their workers. Rank and file workers are often expected to perform the functions that were carried on by their supervisors and middle managers only a few years ago. As more is expected of workers, there emerges a need for companies to provide workers the wherewithal (the authority, resources, skills, etc.) to perform. Following are ten ways some firms are attempting to empower their employees:

Providing the necessary skills to do the job. It's a law of the workplace. Employees can't do what they don't have the skills to do. For workers to have the necessary skills to complete assigned projects, companies need to assess gaps between the current skill levels of employees and current/future job skill requirements. Training, education, and development activities must then be provided to close all discerned skill gaps. Empowerment requires that all workers be trained and retrained in the right skills.

Granting sufficient authority to do the job. A second straightforward method of empowering workers is simply to give them the power to complete their assigned jobs. Employees who have been charged with completing major projects but denied the authority to take the necessary steps to complete their jobs will not feel empowered. Instead they are likely to feel that they are not fully trusted to "handle their jobs." Furthermore, waiting for days for others to make decisions and take actions can cause major delays in projects and lead to almost unbearable frustration.

Articulating a vision of the completed job. A third way to empower employees is help them visualize the end results of their work before they actually begin a project. This way workers can use more of their own skills, past work experience, and ingenuity to achieve the desired outcome. Employees can better weigh all alternative decisions and actions in terms of the potential contributions they might make to the desired end product.

Explaining how a project fits into the big picture. An affliction affecting many organizations is that "the left hand doesn't know what the right hand is doing." The resulting lack of coordination limits the effectiveness of individual workers and prevents work groups from achieving any kind of synergy. An antidote to this workplace malady is to explain to employees how their jobs and work projects fit into the big organizational picture. Only by knowing the big picture can workers identify with it and feel they are making a contribution to it. The resulting expanded sense of accomplishment and pride can be empowering.

Stating the relative importance of a project. The nature of most jobs requires workers to be excellent stewards of their time. Among other things, this entails spending the most time on projects that are of the utmost importance to the company at any given time. No one benefits when employees unknowingly spend 50 percent of their time on a project that has dropped from number 1 to number 6 in priority. Therefore, managers need to tell their subordinates the current priority status of every project. This will enable employees to exercise more effective control over their time and their own individual productivity.

Supplying adequate information to do the job. Traveling down a narrow, unfamiliar, twisting mountain road during a driving rainstorm is not apt to instill a sense of power in many individuals. The lack of information about the road and the surrounding area is likely to cause a driver to bring her/his excursion to a sudden halt. It could even result in a serious accident. So it is with work projects. Their successful conclusion depends on workers being able to secure relevant, accurate, and up-to-date information on all aspects of the project. It really is so: Information is power, and nothing empowers workers more than power.

Allocating ample resources to do the job. Care to travel in a small plane from coast to coast on one tank of gas? Of course not! One tank is insufficient fuel to make such a trip. However, workers are often expected to accomplish similar feats with inadequate resources. It is intimated that their personal commitment and creativity will more than make up for any shortfall in resources. Nothing could be further from the truth. If firms truly want to provide workers the wherewithal to bring important projects to fruition, they can empower them by allocating ample resources to do the job.

Building employees' self-confidence to do the job. Expectancy theory holds that employees who believe they can achieve a certain result are more apt to attempt it and be successful at it. Thus, building employees' confidence in their own abilities is yet another way they can be empowered. This can be accomplished over time by: (1) providing workers opportunities to grow and develop through training and incrementally more challenging work assignments, (2) acknowledging and rewarding past accomplishments, and (3) exhibiting trust in employee's abilities and judgment.

Extending permission to take acceptable risks. An old adage claims that if "nothing is ventured" then "nothing is gained." So it is in business. If companies want to increase market share they must be willing to take a few risks and attempt to create new products and/or services. Realizing that certain ventures will be highly successful but many new endeavors are likely to be miserable flops, firms must also allow their employees to take risks that it feels are "acceptable." They can empower their workers by not always insisting that they "play it safe."

Giving feedback as to how the job is progressing. The former mayor of New York City, Ed Koch, became well known for his question, "How am I doing?" Almost everywhere he traveled in the Big Apple he would ask the citizens, "How am I doing?" So it should be in the workplace. Workers need be encouraged to ask about how they are doing. They must be given continuous feedback on the progress they are making on all important projects. Feedback helps employees to remain on the "right track," build their self-confidence, and develop professionally.

EMPOWERMENT PUZZLE

Directions: Decipher and write the characteristics of empowered employees in the spaces below the puzzle.

PROVIDING NECESSARY SKILLS

BUILDING EMPLOYEE'S SELF-CONFIDENCE

ARTICULATING A VISION

EXTENDING PERMISSION TO TAKE ACCEPTABLE RISKS

GIVING FEEDBACK

SUPPLYING ADEQUATE INFORMATION

ALLOCATING AMPLE RESOURCES

SUFFICIENT GRANTING AUTHORITY

STATING RELATIVE IMPORTANCE OF PROJECTS

EXPLAINING HOW A PROJECT FITS INTO THE BIG PICTURE

1. _____
2. _____
3. _____
4. _____
5. _____
6. _____
7. _____
8. _____
9. _____
10. _____

FEEDBACK FUMBLES #1

TOPIC Behaviors That Hamper the Giving of Performance Feedback

LEARNING OBJECTIVE Participants will be able to identify five diversionary behaviors that often obstruct the sending of job performance feedback.

NUMBER OF PARTICIPANTS Any number of players divided into two teams of similar size

PLAYING TIME 20-30 minutes

REFERENCE McLagan, P. and Krembs, P. (1988). *On-the-level.* St. Paul, MN: McLagan International, Inc.

REQUIRED MATERIALS Pencils, the case study Helen Morgan, the Performance Inventory worksheet, and the Diversionary Tactics Scoresheet #1.

TO PLAY

  1. Introduce players to the notion of diversionary tactics.

  2. Go over the learning objective for the game.

  3. Explain to participants that they are going to read a brief case study and evaluate the main character's job performance. Afterwards, volunteers will engage in friendly but competitive role plays. The goal of the role plays (two mock performance reviews) is for the persons playing Mr. Kelly to candidly discuss Helen's job performance without employing any diversionary tactics.

  4. Pass out the game materials (a pencil, copies of the case study Helen Morgan, and the Performance Inventory worksheet) to each participant.

  5. Ask participants to take 10 minutes to read the case study and complete the worksheet.

  6. After 10 minutes, ask someone from the audience to serve as the scorekeeper for the upcoming competition. Hand the scorekeeper a copy of Diversionary Tactics Scoresheet #1 to study.

  7. Draw an imaginary line down the middle of the large group, dividing it into two groups of similar size. Ask each group to give itself the name of a professional football team.

  8. Recruit two volunteers from each team.

  9. Ask one volunteer from each team to pick up her/his Performance Inventory sheet, come to the front of the room, and be seated on a chair facing the audience. Assign the role of Mr. Kelly to the person on the audience's right and that of Helen to the individual on the left.

  10. Inform Mr. Kelly that he is to hold a five-minute mock performance review with his subordinate Helen. He is to briefly mention Helen's strengths and then go on to directly

point out areas where Helen needs to improve. He is to avoid the use of any diversionary tactics. Helen is to respond to her supervisor's criticisms with a moderate amount of defensiveness.

11. Direct the scorekeeper to record each time Mr. Kelly uses one of the diversionary tactics.

12. Advise players that, after five minutes have passed, the second string of volunteers will come forward and perform another mock review. This time the roles will be reversed for each team. The side with the lowest score at the end of the game will be considered the winning team.

13. Direct the volunteers to begin the first mock performance review.

14. After five minutes, ask the second pair of volunteers to come forward. This time have the player on the audience's left play Mr. Kelly and the person to the right play Helen.

15. Begin the second mock performance review.

16. After five minutes, ask the scorekeeper to add up each team's score (i.e., the number of times the first and the second Mr. Kelly used diversionary tactics during their mock performance reviews).

17. Declare the team with the lowest score the winner.

18. Debrief players. Go over the five diversionary tactics often used by senders of performance feedback. Ask players to share instances in which they have used a particular diversionary tactic when providing a subordinate feedback regarding her/his job performance. Have them explain why they resorted to the tactic. Discuss ways supervisors can bring themselves to provide more honest performance feedback to subordinates.

Directions: Place a tally mark in the right-hand column (Number of Times Used) each time a feedback sender uses the diversionary tactic in the left-hand column (Diversion). Record the total number of times the sender used the respective tactics at the bottom of the right column.

Diversion	Number of Times Used
It's My Duty Diversion: The sender gives performance feedback totally out of obligation. The supervisor completes forms and adheres to company procedures pertaining to performance reviews. However, the sender may neglect to share her/his personal observations or get involved in solving any performance problems. Consequently, real performance issues are seldom addressed.	
Junk Dealer Diversion: The tactic involves burying any constructive criticism. Important information is wrapped in qualifiers, reservations, or irrelevant facts. The sender may exclaim, "You don't have to necessarily agree with me," or "There's a good chance that you might want to get a second opinion on this." Consequently, the subordinate has great difficulty in receiving the message or knowing what to do about it. The sender avoids having to be direct and clear regarding the criticism.	
Lifesaver Diversion: The sender downplays the seriousness of her/his criticism. After sending negative feedback, the supervisor may feel remorseful about smothering the receiver in bad news. He/she may then throw the subordinate a "lifesaver." The lifesaver might come in the form of such comments as, "Well, I wouldn't worry about it," "It's actually not all that important," or "Overall, you do very good work." These diversionary remarks lessen the importance of the criticism and the need to take corrective actions.	
Detective Diversion: The sender refuses to get to the point regarding a subordinate's job performance. Instead the supervisor poses leading and unnerving questions. She/he may ask, "Didn't you know that this would happen?" Consequently, trust between the two parties begins to erode and the receiver may become very defensive.	
Swami Diversion: The tactic may aptly be called the "mind reading game." The sender delivers indirect messages about the feedback, expecting the receiver to be able to know what she/he is thinking. The sender is thinking, "She should know this is a problem without my telling her" or "He must be blind not to see he's off in left field." Consequently, the subordinate may never know the real message. The sender may use her/his anger about the problem as a reason for not giving any direct feedback.	
Total	

SOURCE: Published with permission of McLagan Learning Systems, Inc., 1700 West Highway 36, St. Paul, MN 55113.

Helen Morgan has been a secretary in the college's Business Department offices for the past 10 years. This friendly, well-liked lady can be found at her desk every morning promptly at 8:00 A.M. The department coffee pot is always filled and brewing, a task she has taken on even though it is not part of her official duties. Beside her desk is a perfectly arranged bookcase full of manuals covering topics ranging from school policies to computer operation and repair. Helen's desk is meticulously organized and neat.

At 8:05, Helen is busily typing a letter on her computer from an audio tape the department head, Mr. Kelly, gave to her at 4:50 yesterday afternoon. By 8:40, four perfectly prepared letters are ready for Mr. Kelly's signature. While she is working on the letters, the personnel office calls wanting information on the number of tax exemptions a new instructor wishes to claim. The information is needed before they can issue a paycheck for him. The instructor is not in; so Helen tells the personnel secretary to put down two exemptions and the instructor can change it later if he wishes. It will later be discovered that the new instructor has six children and needs to claim all the exemptions he can get. Because Helen was in a hurry and did not take the time to get the correct information, problems will be created later in changing the forms.

As Helen gets up from her desk to take the completed letters to Mr. Kelly's office, the phone rings again. It's Helen's daughter, who is upset over personal problems with her boyfriend. Helen spends 20 minutes talking to her on the phone. For 15 of those minutes, the accounting instructor, Ms. Gunderson, waits to pick up her course syllabi that she left with Helen to be reproduced. Helen quickly locates the appropriate folder and hands it to Ms. Gunderson with a smile. Ms. Gunderson knows without looking that the copies will be of the highest quality, even though she had to wait 15 minutes for Helen to get off the phone.

A new secretary, in another department office down the hall, calls Helen for advice on operating a computer program that doesn't seem to work properly. Helen goes down the hall, leaving her desk unattended for 12 minutes. Helen finds and corrects the glitch in the computer program. However, while she's gone the phone rings several times, going unanswered unless a faculty member happens to come into the office looking for Helen.

Around 9:30 A.M., the chair of the curriculum committee, Mr. Jenkins, brings in his notes from an early meeting this morning and asks Helen to put them into report form so that he can distribute copies to committee members this afternoon. A problem has arisen that needs to be acted on quickly and the group plans to meet again tomorrow morning. As he starts to explain how he wishes the report to be prepared, the phone rings. It's Helen's elderly mother-in-law wanting to know about Helen's husband's visit to the doctor yesterday. Helen tells her that her son is fine and she will have him call her this evening. The old lady goes into a long narrative about a neighbor's illness, while a busy Mr. Jenkins waits. Finally, Helen sees that Mr. Jenkins is getting impatient. She quickly ends the conversation and resumes her work.

Helen sets to work on Mr. Jenkins report at 10:15 A.M., finishing it quickly and accurately in spite of being interrupted several times by the phone and people coming into the office needing assistance. Helen never seems to lose patience with people, always speaking kindly and respectfully to whoever calls or comes into the office.

The report completed and copied for Mr. Jenkins, Helen adds last-minute items to the office supply order she started yesterday. She needs to have it ready for the interoffice mail when the mail carrier arrives at 11:00. That completed, Helen makes copies of a budget report she knows Mr. Kelly will need the day after tomorrow. She puts them in a bin on her desk as the mail person comes into the office. Helen quickly sorts the mail and puts it into the appropriate department members' boxes.

The phone rings as she finishes the mail. It's that know-it-all Mr. Clark from the state education office wanting to talk to Mr. Kelly immediately. Mr. Kelly came in a short time ago, and Helen knows that he is trying to finish a grant proposal and would not welcome a lengthy interruption, especially from "that man." She tells Mr. Clark that Mr. Kelly is not available at present and that she would take a message. Mr. Clark sarcastically tells Helen to have Mr. Kelly call him back as soon as possible. Helen maintains her poise and assures Mr. Clark that she will pass on the message.

Helen leaves for lunch at noon and returns at 1:20. She is late getting back because she stopped by her sister's house to return a dress that she borrowed and was dragged into a dispute her sister was having with a neighbor. On her return, Helen finds several requests left on her desk by various department members. Helen immediately starts work on the projects, putting them in order according to the time they are needed. She guesses that Ms. Davis' report was due this morning so she completes that one first. Helen is midway through the remaining tasks left for her when Mr. Kelly requests that she deliver a few top priority memos to offices down the hall.

It takes Helen 20 minutes to deliver three memos. She runs into another secretary from the Health Education Department who has a really juicy piece of gossip. One of the instructors in health education has been having an affair with a math instructor. The math instructor's wife found out and came into the health education instructor's office and made a scene. Mr. Kelly is looking unhappy when Helen returns. The phone has been ringing off the hook and he has had to answer it. To make matters worse, Mr. Clark called and finally caught up with him. Helen apologizes and relates her piece of gossip to an appreciative Mr. Kelly. Helen believes that a good secretary always keeps her boss informed.

Mr. Kelly reminds Helen of the budget report he will need copies of in two days. Helen hands him the folder containing the copies. It never ceases to amaze him how much Helen gets done.

Helen spends the remainder of the afternoon completing the projects she was working on before the top priority memos. Next she calls the Maintenance Department to come and fix the door on Mr. Meadows' office, which makes an ear piercing shriek when opened or closed. Mr. Meadows has not complained, but Helen is sure that others in offices close to his would appreciate a quieter environment.

That done, Helen works on a couple of documents that won't be needed until the end of the week. As Helen's mother often said, "It always pays to plan ahead."

At 4:55 a student comes into the office requesting to see Mr. Philpot, the management instructor. Mr. Philpot is at a professional conference and will not be back until Friday. The student wishes to speak to Mr. Philpot about turning in his term paper on Monday instead of Friday. He has just located a book containing some information he needs to complete the paper and it will take extra time to finish. Helen tells the student that it would be all right to turn the paper in on Monday or even a day or two later if he runs into problems getting it typed. Helen is certain that Mr. Philpot, being such a kind man, would be understanding of the student's dilemma.

At 5:00 Helen puts on her jacket to go home. Mr. Kelly doesn't need anything extra done at the last minute, so Helen will be able to leave on time today. Helen is always willing to stay if she's needed, but appreciates getting home to start dinner before her husband gets home. She checks to make sure that the coffee pot is off and rinsed out and that all machinery in the office that should be turned off is indeed off. Everything is in order for tomorrow morning.

Employee *Helen Morgan*   Evaluation Period _____ 199 ____ to _____ 199 ____

Directions: Use the following five-point scale to rate the employee's job performance.

1	2	3	4	5
Unsatisfactory	**Marginal**	**Satisfactory**	**Superior**	**Outstanding**
Does Not Meet Expectations	Comes Close to Meeting Expectations	Meets Expectations	Surpasses Expectations	Greatly Surpasses Expectations

1. *Knowledge of Work* ....
Understanding of the work assignment, mastery
of job skills.   1   2   3   4   5

2. *Dependability* ....
Can be relied on to meet work schedules, job
responsibilities and commitments.   1   2   3   4   5

3. *Productivity* ....
Volume of work accomplished during this evalu-
ation period.   1   2   3   4   5

4. *Quality of Work* ....
Work is thorough, and accurate, and meets
specified standards.   1   2   3   4   5

5. *Works with Others* ....
Shows respect for, cooperates with, and assists
others.   1   2   3   4   5

6. *Initiative* ....
Displays energy and determination in over-
coming obstacles, solving problems, and
keeping the work flowing.   1   2   3   4   5

7. *Organizing and Planning* ....
Systematically plans time and work assignments
resulting in minimal delays, waste, and duplication of efforts.   1   2   3   4   5

8. *Judgment* ....
Actions and decisions are appropriate, based
on sound reasoning and common sense.   1   2   3   4   5

Summary Comment (continue on reverse side)

SOURCE: Published with permission of the Personnel Officer, A-B Technical Community College, 340 Victoria Road, Asheville, NC 28801.

FEEDBACK FUMBLES #2

TOPIC   Behaviors That Hamper the Receiving of Performance Feedback

LEARNING OBJECTIVE   Participants will be able to identify five diversionary behaviors that often obstruct the receiving of job performance feedback.

NUMBER OF PARTICIPANTS   Any number of players divided into two teams of similar size

PLAYING TIME   20-30 minutes

REFERENCE   McLagan, P. and Krembs, P. (1988). *On-The-Level*. St. Paul, MN: McLagan International, Inc.

REQUIRED MATERIALS   Pencils, the case study Ed Burns, Performance Inventory worksheet, and Diversionary Tactics Scoresheet #2

TO PLAY
1. Introduce players to the notion of diversionary tactics.
2. Go over the learning objective for the game.
3. Explain to participants that they are going to read a brief case study and evaluate the main character's job performance. Afterwards, volunteers will engage in friendly but competitive role plays. The goal of the role plays (two mock performance reviews) is for the persons playing Ed to discuss their job performance without employing any diversionary tactics.
4. Pass out the game materials (a pencil, a copy of the case study Ed Burns, and the Performance Inventory worksheet) to each participant.
5. Ask participants to take 10 minutes to read the case study and complete the worksheet.
6. After 10 minutes ask someone from the audience to serve as the scorekeeper for the upcoming competition. Hand the scorekeeper a copy of Diversionary Tactics Scoresheet #2 to study.
7. Draw an imaginary line down the middle of the large group, dividing it into two groups of similar size. Ask each group to give itself the name of a professional football team.
8. Recruit two volunteers from each team.
9. Ask one volunteer from each team to pick up her/his Performance Inventory sheet, come to the front of the room, and be seated on a chair facing the audience. Assign the role of Ed to the person on the audience's right and that of Ed's supervisor, Charlotte Wimpole, to the individual on the left.
10. Inform Ed and his supervisor that they are to hold a five-minute mock performance review. The supervisor is to briefly mention Ed's strengths and then go on to aggressively point out areas where Ed needs to improve. Ed must respond to his supervisor's criticisms without using any of the five diversionary tactics previously discussed.

11. Direct the scorekeeper to record each time Ed uses one of the diversionary tactics.

12. Advise players that, after five minutes have passed, the second string of volunteers will come forward and perform another mock review. This time the roles will be reversed for each team. The side with the lowest score at the end of the game will be considered the winning team.

13. Direct the volunteers to begin the first mock performance review.

14. After five minutes, ask the second pair of volunteers to come forward. This time have the player on the audience's left play Ed and the person to the right play Ed's supervisor.

15. Begin the second mock performance review.

16. After five minutes, ask the scorekeeper to add up each team's score (the number of times the first and the second Eds used diversionary tactics during their mock performance reviews).

17. Declare the team with the lowest score the winner.

18. Debrief players. Go over the five diversionary tactics often used by receivers of performance feedback. Ask players to share instances in which they have used a diversionary tactic during the course of a performance review. Have them explain why they resorted to the tactic. Discuss ways employees can keep themselves from being overly defensive during performance reviews.

Directions: Place a tally mark in the right-hand column (Number of Times Used) each time a feedback receiver uses the diversionary tactic in the left-hand column (Diversion). Record the total number of times the receiver used the respective tactics at the bottom of the right column.

Diversion	Number of Times Used
Wounded Animal Diversion: The aim is to make the sender of the criticism feel so guilty that she/he avoids giving any type of constructive criticism in the future. The receiver deliberately interprets the feedback to apply more broadly than the supervisor intends. The employee pretends that she/he is extremely hurt. She/he may pout or sulk for weeks.	
Changing the Scent Diversion: This is a very old and common diversionary tactic. When presented with criticism about her/his job performance, the receiver quickly changes the subject. Little benefit is derived from the feedback because issues are seldom discussed and conclusions about the receiver's work are never drawn.	
Counterattack Diversion: The deployment of this tactic involves going on the defensive. Sometimes it takes the form of a preemptive criticism. Upon receiving criticism about her/his job performance, the receiver often accuses the sender of not understanding, being misinformed about matters, or actually being responsible for any performance problems. The receiver claims that the supervisor would probably do the very same thing if she/he were in the receiver's shoes. The performance review turns into a session of charges and countercharges.	
Ally Building Diversion: Operating on the principle that there is safety in numbers, the ally building diversion is another highly defensive tactic. The objective is for the receiver to get as many people as possible on her/his side so that she/he doesn't have to deal with feedback. A large alliance of employees thus proves the feedback is wrong. The receiver thus avoids listening to and acting on any feedback.	
Masochist Diversion: The masochist diversion is most commonly played by overachievers who are chronically harder on themselves than anyone else. The receiver punishes herself/himself so that the supervisor won't have to. It often occurs when the receiver fears the worst and does not check to see what the supervisor really thinks. This tactic can also be used to manipulate the sender into giving positive feedback. For instance, a supervisor may begin to give constructive criticism to a masochist but end up acting as a lifesaver instead. The supervisor may tell the masochist, "It's not as bad as you think. Let's look on the bright side."	
Total	

SOURCE: Published with permission of McLagan Learning Systems, Inc., 1700 West Highway 36, St. Paul, MN 55113.

Ed Burns has been an English Instructor at the college for 25 years, going there directly after graduate school. Ed has clearly settled in and has never given even a passing thought to changing jobs. He and his wife Barbara, a secretary in the administration office, have been married 20 years with no children.

On a typical day, after dropping Barbara off at her office, Ed arrives at his office around 7:55 A.M. His first class isn't until 10:00; so Ed has plenty of time to do several little things held over from yesterday. Ed, looking for his notes on Chaucer, found one student's class drop form, another student's missing midterm report, and a questionnaire sent by a colleague three weeks ago. Before he starts tackling these tasks, he decides to check his mail.

Ed receives a letter from his publisher containing an advance check for his new spy novel. Of all of Ed's activities, writing the Justin Bean spy novels is closest to his heart. The escapades of the heroic Justin give Ed the adventure and glory he would love to have in his own life, without the danger of real life spying. Since there's not much mail, Ed quickly gets back to his other work.

Ed begins by signing the student's class drop form, adds an apologetic note for its lateness, and sends it over to the registrar's office. Next he reads the previously missing midterm report. It is a very well written paper done by a freshman comp student. This student shows great promise and Ed looks forward to having her in his creative writing class.

As Ed picks up a pencil to start work on the questionnaire sent to him by an English professor doing research at the university, he is startled by a loud knock on his office door. It's Bill Jones' turn to collect Ed for the department's strategic planning committee meeting. It's no secret; everyone in the department knows that Ed sincerely does not mind meetings. He notes the appointments on his calendar, but either loses the calendar for a period of time or forgets to look at it on any regular basis. Ed's co-workers feel that taking turns getting him to meetings is a small price to pay for having him on committees. Ed often comes up with brilliant insights into problems and invariably offers to write reports for the meetings, turning out "masterpieces."

The meeting lasts for 50 minutes and Ed has to hurry to get to his 10:00 class. He rushes into his office, grabs a folder of materials for English Literature 101, and speeds up the stairs to his classroom. Today he would be introducing the works of Jane Austen to his students.

Making it to the classroom with three minutes to spare, Ed opens the folder to discover not his Jane Austen materials, but his notes from yesterday's curriculum committee meeting. Ed knows the material for all his classes so well that he doesn't need his notes, but he does need the outline he prepared to help the students follow along with the lesson. Ed creates wonderful activities and learning aids for all his classes, which helps each student get the greatest possible benefit from the classes. Ed sets the class to work reading a section from their textbooks while he runs to get the proper folder. On his return, Ed launches into a discussion of the society in which Miss Austen lived and the impact it had on her writings. Ed's comprehensive subject knowledge, enthusiasm, and natural wit keep his students in the palm of his hand during his lectures.

After class, two students stop to ask Ed for assistance. One student is having trouble finding an information source for her report. Ed tells her exactly where the information can be found in city library, rather than the college library. He also tells the student of a person in the community that she might like to interview. The person, an older lady, has done extensive research into the student's chosen subject. The student thanks Ed and hurries away to get the information and call the lady.

The other student, a young man, is having significant family problems. The student likes and respects Ed and feels that he can give some helpful advice on what to do with his problems at home. Ed, known for his sound judgment and caring nature, quickly sees that the student's problem is beyond his expertise. He takes the young man back to his office where he makes a phone call to John Mullens, a good friend of his in the counseling center. John is available now; so Ed personally takes the young man over to his office. He introduces the student to John and leaves the two to sort out the problems.

On his way back to his office, Ed stops at the library to check on the new books he asked to be ordered. The books are not in yet, but are due to arrive by the end of the week. As Ed arrives back at his office, his phone rings. His colleague, Mark Carroll, an instructor in the Math department, wants to meet Ed for lunch. Ed agrees and meets Mark at a little cafe near the campus. On the surface, Ed and Mark seem to be odd companions, but they are close friends. Ed is the only person on campus who knows that Mark writes romance novels under the name of Georgia Gilroy. Ed is a loyal friend and has kept Mark's secret for the many years they have known each other. Ed is always flattered when Mark asks for advice on his books. Ed frequently helps other instructors who are writing journal articles or books.

Ed and Mark get involved in a discussion of publishing guidelines and lose all track of time. This doesn't cause a problem for Mark, but Ed has a 1:00 P.M. class. Ed rushes back to his office, scoops up his class materials, and races to his class, arriving 13 minutes late. Ed's students are accustomed to his being late about once every two weeks. This is the only fault the student's have found with the classes that Ed teaches.

Ed has a 2:00 meeting with a group of citizens who wish to establish a community theater. On his way to the meeting, he stops by his office to drop off papers he collected from his class and pick up some materials he feels would be of interest to the theater group. He finds a memo from the department head, Ms. Charlotte Wimpole. Ms. Wimpole wants a copy of Ed's American Literature course syllabus no later than this afternoon. Since Ed has to get to the meeting, the syllabus will have to wait for his return.

After the community theater group meeting, Ed runs into Jack Richards who teaches history. Jack wants advice on putting together some supplemental materials for one of his World History classes. Ed is delighted to help and spends an hour and a half with Jack developing some high-quality materials. Ed has completely forgotten about Ms. Wimpole's request.

At 4:45 Ed returns to his office. A few minutes later, Ms. Wimpole comes to Ed's office door and peers inside to find him completely absorbed in a book that has just arrived in the afternoon mail. Ms. Wimpole, though by no means immune to Ed's charm, needs the syllabus today. Because she has been waiting patiently all afternoon and now it is almost time to go home, Ms. Wimpole speaks a bit louder and sharper than is usual for her. Ed is startled and jumps up, knocking over his chair. Setting the chair back up and with heart still pounding, Ed remembers Ms. Wimpole's memo. He starts searching through his files for the needed syllabus and finds one that is three years old. He has intended to write a new one, but has just never gotten around to it. Ms. Wimpole insists that Ed write a new syllabus and have it on her desk by 8:30 tomorrow morning. As she leaves his office, the idea of using a character fashioned after Ms. Wimpole in his next book crosses Ed's mind. The facade of a sweet little older lady covering up the personality of a storm trooper would be an excellent addition to his cast of characters.

The syllabus will have to be done in the morning. It is now 5:10 P.M. and time to pick up Barbara. There is just enough time to get a quick bite to eat before going to his evening class at 7:30. Even though Ed teaches 120 students a semester and advises 60, he volunteers his time to teach remedial grammar to 15 more students. The class meets once a week at the YMCA. The students are difficult to teach; so Ed does not really enjoy the class. However, his creative teaching style has done wonders with the group of students. The students, enjoying the class, are inspired to do much better than even Ed had anticipated. Ed always puts his heart into every class he teaches, but this class takes much extra time and energy. He is uncertain as to whether he will volunteer for this class again next semester.

Employee _Ed Burns_ Evaluation Period _____ 199 ____ to _____ 199 ____

Directions: Use the following five-point scale to rate the employee's job performance.

1	2	3	4	5
Unsatisfactory	**Marginal**	**Satisfactory**	**Superior**	**Outstanding**
Does Not Meet Expectations	Comes Close to Meeting Expectations	Meets Expectations	Surpasses Expectations	Greatly Surpasses Expectations

1. *Knowledge of Work* ....
   Understanding of the work assignment, mastery of job skills.
       1   2   3   4   5

2. *Dependability* ....
   Can be relied on to meet work schedules, job responsibilities and commitments.
       1   2   3   4   5

3. *Productivity* ....
   Volume of work accomplished during this evaluation period.
       1   2   3   4   5

4. *Quality of Work* ....
   Work is thorough, and accurate, and meets specified standards.
       1   2   3   4   5

5. *Works with Others* ....
   Shows respect for, cooperates with, and assists others.
       1   2   3   4   5

6. *Initiative* ....
   Displays energy and determination in overcoming obstacles, solving problems, and keeping the work flowing.
       1   2   3   4   5

7. *Organizing and Planning* ....
   Systematically plans time and work assignments resulting in minimal delays, waste, and duplication of efforts.
       1   2   3   4   5

8. *Judgment* ....
   Actions and decisions are appropriate, based on sound reasoning and common sense.
       1   2   3   4   5

Summary Comment (continue on reverse side)

SOURCE: Published with permission of the Personnel Officer, A-B Technical Community College, 340 Victoria Road, Asheville, NC 28801.

HOCUS FOCUS

TOPIC   Goal Setting

**LEARNING
OBJECTIVE**   Participants will be able to explain the relationship between the clarity of a career goal and the motivation to achieve it.

**NUMBER OF
PARTICIPANTS**   Any number of players divided into two teams of similar size

PLAYING TIME   10-15 minutes

REFERENCE   None

**REQUIRED
MATERIALS**   Overhead projector, Goal Setting Statements, and a transparency of the Mystery Statement

TO PLAY

1. Prior to the beginning of the training session, place a transparency of the Mystery Statement on the overhead projector. The focus knob on the projector should be turned so that the saying is almost a total blur.

2. Familiarize participants with the concept of setting career goals.

3. Go over the learning objective for the game.

4. Inform players that they will be divided into two competing teams to engage in a fun game pertaining to goal setting.

5. Divide the players into two teams, with one group seated on the left side of the room and the other seated on the right side of the room.

6. Inform players that you will read up to ten statements about the setting of goals. When it is their team's turn to play, they may, through their spokesperson, declare whether a statement is true or false. While the members of the respective teams can discuss what they consider to be the correct response, only the spokesperson can officially give the team's answer.

7. Advise participants that if they give a correct answer, their team gets a chance to guess the Mystery Statement. The first team to correctly guess the Mystery Statement on the overhead will be considered the winner. Again, only the spokesperson for the group can offer a team's official solution to the Mystery Statement.

8. Tell players that the mystery statement will first appear very blurry on the screen. However, after a team has made an attempt to solve the mystery saying, the saying will be brought into a little better focus.

9. Turn on the overhead projector.

10. Read the first goal setting statement to the team who first gave the name of their spokesperson. Allow up to 30 seconds to answer.

11. If answered correctly, give the team a chance to solve the blurred Mystery Statement.

12. Continue alternating play from one team to another. After a team incorrectly guesses the Mystery Statement, turn the focus knob on the overhead projector so that the image becomes slightly more in focus.

13. When a team's spokesperson correctly reads the Mystery Statement, declare that team the winner.

14. Debrief players. Ask players to give the characteristics of a well stated goal. Discuss why a clearly stated goal might be more motivating than a fuzzily stated goal.

GOAL SETTING STATEMENTS

1. Trying to reach specific goals sometimes makes a person's career more fun than it might otherwise be.

2. Having a suitable action for reaching one's goals is relatively unimportant. The critical thing is to have a goal.

3. It's a good idea to periodically chart one's progress toward a given goal.

4. To make goal setting work, sufficient resources (such as time, money, equipment) must be committed to the goal's achievement.

5. Any goal worth having must be very difficult to reach.

6. There is no such thing as too many goals. The more goals one has, the better.

7. It is a good idea to avoid conflicting goals.

8. Goals should be both short-range and long-range.

9. Excessive external pressures to achieve goals can lead to considerable dishonesty and cheating.

10. It is not a good idea to reward yourself for achieving an important goal. The achievement of a goal should serve as its own reward.

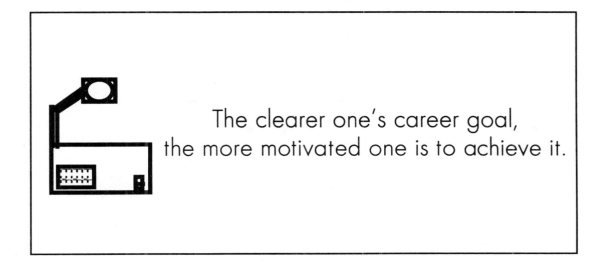

The clearer one's career goal,
the more motivated one is to achieve it.

PATHWAYS PUZZLE

TOPIC Career Paths

LEARNING OBJECTIVE Participants will be able to identify selected career paths.

NUMBER OF PARTICIPANTS Any number of players

PLAYING TIME 5–8 minutes

REFERENCE None

REQUIRED MATERIALS Crayons and copies of the Pathways Puzzle Sheet

TO PLAY

1. Familiarize participants with the concept of career paths.

2. Go over the learning objective for the game.

3. Inform players that they are about to receive a copy of the Pathways Puzzle Sheet, which contains six different career paths. Explain that they will have three minutes to find as many paths as they can. The person(s) finding the most paths will be considered the winner(s).

4. Provide each player with six crayons of different colors and a copy of the Pathways Puzzle Sheet face down.

5. Ask players to turn their puzzles over and follow along as you read the directions. Ask that no one begin until you say "go."

6. When everyone is clear on the directions, call, "Go." Remind participants that they have three minutes to find as many paths as possible.

7. Three minutes later call, "Stop."

8. Give players the correct answers as they check their own puzzles.

9. Declare the person(s) with the most correct answers the winner(s).

10. Debrief players. Ask participants to identify some traditional career paths within their organizations. Discuss some less traditional career paths employees might pursue if the more traditional paths disappear or are blocked.

Directions: This puzzle contains six career paths. Beginning at each of the start positions, draw a line up and through the cells containing the various career stops along a given path. Use a different color crayon for each path.

Director of Nursing	Company Vice President	Supreme Court Justice	General	State Senator	Full Professor
Appellate Judge	Associate Professor	District Manager	State Representative	Ward Supervisor	Major
Registered Nurse	County Commissioner	Lieutenant	District Judge	Assistant Professor	Plant Manager
Mayor	District Attorney	Instructor	Operations Manager	Sergeant	Licensed Practical Nurse
Graduate Assistant	Alderperson	Nurse's Aide	Private	Line Supervisor	Lawyer
START #1	START #2	START #3	START #4	START #5	START #6

PLATEAUED PLAYOFFS

TOPIC   Career Plateauing

LEARNING OBJECTIVE   Participants will be able to identify appropriate interventions for four types of career plateauing.

NUMBER OF PARTICIPANTS   Any number of players divided into groups of four

PLAYING TIME   15-20 minutes

REFERENCE   Kaye, Beverly. (1989, August). Are plateaued performers productive? *Personnel Journal.*

REQUIRED MATERIALS   Plateauing Boards, Plateaued Playoffs Role Cards, Plateaued Playoffs Intervention Cards, and multicolored candy lifesavers

TO PLAY

1. Familiarize participants with the concept of career plateauing and the four types of plateaued employees described on the Plateaued Playoffs Role Cards.

2. Go over the learning objective for the game.

3. Divide participants into groups of four members each.

4. Pass out a set of game materials to each group (one Plateauing Board, a set of Plateaued Playoffs Role Cards, and a set of Plateaued Playoffs Intervention Cards).

5. Ask players to place their Plateauing Boards in the center of their respective groups.

6. Explain that the goal of the game is to be the first plateaued employee to reach the "Development Zone" on the board.

7. Request that someone in each group shuffle the Plateaued Playoffs Role Cards. Have each player draw a card and carefully read it aloud. Explain that this is the role she/he will be playing in the game.

8. Pass out candy lifesavers to each player. Make certain that players in the same group have different color lifesavers.

9. Direct players to place their lifesavers on the bottom line of the playing board over the type of plateaued employee they are playing in the game (productively, partially, pleasantly, or passively plateaued).

10. Have someone in each group sort the Plateaued Playoffs Intervention Cards into four different piles, with each containing one productively, one partially, one pleasantly, and one passively plateaued card.

11. Direct someone in each group to shuffle one pile of cards and place each card face down in a separate cell across the bottom row of arrows.

12. Repeat step 11 for the remaining piles of cards and rows of arrows.

13. Inform players that the order of play will begin with the productively plateaued employee going first, followed by the partially, pleasantly, and the passively plateaued.

14. Advise participants that, when it becomes their turn to play, they are to pick up any intervention card from the row directly above their marker. If the card contains an intervention that is appropriate for their role type (i.e., has their type printed at the top of the card), they are to: (a) read the card aloud and (b) move their marker to the cell from which the card was drawn. If the card is of a different role type than theirs, they are to return the card face down to its original cell and their turn ends. They are not to reveal the contents of the card to any other player.

15. Tell groups to begin play. Play is to continue in each group until a plateaued worker has drawn all four of her/his intervention cards and arrived at the Development Zone.

16. When a player in each group has arrived at the Development Zone, ask these plateaued workers to stand and declare them winners.

17. Debrief players. Discuss some of the structural and psychological factors leading to plateauing. Ask participants to come up with additional interventions for workers who are productively, partially, pleasantly, and/or passively plateaued.

Development Zone

Productively Plateaued	Partially Plateaued	Pleasantly Plateaued	Passively Plateaued
↑	↑	↑	↑
↑	↑	↑	↑
↑	↑	↑	↑
↑	↑	↑	↑

PLATEAUED PLAYOFFS ROLE CARDS

To make a set of Plateaued Playoffs Role Cards, photocopy the following items using card stock paper and cut them out.

Productively Plateaued
 	
I am:
    a performer.
    loyal to my company.
    indispensable in my job.
    appreciated by my boss and co-workers.
	Partially Plateaued
	
	I am:
	    excited about my pet projects.
	    an expert in my field.
	    active in my professional organization.
	    a network person.

Pleasantly Plateaued
 	
I am:
    not interested in promotion.
    happy with my job.
    intending to remain with the company.
    not comfortable with change.
	Passively Plateaued
	
	I am:
	    in a rut and feel powerless.
	    not very creative.
	    given good performance reviews for longevity.
	    not interested in training or skill upgrading.

PLATEAUED PLAYOFFS INTERVENTION CARDS

Directions: To make a set of Plateaued Playoffs Intervention Cards, photocopy the following items using card stock paper and cut them out.

Productively At your boss's request, you are developing an entirely new system for doing your job using cutting edge technology.	**Productively** You have been assigned the task of creating productivity skills workshops to be facilitated by you on a companywide basis.	**Productively** You have been appointed the first official mentor and coordinator of a new company mentoring program.
Productively You have developed your own field of expertise and keep your skills up-to-date with the full support of your superiors.	**Partially** You are participating in your company's skill diversity training program and have mastered the last step in this job skill sequence. Move on to the next in the series.	**Partially** You have developed networks in other company departments. You are now included in many interdepartmental projects.
Partially Your involvement in local politics and your newfound hobby of collecting antiques has added zest to your life.	**Partially** Your company has given you a six-month paid sabbatical to do research on a facet of your job that is of great interest to you.	**Pleasantly** Your superiors have included you in a new job rotation program. You will be working in company divisions all over Europe.

Pleasantly

Team projects are now the order of the day in your company. The team you will be a member of may change with each project.

Pleasantly

To allow for more flexibility and autonomy in work performance, several jobs have been redesigned—including yours. You have a variety of added responsibilities.

Pleasantly

Your boss, whom you like very much, has given you some very constructive feedback about your work. His/her observations have inspired you to greater heights.

Passively

Your company's new incentive program, which pays super bonuses for outstanding performance, really motivates you. That new car may not be out of reach!

Passively

At the company awards banquet last night, your supervisor highly praised your experience and skill in job performance. You are motivated to live up to this praise.

Passively

Your participation on a high-visibility project has brought you recognition from higher-ups and other influential people. Keeping yourself visible could bring great rewards.

Passively

Your work with product innovation has not gone unnoticed by company bigwigs. You have been chosen to represent the company at a national conference.

SOURCE: Published with permission of Career Systems, 3545 Alana Drive, Sherman Oaks, CA 91403-4708.

SATISFACTION 21

TOPIC	Job Satisfaction, Need Motivation
LEARNING OBJECTIVE	Participants will be able to identify and distinguish job satisfiers from job dissatisfiers.
NUMBER OF PARTICIPANTS	Any number of players divided into small groups containing three or four members each
PLAYING TIME	15-20 minutes
REFERENCE	Herzberg, F., Mausner, B. and Snyderman, B. (1959). *The motivation to work.* New York: Wiley.
REQUIRED MATERIALS	Satisfaction 21 Playing Deck for every four players
TO PLAY	

1. Introduce players to Frederick Herzberg's Motivation-Hygiene Theory.

2. Go over the learning objective for the game.

3. Divide learners into small groups of three or four players each.

4. Designate a dealer for each group by handing her/him a deck of Satisfaction 21 playing cards.

5. Explain that the object of play is to be the first person in each group to reach exactly 21 points. Hygiene satisfier cards are worth 6 points each and dissatisfier cards are worth 3 points each. All other cards count 0 points.

6. Inform participants that play begins with dealing each player four cards. The remainder of the cards are placed on a draw pile, face down.

7. Tell participants that the first player picks up the top card from the draw pile and discards a card of her/his choosing face up on a discard pile. Subsequent players may either draw a top card from the draw pile or the discard pile. No player can keep more than four cards in her/his hand.

8. Advise participants that the first player to get precisely 21 points and calls "Satisfaction 21" becomes the winner in her/his small group.

9. Explain that the player calling "Satisfaction 21" must have the accuracy of her/his hand confirmed by the facilitator to be declared the official winner.

10. Debrief players. Discuss whether the five items Herzberg classifies as motivators are the items that most strongly motivate them to do a better job or to work harder.

HERZBERG'S MOTIVATION-HYGIENE THEORY

Guided by the concepts found in Maslow's Need Hierarchy Theory, Herzberg developed a motivation-hygiene theory. The theory places work incidents into two general categories:

hygiene factors and motivators. The *hygiene factors* (extrinsic variables) are held to be more associated with job dissatisfaction and include policy and administration, supervision, salary, interpersonal relations, and working conditions. Such incidents are considered to have more to do with the environment in which work is performed than with the work itself. *Motivators* (intrinsic variables), the second category, are assumed to be sources of job satisfaction. They relate to the job itself and include achievement, recognition, work itself, responsibility, and advancement. Thus, the theory argues that job dissatisfaction and job satisfaction ensue from different sources; satisfaction depends on intrinsic factors, while dissatisfaction is the result of extrinsic factors.

CONSTRUCTION OF SATISFACTION 21 PLAYING DECK

Make photocopies of satisfaction, dissatisfaction, and decoy cards on card stock paper. Cut out the appropriate numbers of each card. A complete deck suited to a playing group of three or four players consists of 20 satisfaction cards (four of each kind), 30 dissatisfaction cards (six of each kind), and 15 decoy cards (three of each kind).

SATISFIERS	DISSATISFIERS	DECOY CARDS
Achievement	Policy and Administration	Rituals
Recognition	Supervision	Training
Work Itself	Salary	Visibility
Responsibility	Interpersonal Relations	Longevity
Advancement	Working Conditions	Company Size

STRESSBUSTERS

TOPIC Recognizing and Reducing Stress

LEARNING OBJECTIVE Participants will be able to identify three job-related stressors.

NUMBER OF PARTICIPANTS 12 to 25

PLAYING TIME 10-15 minutes

REFERENCE Robinson, Jerry W. (1980). *Understanding and managing stress.* Urbana, IL: self-published.

REQUIRED MATERIALS Pencils, small strips of paper (2.5 by 0.5 inches), and party balloons

TO PLAY

1. Introduce players to the concept of stress (its causes and symptoms, and potential stress reducers).
2. Pass out game materials (one pencil, three small strips of paper, and three party balloons) to each participant.
3. Ask players to think of three things at their jobs that are causing them a great amount of stress. Have them write one stress producer on each of the small pieces of paper.
4. Direct participants to place their small pieces of paper into three separate balloons.
5. Have players blow up and tie the ends of each of their balloons. They should be blown up as much as possible without bursting. Furthermore, the ends of balloons must be securely tied so as not to allow any air to escape.
6. Inform players that they are going into the "stressbusting" business. Advise them that when you call, "Stressbusters," they are to attempt to burst their three balloons as quickly as possible by sitting on them. The first player to break all her/his balloons will be declared the winner. If they so choose, players may attempt to break more than one balloon at a time.
7. Call, "Stressbusters."
8. After a player has broken all of her/his balloons, declare her/him the winner and "Master Stressbuster."
9. Debrief the players. Besides bursting balloons, ask participants to suggest ways workers can reduce job-related stress.

When someone is under severe job-related stress, behavioral, cognitive, emotional, and physical changes may occur. The following symptoms may be evident in varying degrees and combinations.

Figure 2.1. Common signs and symptoms of severe stress.

Behavioral Symptoms	Cognitive Symptoms
■ Crying ■ Withdrawal ■ Retardation ■ Agitation ■ Misplaced aggression ■ Hallucination	■ Negative self-concept ■ Negative view of world ■ Negative expectations of the future ■ Self-blame ■ Indecisiveness ■ Helplessness ■ Hopelessness ■ Worthlessness ■ Delusions (of guilt, sin, worthlessness)
Emotional Symptoms	**Physical Symptoms**
■ Sadness ■ Guilt ■ Anxiety ■ Anger ■ Diurnal mood variation ■ Nervousness or tension	■ Frequent migraine headaches ■ Sleep disorder ■ Low back pain ■ Eating disorder ■ Constipation or diarrhea ■ Menstrual irregularity ■ Impotence/frigidity ■ Rapid weight loss ■ Easily fatigued ■ Other pain of unexplained origin ■ Diminished sexual drive

To reduce stress, it is often recommended that individuals do what is recommended in Fig. 2.2.

Figure 2.2. Stress reducers.

✓ Be proactive.
✓ Exercise.
✓ Eat a balanced diet.
✓ Get a good night's sleep.
✓ Engage in deep relaxation.
✓ Have a support group.
✓ Keep a positive mental attitude.
✓ Plan and get recreation.

SOURCE: Published with permission of Jerry Robinson, Room 130 Ewing Hall, P.O. Box 3134, Cleveland, MS 38733.

THE HAPPY HIERARCHY

TOPIC   Need Motivation Theory

**LEARNING
OBJECTIVE**   Participants will be able to identify and appropriately sequence Maslow's five universal needs.

**NUMBER OF
PARTICIPANTS**   Any number of players in multiples of five

PLAYING TIME   10-15 minutes

REFERENCE   Maslow, A. (1954). *Motivation and personality.* New York: Harper & Row.

**REQUIRED
MATERIALS**   Felt-tip markers, straight pins, and Maslow's Smiley Faces Name Badges

TO PLAY
1. Familiarize participants with the general concept of need motivation.
2. Go over the learning objective for the game.
3. Pass out the game materials. Each person should receive a Maslow's Smiley Faces Name Badge and a straight pin.
4. Circulate felt-tip markers among participants. Ask players to print their names on their badges and pin the badges to their clothing.
5. Advise players that the goal of the game is be the first group of five participants to correctly assemble themselves at the front of the room.
6. Explain that a correctly constituted group will contain five members wearing badges that include all of Maslow's need motivators. The group must stand at the front of the room, with the person with the lowest need in Maslow's hierarchy being the first one in the line and the person with Maslow's highest need being the last one in the line. All players between the first and last players must be standing in the correct order.
7. Direct players to assemble themselves as quickly as possible.
8. Declare the first group of players assembling themselves correctly the winning group.
9. Debrief players. Review Maslow's Hierarchy of Needs theory. Ask players to identify specific ways their organizations might provide opportunities for employees to satisfy some of the universal needs identified by Maslow.

To prepare a set of Maslow's Smiley Faces Name Badges, photocopy the following items on card stock paper and cut out the individual cards.

SURVIVAL

SAFETY

BELONGINGNESS

SELF-ESTEEM

SELF-ACTUALIZATION

Chapter Three
CAREER DEVELOPMENT GAMES

The games in Chap. 3 pertain to career development. The authors believe that instruction in career building should begin with helping highly motivated learners understand themselves (their interests, skills, and values), the process of choosing an occupation, and how people develop careerwise over their life spans. Three games are based on John Holland's Occupational Congruence Theory. They include *Class Elections, Morrow's Mirrors,* and *RIASEC Bingo.* Others games, like *Anchor Actups* and *Super-O,* relate to Edgar Schein's well-known theory concerning "career anchors" and Donald Super's Career Development Theory. *Values Swap Shop* is based on items appearing on the Minnesota Importance Questionnaire. *Matching Orientations* is based on Brooklyn Derr's Career Success Map. An understanding of these theories provides participants a solid framework in which to think about and discuss their own career development.

Because choosing a career requires knowledge of occupations in addition to an understanding of oneself, the remaining games in Chap. 3 focus on job analysis skills. For example, the game *Jobs Analyst* assists players in analyzing occupations in terms of people, data, things, and ideas. *Lovers and Fighters* involves players in a task analysis of their current jobs. *Secretary's Dream Job* can be used to help players imagine or focus on the types of jobs they "really want."

ANCHOR ACTUPS

TOPIC

Career Anchors

LEARNING OBJECTIVE

Participants will be able to associate various career behaviors to Schein's career anchors.

NUMBER OF PARTICIPANTS

Any number divided into groups of 10-12 players each

PLAYING TIME

20-25 minutes

SOURCE

Schein, E. H. (1993). *Career anchors: Discovering your real values*, rev. ed. San Diego: Feiffer.

REQUIRED MATERIALS

Career Anchor Name Cards (see App. B), straight pins, Sea Creature Cards (50 for each Sea Bag), One Sea Bag for each group (small brown paper bags), and one Career Anchor Score Card for each group

TO PLAY

1. Introduce participants to Schein's career anchors. Carefully explain Schein's five career anchors.
2. State the learning objective for the game.
3. Pass out Career Anchor Name Cards. Have participants record their *names* and the *two anchors* which best characterize their past career behaviors. Have players pin Career Anchor Name Cards to their blouses or shirts.
4. Divide participants into groups of 10-12 players each. Each group must have members with a variety of career anchors.
5. Ask each group to form a circle and choose a "Sea Captain" from among its members. The Captain will be responsible for keeping score and enforcing the rules within the group.
6. Supply each group with a Sea Bag and and a Career Anchors Score Card (see below for contents of Sea Bag).
7. Tell players that the object of the game is to be the first person to get 9 points in her/his group. Points are earned when a player draws a Sea Creatures Card from the Sea Bag that matches one of the two anchors on her/his Career Anchor Name Card and then acts out the story line on the card.
8. Inform participants that the game begins with the person to the left of the Captain drawing first. If the card matches one of the anchors of the person drawing it, she/he acts out what is on the card and receives the number of points printed on it. Play continues clockwise around the group. The Captain collects the cards drawn from the Sea Bag for safekeeping.
9. Advise players that, if an individual draws a Sea Creature Card of a different anchor than what she/he is wearing, she/he has the option of either putting the card back in the bag and letting the next person draw or handing the card to any other person in her/his group who is wearing a corresponding Career Anchor Name Card. If that

person acts out what is on the card, she/he receives the number of points printed on it and play continues with the person to her/his immediate left. Make sure that participants understand that passing a Sea Creature Card to another player may afford that player an opportunity to score points and at the same time deny other players the opportunity to draw a Sea Creature Card during that round.

10. When a member of a group earns 9 points, declare her/him the winner.

11. Debrief players. Discuss with players the analogy of a ship's anchor to Schein's career anchors. Ask participants if they believe their career anchors have helped or thwarted their own career development.

SCHEIN'S ORGANIZATION CAREER DEVELOPMENT MODEL

Managing one's career involves balancing individual needs and strengths with the realities of the workplace (employing organization). Schein, in his organization model, attempts to mesh individual and organizational aspects of career development. With respect to the external dimensions of a worker's career (i.e., one's employing organization), Schein recognizes three types of career moves. They include hierarchical (mostly up in the managerial ranks as a result of promotions), functional or technical (along the dimension of technical or professional expertise), and toward the "inner circle" (access to organization's decision makers, privileges, and secrets).

Schein believes that individuals and organizations interact in ways to meet their respective needs. Through these interactions, individuals develop occupational self-concepts, which become "career anchors." Embodied in the anchors are self-perceived talents, abilities, motives, needs, attitudes, and values. Career anchors greatly influence the career choices and decisions workers make. Common career anchors include:

- *Technical competence.* Perceptions of and concerns about one's technical abilities.
- *Managerial competence.* Perceptions of and concerns about managerial tasks, challenges, and responsibilities.
- *Security and stability.* Perceptions of and concerns about being trusted in one's organization.
- *Creativity.* Perceptions of and concerns about creating new products and/or processes.
- *Autonomy.* Perceptions of and concerns about freedom from organizational constraints.

CONSTRUCTION OF SEA BAGS

Decorate plain brown paper bags (about the size of a lunch bag or a little larger) with symbols or pictures of objects related to the sea. Photocopy the Sea Creature Cards on card stock paper and cut out the individual items. Place two sets of the 25 cards into each bag.

TECHNICAL CREATURE CARD

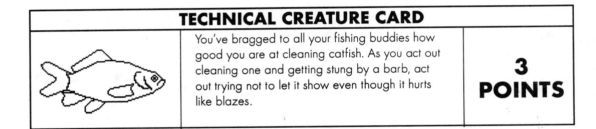

You've only sailed in calm waters, but now a ferocious storm is blowing up. Act out getting your boat to safe harbor.

5 POINTS

TECHNICAL CREATURE CARD

You are deep sea fishing when what feels like a whale takes your hook. Act out landing the fish.

4 POINTS

TECHNICAL CREATURE CARD

You've bragged to all your fishing buddies how good you are at cleaning catfish. As you act out cleaning one and getting stung by a barb, act out trying not to let it show even though it hurts like blazes.

3 POINTS

TECHNICAL CREATURE CARD

Because you are such a talented octopus, your boss has given you the task of providing music for the lobster/crab wedding. Act out playing all your instruments simultaneously.

2 POINTS

TECHNICAL CREATURE CARD

As an expert diver you are to retrieve gold from a haunted sunken ship. Act out getting the goods while avoiding the "ghoulies."

2 POINTS

MANAGERIAL CREATURE CARD

| 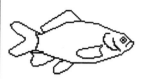 | You are captain of the south sea's nastiest pirate ship. Lead your band of cutthroats in plundering a ship loaded with treasure. | **5 POINTS** |

MANAGERIAL CREATURE CARD

| 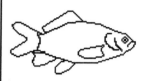 | You are head fish in a school of tuna when you see a net looming ahead. Lead your group to safety. | **4 POINTS** |

MANAGERIAL CREATURE CARD

| 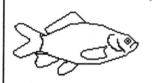 | You are commander in chief of a fleet of new recruit whales. Demonstrate to them the proper method of spraying water out of the tops of their heads. | **3 POINTS** |

MANAGERIAL CREATURE CARD

| 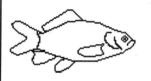 | You are an electric eel in charge of the annual ocean creatures parade. Act out getting the participants lined up in proper order while maintaining peace between natural combatants. | **2 POINTS** |

MANAGERIAL CREATURE CARD

| 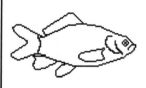 | You are captain of a cruise ship. All of your crew have succumbed to a mysterious stomach ailment after a stop at the last port. Act out trying to stay awake and on course. | **2 POINTS** |

SECURITY CREATURE CARD

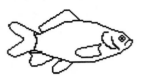

You are a lovely mermaid who has just found a shipwrecked sailor floating on a raft. Without words, convince this disoriented man to trust you to get him to safety.

5 POINTS

SECURITY CREATURE CARD

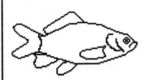

Crabs walk sideways and lobsters walk straight, but you are a crab who wants to be friends with a lobster. Show the lobster that, even though you're different, you can be trusted.

4 POINTS

SECURITY CREATURE CARD

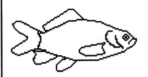

Last week was your turn being lead porpoise in your group and you almost got the group "beached." Now they won't have anything to do with you. Act out winning back their acceptance.

3 POINTS

SECURITY CREATURE CARD

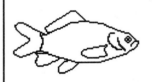

You are a cowardly skinny shark who is laughed at by the other sharks because you are afraid of the very creatures you must catch to eat. Act out overcoming your fears to gain the respect of your peers.

2 POINTS

SECURITY CREATURE CARD

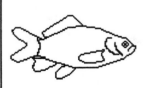

You are seen as just the wimpy little cook on a ship of nasty pirates. Act out grabbing a cutlass and saving the life of one of your "mates" during battle in a very awe-inspiring performance.

2 POINTS

CREATIVITY CREATURE CARD	
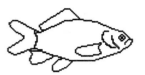 You are a porpoise at sea world and your trainer is holding some prize perch over your head. Show him some very creative tricks so that you'll get the fish.	**5 POINTS**

CREATIVITY CREATURE CARD	
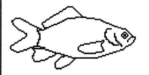 You are Charlie Tuna and wish to be caught by Starkist, but they keep throwing you back. Try some new tactics so that they'll take notice of you.	**4 POINTS**

CREATIVITY CREATURE CARD	
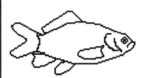 Sea turtles glide through the water with the aid of streamlined bodies and powerful flippers. Demonstrate how to swim gracefully with an arthritic left flipper.	**3 POINTS**

CREATIVITY CREATURE CARD	
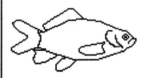 You have been adrift on a life raft for three days. With the sharks circling, act out ways of getting the attention of planes overhead and ships in the distance without becoming lunch.	**2 POINTS**

CREATIVITY CREATURE CARD	
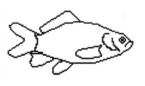 As a tropical fish, you have a passion for the taste of curly sea ivy and have developed a system of cultivating it in an underwater garden. Demonstrate how this might be done.	**2 POINTS**

AUTONOMY CREATURE CARD

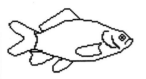

You're tired of swimming around in circles with a bunch of smelt. Act out breaking free from this school of bores and exploring the ocean around you on your own.

5 POINTS

AUTONOMY CREATURE CARD

You are a marine biologist who is trying to collect plant life specimens from the ocean floor. Act out doing this while a large snapping turtle is pestering you.

4 POINTS

AUTONOMY CREATURE CARD

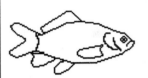

As a bigger-than-average oyster, you are trying to create a large perfect pearl, but a fisherman wants you and the pearl. Show him that you don't want to be bothered.

3 POINTS

AUTONOMY CREATURE CARD

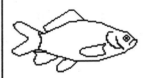

As low man on a seagoing vessel, you are tired of swabbing decks and the idiot who keeps telling you how to do it. Show him how you'd like to use the mop.

2 POINTS

AUTONOMY CREATURE CARD

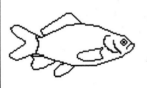

You are captain of a Spanish galleon filled with treasure, and another one of those pesky pirate ships is on your tail again. Show how you'd deal with the nasty little creeps.

2 POINTS

SCORE CARD		ANCHOR ACTUPS						
Players	Points							

SCORE CARD		ANCHOR ACTUPS						
Players	Points							

SCORE CARD		ANCHOR ACTUPS						
Players	Points							

CLASS ELECTIONS

TOPIC
Holland's Six Personality Types and Corresponding Work Environments

LEARNING OBJECTIVE
Participants will be able to associate selected jobs with John Holland's six personality types.

NUMBER OF PARTICIPANTS
8 to 24 players

PLAYING TIME
20-25 minutes depending on the number of players

REFERENCES
Gottfredson, G. D., & Holland, J. L. (1989). *Dictionary of Holland occupational codes*, 2nd ed. Odessa: Psychological Assessment Resources.

Holland, J. L. (1985). *Making vocational choices: A theory of vocational personalities and work environments*. Englewood Cliffs: Prentice-Hall.

REQUIRED MATERIALS
Overhead projector, Class Officers Transparency, list of Officers' Responsibilities, and a small piece of scratch paper.

TO PLAY

1. Introduce players to the notion that people's personalities make them more or less suited for various types of occupations.

2. Go over the learning objective for the game.

3. Explain that there is going to be an election of class officers two weeks from today. However, before an election can be held, the class needs to come up with a slate of candidates.

4. Place the Class Officers transparency on the overhead projector. Tell participants that these are the offices that may be filled.

5. Advise players that they will soon be divided into pairs. As partners they will have the opportunity to interview each other for 10 minutes. After 10 minutes, each person will place her/his partner's name in nomination for one of the six class offices and explain why they believe the partner is well suited for this job.

6. Inform players that during the interviews they cannot ask their partner's preference for serving in an office, nor can they reveal to their partners the specific office for which they are going to nominate them.

7. Go over the responsibilities for each office. Feel free to expand the responsibilities listed under "Office Responsibilities."

8. Divide the group into pairs. Provide them 10 minutes to interview each other. Explain that the purpose of the interviews is to find out more about their partner's personality (interests, competencies, and other traits).

9. After 10 minutes of interviewing, go around the room permitting each person to nominate her/his partner for one of the six class offices. Give her/him 30 seconds to state why she/he believes her/his partner is suited for an office. Keep track of the number of individuals nominated for each position.

10. Explain that the six respective offices are examples of jobs from Holland's six personality types. AV Equipment Operator is a Realistic type of occupation. Research Consultant is an Investigative type. Classroom Decorator is an Artistic type. Social Coordinator is a Social type. Class President is an Enterprising type. And Record Keeper is a Conventional type.

11. Tell players that you are about to read brief descriptions of these types and that they are to decide which type best describes them.

12. Read a description of Holland's six personality types (see the game Morrow's Mirrors for a description of the types).

13. Ask players to write down on pieces of scratch paper the personality types they believe most closly matches their own personalities.

14. If the types they write down are the same types as the offices for which their partners nominated them, award the partners 5 points each. Congratulate these players for being keen observers of people's personalities.

15. If both partners of a pair receive 5 points in step 12, declare them winners and refer to them as "terrific type tellers."

16. Debrief players. Discuss some of the difficulties players had in matching their partners to a suitable office. Speculate on the reasons why some of the offices had several nominees and others had fewer or none. Inquire into what this says about the class. Ask players if they think the personality types are distributed similarly throughout the greater society.

To make the Class Officers Transparency, photocopy the following item onto a blank transparency sheet.

Class Officers

❶ AV Equipment Operator

❷ Research Consultant

❸ Classroom Decorator

❹ Social Coordinator

❺ Class President

❻ Record Keeper

OFFICE RESPONSIBILITIES

- **AV Equipment Operator.** Take care of all audiovisual equipment including the set-up and repair of overhead projectors, slide equipment, film projectors, and other apparatus.

- **Research Consultant.** Assist classmates in locating research information, accessing computerized databases, and performing statistical analyses of data.

- **Classroom Decorator.** Beautify the classroom by means of plants, attractive posters, special lighting, and pleasant room arrangements.

- **Social Coordinator.** Arrange social gatherings, send greeting cards, and see to it that all participants know each other by the end of the course.

- **Class President.** Act as the leader and spokesperson for the class.

- **Record Keeper.** Prepare a class roster, maintain accurate attendance records, and oversee sign-up sheets.

JOBS ANALYST

TOPIC   Job Analysis

**LEARNING
OBJECTIVE**   Participants will be able to identify occupations that predominantly involve working with
                     people, data, things, and ideas.

**NUMBER OF
PARTICIPANTS**   Any number

PLAYING TIME   25–30 minutes

REFERENCE   Prediger, D., Swaney, K,. and Mau, W. (1993). The world-of-work map. *Journal of Coun-
                     seling & Development, 71, 425.*

**REQUIRED
MATERIALS**   Pencils and Job Analysis Worksheet

TO PLAY

1. Introduce players to the skill of task analysis. Discuss how the skill might be used in selecting an appropriate career.

2. Go over the learning objective for the game.

3. Provide definitions and examples of people, data, things, and ideas involved in many
   work tasks.

4. Explain to participants that they are about to try their hands at job analysis and that
   they will be divided into small teams of four members each.

5. Divide the larger group into small groups of four members each.

6. Pass out a pencil and Job Analysis Worksheet to each participant.

7. Go over the directions at the top of the worksheet. Advise players that the goal is to
   come up with as many occupations as they can to fit into the 16 cells.

8. Tell players they will have 15 minutes to complete their worksheets.

9. Answer any questions players may have and direct the groups to begin.

10. After 15 minutes, call, "Time."

11. Give participants the correct answers while they check the accuracy of their re-
    sponses.

12. Declare the group with the greatest number of correct answers the winners.

13. Debrief the players. Have participants write down what percentage of their current
    job is spent on working with people, data, things, and ideas. Discuss what they would
    like for these percentages to be.

Figure 3.1. Explanations of people, data, things, and ideas tasks

PEOPLE TASKS

Can involve serving, speaking with, persuading, supervising, instructing, negotiating, and mentoring of individuals.

DATA TASKS

Can involve counting, copying, comparing, compiling, and computing of facts and/or information pertaining to people, animals, and objects.

THINGS TASKS

Can involve handling, tending, manipulating, operating, and controlling of inanimate objects.

IDEAS TASKS

Can involve extrapolating, analyzing, synthesizing, and evaluation of information and concepts.

Figure 3.2. Examples of people, data, things, and ideas jobs

PEOPLE JOBS

Counselor
Minister
Police officer
Teacher

DATA JOBS

Accountant
Bookkeeper
Clerk
Secretary

THINGS JOBS

Carpenter
Farmer
Machine operator
Mechanic

IDEAS JOBS

Artist
Architect
Composer
Scientist

Directions: The following table has four columns titled People, Data, Things, and Ideas. There are also four rows headed by the letters J, O, B, and S. In column 1 write in the names of occupations that predominantly involve working with people and in column 2 careers that predominately involve working with data. Do the same in columns 3 and 4 for occupations primarily requiring working with things and ideas. However, all the occupations must begin with the letters J, O, B, or S and be recorded in the row bearing that letter. For example the occupation "Jailer" would be written in column 1 (people) and row 1 (J).

	People	Data	Things	Ideas
J	Jailer			
O				
B				
S				

LOVERS AND FIGHTERS

TOPIC Loves and Hates of Current Job Tasks

LEARNING OBJECTIVE Participants will be able to determine how much they love doing their current job tasks.

NUMBER OF PARTICIPANTS Any number

PLAYING TIME 20–25 minutes

REFERENCE None

REQUIRED MATERIALS Lovers and Fighters playing board, pencils, and Job Task Cards

TO PLAY

1. Introduce players to the concept of jobs tasks (i.e., the job itself).

2. Go over the learning objective for the game.

3. Pass out a pencil and 20 Job Task Cards to each player.

4. Ask players to write on the cards major tasks they do at work. Have them write down tasks that they do frequently and that take up a significant portion of their time. Advise them to write down the tasks in short phrases like, "Make cold sales calls," "Resolve customer complaints," and "Write monthly sales reports."

5. After players are satisfied that their cards are representative of the tasks they perform, pass out the Lovers and Fighters playing board.

6. Explain that they are about to find out if they spend most of their time on the job being lovers of their work or fighters of their work. Ask them to now place their Job Task Cards on the board according to two criteria. First have players place their cards in the appropriate column. If they love to perform the task on a card, then it goes in column 1, "Love Doing." If they strongly dislike doing a task and usually have to make themselves do it, then the card goes in column 3, "Fight Doing." If they neither love nor hate doing a task, the card is placed in column 2, "Do."

7. Now have players place their cards in the appropriate row. If they spend more than 10 percent of their total work time performing a task then it goes in row 1, "10+%." If they spend 7–10 percent of their time on the task, the card goes in row 2, "7–10%," and so on. All cards should end up being in one of the 12 rectangles on the board. The tasks players love doing the most and spend an appreciable amount of their time performing will be clustered in the upper left corner of the board. The tasks that players fight doing the most but spend a great portion of their time performing will be clustered in the upper right corner of the board.

8. Have players add up the number of cards they placed in rows 1 and 2 of column 1 (the top two left cells).

9. Have players count the number of cards they placed in rows 1 and 2 of column 3 (the top two right cells).

70

10. Have players compare the two numbers. Ask players who placed more cards in the upper left cells to raise their hands. These are workers who have more major job tasks that they love doing than they fight doing. Declare them winners and "lovers of their work."

11. Ask players who placed more cards in the upper right cells to raise their hands. These are workers who have more major job tasks that they fight doing than they love doing. Declare them "fighters of their work."

12. Debrief players. Discuss what is more important to the players, the job itself (i.e., how much they enjoy performing the tasks they do everyday) or the context of a job (i.e., working conditions, salary, job security, and other circumstances).

JOB TASK CARDS

To make a set of Job Task Cards, photocopy the following page and cut out the 20 rectangles.

LOVERS AND FIGHTERS

	LOVE DOING	DO	FIGHT DOING
10+%			
7–10%			
4–6%			
1–3%			

MATCHING ORIENTATIONS

TOPIC Brooklyn Derr's Career Orientations

LEARNING OBJECTIVE Participants will be able to identify the career orientations held by various individuals.

NUMBER OF PARTICIPANTS 10-20 players divided into competing teams of five players each

PLAYING TIME 25-30 minutes

REFERENCE Derr, C. B. (1988). *Managing the new careerists.* San Francisco: Jossey-Bass.

REQUIRED MATERIALS Set of Orientation Cards for each player and Orientation Case Studies

TO PLAY
1. Give the learning objective for the game.
2. Briefly describe Derr's five career orientations (descriptions follow).
3. Divide participants into teams of five players each.
4. Supply each player a set of Orientation Cards.
5. Assign someone who is not a member of any team to be the scorekeeper.
6. Arrange opposing teams into facing parallel rows seated approximately 4 feet apart.
7. Inform participants that they will be read 12 case studies. After the reading of each case study, they will have 10 seconds to select an orientation from their Orientation Cards that they believe most closely matches the orientation of the person in the case.
8. Explain that for a team to score, at least three of five members must come up with the correct orientation. Since 12 case studies will be presented, 12 is the highest score obtainable by any team.
9. Tell players that, after a case study is read, they are to: (a) pull the correct Orientation Card from their decks of cards as quickly as possible, (b) place the card face down on their laps, and (c) wait until the facilitator calls, "Match." Let players know that, when "Match" is called, they are to hold up their cards so that the scorekeeper can determine if at least three persons on their team have selected the correct orientations.
10. Read one of the case studies for practice.
11. After contestants have held up their cards, give the correct answer aloud.
12. Have the scorekeeper score the round for practice. Each team who has three of its five members with the correct orientation should receive 1 point.
13. Begin playing the game according to the directions provided in steps 7-12.
14. At the end of 12 case studies, members of the team with the greatest number of points are declared winners. If necessary read an additional case study to break any ties.

15. Debrief players. Ask players to identify which of Derr's orientations most closely resembles their own career orientation. Discuss a few of the strategies Derr offers for implementing some of these orientations (see Fig. 3.3).

DESCRIPTION OF DERR'S FIVE CAREER ORIENTATIONS

Derr believes that individuals hold varying orientations toward work. One orientation is often dominant. It is not uncommon for persons to switch from one orientation to a similar orientation. The five orientations include:

1. *Getting ahead.* These individuals are interested in climbing the corporate ladder. They are turned on by status, money, and power. They are fiercely competitive. While many individuals hold this orientation in the earlier stages of their careers, few are willing to make the personal sacrifices necessary to be successful at it. Assessment centers are considered by Derr to be a particularly appropriate organization career development/management intervention for identifying getting ahead individuals. Holders of this orientation are perhaps the easiest to manage.

2. *Getting secure.* Holders are willing to give loyalty to the organization in return for a sense of belonging. They are the preservers of the company's collective history. These workers usually take a "local," as opposed to "cosmopolitan," view. While getting secure types are interested in advancing in their organizations, they are often more patient and more willing to wait for promotions than the get ahead types. The getting secure orientation has the fewest fallback orientations.

3. *Getting free.* Persons with this orientation want the freedom to do things their way. They are hard working, creative, and set high standards for themselves. They have little interest in climbing the corporate ladder. They are more interested in finding new and better ways of doing things than adhering to traditional practices.

4. *Getting balanced.* This is perhaps the newest of the orientations to emerge in the American culture. While these individuals want to have challenging and meaningful careers, they do not look to their careers to meet all or even most of their psychological needs. They also want a family life and time to pursue other interests. Individuals of this orientation are most similar to the getting free and getting high types.

5. *Getting high.* In this more than any other orientation, holders define career success in terms of the *content,* not the *context* of work. They look to the work itself as a major source of career satisfaction. They may be highly specialized in their fields. They may also love adventure or be highly successful entrepreneurs. Some may approach their work as a religious calling.

Figure 3.3. Quick reference to personality traits and implementation strategies.

Getting Ahead

Personality
- Wants to be upwardly mobile, member of inner circle.
- Likes lots of responsibility and authority.
- Likes to be very highly rewarded based on results.
- Craves challenge.

Strategies
- Put your job first.
- Have a career plan and move quickly.
- Get a sponsor.
- Punch the right tickets.
- Run on challenge.

Getting Secure

Personality
- Is very loyal to the company—"married to the company."
- Wants to move up but is willing to take a turn.
- Is willing to do about any job to help the organization.
- Highly values job security.

Strategies
- Find the right company.
- Study the company's culture and fit in.
- Put organization's needs first.
- Become member of inner circle.
- Build up social debts.

Getting Free

Personality
- Has a tough streak of independence.
- Hates conformity and compliance.
- Is hard to get to know, aloof.
- Likes to carve out a little niche in which he/she possesses irreplaceable expertise.

Strategies
- Pay your dues.
- Keep one step ahead of the game.
- Hoard, control, and manipulate scarce information.
- When the chips are down, come through.
- Expand your peer group.

Getting Balanced

Personality
- Camouflages his/her orientation.
- Values having a personal life and a career.
- Is hard working and willing to pitch in during a crisis.
- Wants to "smell the roses."

Strategies
- Pay your dues and follow the rules.
- Get a sponsor.
- Keep your career strategy to yourself.
- Resist tempting job assignments.
- Watch your timing.

Getting High

Personality
- Is talented and wants to use his/her talents.
- Is easily bored.
- Is motivated by stimulating work, not by the money.
- Is a good idea person, poor manager.

Strategies
- Be prepared to deliver brilliantly.
- Pay your dues.
- Seek out stimulating tasks.
- Learn the skills of persuasion.
- Be ready to seize opportunities.

SOURCE: Published with permission of Jossey-Bass, Inc., 350 Sansome St., San Francisco, CA 94104.

To make a set of Orientation Cards, photocopy the following items using card stock paper and cut them out.

Getting Ahead

Getting Free

Getting High

Getting Secure

Getting Balanced

1. Laura is a 30-year-old junior attorney who has been working in a large corporate law firm for two years. All through college and law school, she was at the top of her class, working nights and weekends in the library on extra projects for her professors. This drive and ambition have been transferred to the law firm where, working constantly, she always seems one step ahead of her co-workers. Laura spends little time socializing with those who aren't in a position to help her advance. Accurately predicting the next moves of her superiors, Laura seems to know just how to apply that information to her best advantage. What is Laura's career orientation?

2. Alan has been a specialist with a large advertising company for the past six years. At 31, he's already brought in several large accounts with his creativity. His superiors are impressed with his drive and dedication to the company. As a result of his hard work, he has rapidly been promoted to a supervisory level where he manages projects involving people senior to himself. Some of the other employees find Alan aggressive and pushy, but he knows exactly where he wants to go and the ground rules for getting there. He drives the "right" car, belongs to the "right" organizations, and dates only young women who appear to be potential "executive wife" material. What is Alan's career orientation?

3. Matthew, an up and coming manager in his late twenties, knows just how to get where he's going. Though he's only been with the company for three years, early on he sought out a mentor who could help him advance and assiduously courted his approval and sponsorship. He takes work home every night and most weekends. In his spare time, Matthew plays racquetball and tennis and is very competitive in all that he does. Matthew projects a charming personality and is well liked among his co-workers. He sees himself achieving at least two promotions in the next two to three years and an executive position by the time he's in his middle forties. What is Matthew's career orientation?

4. Ralph started working for a large accounting firm when it was founded 25 years ago. Over the years, he has risen to middle management as supervisor over dozens of projects. He enjoys doing all the paperwork involved in his job and is very proud of the part he's played in the steady growth of the company. Ralph likes nothing better than expounding on the origins and traditions of the organization to new employees. He sees those who would stray from the paths of tradition as traitors and unworthy of working in such a fine organization. What is Ralph's career orientation?

5. Albert has been with the same international banking company for 30 years. His father and grandfather also worked for "the company" all their working lives. Though all three of the men started out "at the bottom," only Albert achieved a senior management position. This brings his father enormous pride and would have brought great joy to his grandfather were he still living. As a child, Albert learned about "company traditions" and that hard work and company loyalty brings great rewards and recognition, and he follows those maxims to the letter. Albert is well liked by his co-workers, but they sometimes jokingly say behind his back that he must be the reincarnation of old man Johnson, the man who founded the company in 1893. What is Albert's career orientation?

6. At 50, Sarah is the Assistant to the Vice-President of a medium-sized textile firm. She started out in the steno pool 28 years ago, and her loyalty to the company helped her to rise to her present position, which she's held for the past 15 years. Sarah doggedly works to make sure that everything in the VP's office runs smoothly, reflecting not only the dignity of her esteemed superior, but also the high standards of the company. Sarah is always early to work, often going home late, agreeable to any task asked of her, and devoted to her boss's interests. A few years ago, when a new computer network was installed in the company offices, she took several courses in computer operations and programming. Though working the classes into her already busy schedule was difficult, she felt that not making the extra effort would be letting her boss and the company down. What is Sarah's career orientation?

7. Gary is a political reporter with a major metropolitan newspaper. His genius for getting the inside scoop is legendary. He constantly turns in expense requests for high-priced political dinners, country club bar tabs, first class airline tickets, and many other such items to the distraction of his supervisor. Gary is rarely found at his desk at the newspaper office—again, much to the dismay of his superiors. Gary's writing talent and political savvy attracted the attention of a high-ranking official at the White House, who promptly offered Gary a prestigious job with the President's staff. Gary graciously declined, saying that, though he was honored, he felt that he would prefer to stay in his less prestigious and very much less restrictive job. What is Gary's career orientation?

8. Larry is an account salesman with a medical supply company. He has occupied this position for five years. For the past four years he has held the record for yearly sales for the entire company, bringing in millions of dollars in business. Rather a flamboyant character, Larry is well liked and respected by his co-workers and clients. His charm has gotten him a top-of-the-line car to drive, complete with cellular phone and portable computer at company expense. The only point of contention between him and his supervisor is Larry's frequent failure to attend department meetings, often not coming into the office for days. Instead, he will call in orders to secretaries, causing them extra work. Larry knows that, if the company forced him to "punch a time clock," he would have to find another company that would let him "do his thing." What is Larry's career orientation?

9. John is a project manager with a large engineering firm. He is a genius at his craft. State-of-the-art equipment, cutting edge technology, constantly learning new things, and affiliation with those in his field are some of the things that turn John on, but being able to do his work in his own way is the most important thing in his life. Because the company gives him access to some of the most challenging work anywhere, and supplies him with the latitude to work without someone looking over his shoulder, he enjoys working for his present employer. He goes after the most challenging projects with fervor, becomes completely absorbed in his work, and never fails to put out top-quality work. What is John's career orientation?

10. Karen, a working mother of two small children, loves her work and is brilliant at it. During her pregnancies, she negotiated for and got a home workstation so that she could at least work part-time. Since she isn't interested in the friendly fellowship of her co-workers, that arrangement suited her quite well. She goes after the most challenging projects with a vigorous determination and puts her heart into them when she lands them. In her eyes, an exciting assignment is much better than any promotion and has, in fact, turned down two impressive promotions so that she could continue doing what she likes best. What is Karen's career orientation?

11. George, at 35, has worked for a large metropolitan police force for the past 13 years. In that period of time, he has worked in several different capacities, starting out as a patrol officer and recently promoted to head of the homicide investigation team. His natural abilities, enhanced by his taking advantage of every training class or program that comes along, and his love for his work have made George a valuable member of the force. He feels that, when he has experienced all the professional growth he can from this job, perhaps he'll try for a position with the FBI or CIA. George has remained single by choice. He spends his spare time and vacations sky diving, hang gliding, or engaged in one of the many challenging activities that has caught his interest. What is George's career orientation?

12. Martin, at 50, has the money and success that most people dream of. The money itself is not important to him. Rather, it's the thrill of the challenge and winning. Martin is an entrepreneur in the greatest sense. His entire adult life has been spent on starting up new businesses, making them extremely profitable, selling them for obscene amounts of money, and moving on when the challenge subsides. He works long hours and, even when he is at home, seems distracted. This is usually because his mind is busy with solutions to problems in his current endeavor or an idea for a new venture has presented itself. Martin doesn't have many close friends, but rather business associates. He sometimes regrets not being home much when his kids were growing up, but thinks perhaps he'll be able to spend more time with his grandchildren. This thought gives him an idea for a new chain of child care centers. What is Martin's career orientation?

13. Carol is a music teacher at a high school in a medium-sized Midwestern city. She has a lovely voice and sings occasionally with a local band. Her husband, Don, is a language arts instructor at the community college. He is also a talented musician, playing several instruments masterfully. Friends have encouraged the couple to form a duo act and try for the "big time," but Carol and Don can' t see themselves pursuing that kind of lifestyle. Now that they have both settled in their jobs, they'd like to start a family, but still have time for Carol's watercolor painting and Don's work with the community theater group. What are Carol's and Don's career orientations?

14. Glen and Mary seem to be the "all-American" couple. Living in the South, they both have good jobs. Glen is a sales manager with a large national company, while Mary is head librarian at the city library. They have two children, now both in high school. Glen and Mary are involved in assorted community and school activities. Both of their parents and most of the other family members live nearby, allowing for lots of family get-togethers. The company Glen works for recently decided to open a branch office in the Northeast and offered Glen an excellent promotion as head of the new office. After careful consideration, Glen turned down the promotion because it would mean changing high schools for the children, leaving behind a close-knit family group, Mary having to find another job, and, perhaps worst of all for a Southerner, having to live in the cold climes of the North. Glen could not let his job take that much precedence over his and his family's lives. What are Glen's and Mary's career orientations?

15. Josh and Janet work for the same company, though in different departments. Both worked extremely hard for the first several years to get established and promoted to the positions where they felt they would get the most satisfaction in working and that would fit into their desired lifestyle. Though at present, they have decided that they do not particularly care to have children, they are leaving that option open. They both have many interests outside of work, and Josh has elderly parents who occasionally need his help. Though they never turn down challenging projects at work, both let it be known that the job comes neither first nor last, but will only get its share of their time so that the other parts of their lives will not have to suffer. What are Josh's and Janet's career orientations?

MORROW'S MIRRORS

TOPIC Holland's Six Personality Types

LEARNING OBJECTIVE Participants will be able to identify their own personality types and those of others.

NUMBER OF PARTICIPANTS Six or more

PLAYING TIME 25-30 minutes depending on the number of players

REFERENCES Holland, J. L. (1985). *Making vocational choices: A theory of vocational personalities and work environments.* Englewood Cliffs: Prentice-Hall.

Morrow, James (1993). *Exercise—becoming familiar with Holland's personality types.* Unpublished manuscript.

REQUIRED MATERIALS Pencils, Morrow's Mirrors Worksheet, and a deck of Morrow's Mirrors Cards

TO PLAY

1. Introduce players to the concept of John Holland's six personality types.
2. Go over the learning objective for the game.
3. Pass out pencils and copies of Morrow's Mirrors Worksheet.
4. Have participants read the brief descriptions of Holland's six personality types.
5. Ask participants to look into Morrow's mirrors (i.e., read each of the descriptions of the personality types again) and compare that image to the personality they see in themselves. Explain that no one type will be an exact reflection of themselves, but one of the types will probably look more like them than the others. Advise players to pay attention to the overall descriptions of the types and not to concentrate on just one or two of its characteristics.
6. As soon as players are satisfied that one type reflects their personality better than the others, have them place a checkmark on that particular mirror.
7. Tell participants that they are now ready to actually play the game, Morrow's Mirrors. Inform them that the goal is to guess the personality type of three other players in the room. For the moment, each player is not to reveal to anyone which personality type he or she has checked.
8. Have the group divide into pairs. Ask each player to pair off with someone he or she knows fairly well.
9. Pass out a deck of Morrow's Mirrows Cards to each player.
10. Explain that they are to guess the personality types of their partners by pulling the correct mirror from their decks and showing it to them. If the mirror is the same personality type that her/his partner has checked on the Morrow's Mirrors Worksheet, the guesser records a 6 on the back of the mirror. If the type does not match that of

her/his partner's, a second guess is made. Guesses continue until the correct mirror has been picked. Second guesses bring 5 points, third guesses bring 4 points, and so on. Points are recorded on the backsides of mirror cards.

11. Repeat steps 8 and 10 two more times.

12. At the end of three rounds, have players total the number of points on the backs of their mirror cards.

13. Declare players with the most points winners and congratulate their partners for making such good "reflections."

14. Debrief players. Identify and discuss the personality codes of individuals whose partners had an easy time guessing their personality types. Elaborate on some of the possible reasons for this ease of identification. Do the same for individuals having personality types that were difficult to identify.

BACKGROUND INFORMATION ON THE RELATIONSHIPS AMONG THE PERSONALITY TYPES

As you read the descriptions of the six personality types, you will see that each type shares some characteristics with some of the other types, but is different from the rest. To help you compare and contrast the six types, Holland's "hexagon," which illustrates the order of the relationships among the types, is shown in Fig. 3.4. Each type shares some characteristics in common with those types adjacent to it on the hexagon. Each type has only a little in common with those types two positions removed from it, and it is very unlike the type opposite it on the hexagon. For example, the Investigative type shares some characteristics in common with the Realistic and Artistic types, has little in common with the Conventional and Social types, and is quite different from the Enterprising type. If you will read the descriptions of the six types once more with the hexagon in mind, the relationships among the types will become clearer.

Figure 3.4. Holland's hexagon. SOURCE: Reproduced by special permission of the Publisher, Psychological Assessment Resources, Inc. from *Making Vocational Choices*, copyright 1973, 1985 by Psychological Assessment Resources, Inc., P.O. Box 998, Odessa, FL 33556. All rights reserved.

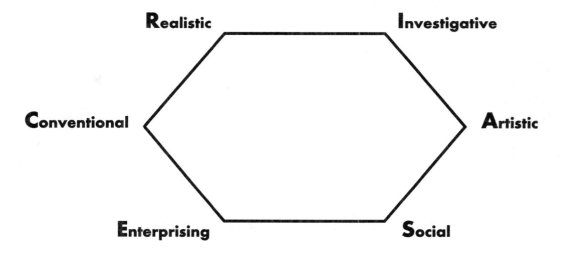

To assist you in further developing an understanding of the relationships among the types, a summary of similarities and differences follows:[1]

- The *Realistic and Investigative types* lack interpersonal skills and have difficulty with emotional expression of feelings. They tend to be reserved and withdrawn in social situations. They differ in the areas of creativity, originality, tolerance for ambiguity, theoretical reasoning, and acceptance of traditional attitudes and values.

- The *Investigative and Artistic types* are original and creative and enjoy abstract tasks. They are independent and prefer to work without supervision. They question traditional attitudes and values. They differ in the areas of self-discipline, logical thinking, and emotional expression of feelings.

- The *Artistic and Social types* are emotional in the expression of feelings. They are idealistic and subjective in outlook. They dislike highly ordered and repetitive activities. They differ in their need for social interaction, helpfulness toward others, and tactfulness in dealing with others.

- The *Social and Enterprising types* are outgoing and friendly. They enjoy being with others, like attention, and are verbally persuasive. They differ in the areas of sensitivity to others' feelings and concern for others' well-being.

- The *Enterprising and Conventional types* are status-conscious and organization-minded. They value physical comfort and material possessions. They differ in the areas of leadership, verbal ability, impulsiveness, orderliness, and tolerance for routine.

- The *Conventional and Realistic types* are conservative and have traditional attitudes and values. They are low on creativity and originality. They are reserved in social interaction situations. They differ in their interests in outdoor, mechanical, and physical activities.

MORROW'S MIRRORS WORKSHEET

Directions: Dr. Jim Morrow's descriptions of Holland's six personality types follow. Which of these types best reflects your own personality? Read over all the descriptions very carefully before making a choice. To indicate your answer, place a checkmark on one of the six mirrors.[2]

[1]SOURCE: Published with permission of Dr. James M. Morrow, 718 Magnolia Street, Mooresville, NC 28115.
[2]Ibid.

82

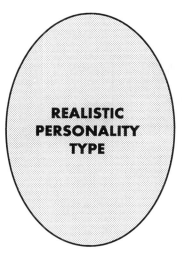

REALISTIC PERSONALITY TYPE

Realistic persons are attracted to outdoor, mechanical, and physical activities, hobbies, and occupations. They like to work with things, objects, and animals rather than with ideas, data, and people. They tend to have mechanical and athletic abilities, and are usually strong and well-coordinated. They like to construct, shape, and restructure things around them and to repair and mend things. They like to use equipment and machinery and to see tangible results from their efforts. Although they are persistent and industrious builders, they are seldom creative and original ones, preferring instead to use familiar methods and to follow established patterns.

They tend to think in terms of absolutes and to have a low tolerance for ambiguity. They have a straightforward and uncomplicated view of life and prefer not to deal with abstract, theoretical, and philosophical issues and problems. They are materialistic and have traditional and conservative values and attitudes.

They do not have strong interpersonal and verbal skills, and are uncomfortable in social situations in which attention is directed at or centered on them. They find it difficult to give emotional expression to their feelings and tend to be regarded as shy.

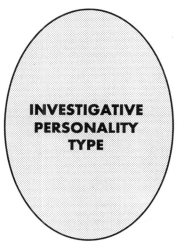

INVESTIGATIVE PERSONALITY TYPE

Investigative persons are naturally curious and inquisitive. They have a need to understand, explain, and predict the things that go on around them. They are scholarly and scientific in their attempts to understand things, and tend to be pessimistic and critical when nonscientific, simplistic, or supernatural explanations are suggested by others. They tend to become engrossed in whatever they are doing, and may appear to be oblivious to everything else around them. They are independent and like to work alone. They prefer neither to supervise others nor to be supervised.

They are theoretical and analytical in outlook, and find abstract and ambiguous problems and situations challenging. They are original and creative, and often find it difficult to accept traditional attitudes and values. They avoid highly structured situations with externally imposed rules, but are themselves internally well-disciplined, precise, and systematic in thought and action. They have confidence in their intellectual abilities, but often feel inadequate in social situations. They lack leadership and persuasive skills, and tend to be reserved and formal in interpersonal relationships. They find it difficult to express themselves emotionally and are not considered to be friendly.

ARTISTIC PERSONALITY TYPE

Artistic persons are very creative, original, and individualistic. They like to be different and strive to stand out from the crowd. They like to express their personalities by creating new and different things with words; with music; with materials, through painting, carving, sculpturing, engraving, crafting, etc.; and with physical expression, as in acting and dancing. They want attention and praise for their artistic endeavors, but are very sensitive to criticism. They tend to be uninhibited and nonconforming in dress, speech, and action. They prefer to work without supervision.

They are impulsive and idealistic in outlook. They place great value on beauty and esthetic qualities, and tend to be emotional in the expression of their feelings. They prefer abstract tasks and unstructured situations. They find it difficult to function effectively in highly ordered and systematic situations.

They seek acceptance and approval from others, but often find the demands of close interpersonal relationships so stressful that they avoid them. They compensate for their resulting feelings of estrangement or alienation by relating to others primarily through the indirect medium of their art.

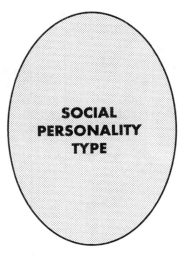

SOCIAL PERSONALITY TYPE

Social persons are friendly and outgoing. They are cooperative and enjoy working with and being around other people. They are understanding and insightful concerning the feelings and problems of others. They like to be helpful to others by serving in facilitative roles such as those of teachers, mediators, advisers, or counselors. They have social skills, express themselves well, and are persuasive in interpersonal relationships. They like attention and enjoy being at or near the center of the group.

They are idealistic, sensitive, and conscientious in their outlook on life and in their dealings with others. They like to deal with philosophical issues such as the nature and purpose of life, religion, or morality. They dislike working with machines, tools, and data and at highly organized, routine, and repetitive tasks.

They see themselves as having social and educational skills, but as lacking in mechanical and scientific abilities. They get along well with others and find it natural to express their emotions. They are tactful in relating to others and are considered to be kind, supportive, and caring.

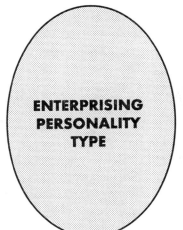

ENTERPRISING PERSONALITY TYPE

Enterprising persons are self-confident, outgoing, and optimistic. They like to organize, direct, and control the activities of groups. They are ambitious and like to be in positions of authority. They place a high value on status, power, money, and material possessions. They like to feel that they are in control of situations and are responsible for making things happen. They are energetic and enthusiastic in initiating and supervising the activities in which they engage. They like to influence the opinions and actions of others and to hold positions of leadership.

They are adventurous and impulsive. They are assertive and verbally persuasive in bringing others around to their point of view. They enjoy social gatherings and like to associate with well-known and influential people. They like to travel and explore, and often have exciting and expensive hobbies.

They see themselves as popular and as having leadership and speaking abilities. They tend to dislike activities requiring scientific abilities and systematic and theoretical thinking. They avoid activities that require attention to detail and adherence to a set routine.

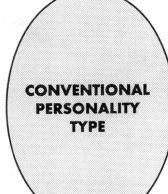

CONVENTIONAL PERSONALITY TYPE

Conventional persons are well-organized, persistent, and practical in their approach to life. They enjoy clerical and computational activities performed according to set procedures. They are dependable, efficient, and conscientious in accomplishing the tasks in which they engage. They enjoy the security of belonging to groups and organizations and make good team members. They are status-conscious but usually do not aspire to positions of highest authority and leadership. They are most comfortable working in situations and at tasks in which they know what is expected of them.

They tend to be conservative and traditional in values and attitudes. They usually conform to expected standards and follow the lead of those in positions of authority, with whom they identify. They like to work indoors in pleasant surroundings and place value on material comforts and possessions.

They are self-controlled and low-key in the expression of their feelings. They avoid intense personal relationships in favor of more casual ones. They are most comfortable in familiar situations and in the company of persons they know well. They like for things to go as planned and prefer not to have their routines changed or upset.

To make a deck of Morrow's Mirrors Cards, photocopy the following graphic on card stock paper and cut out individual items.

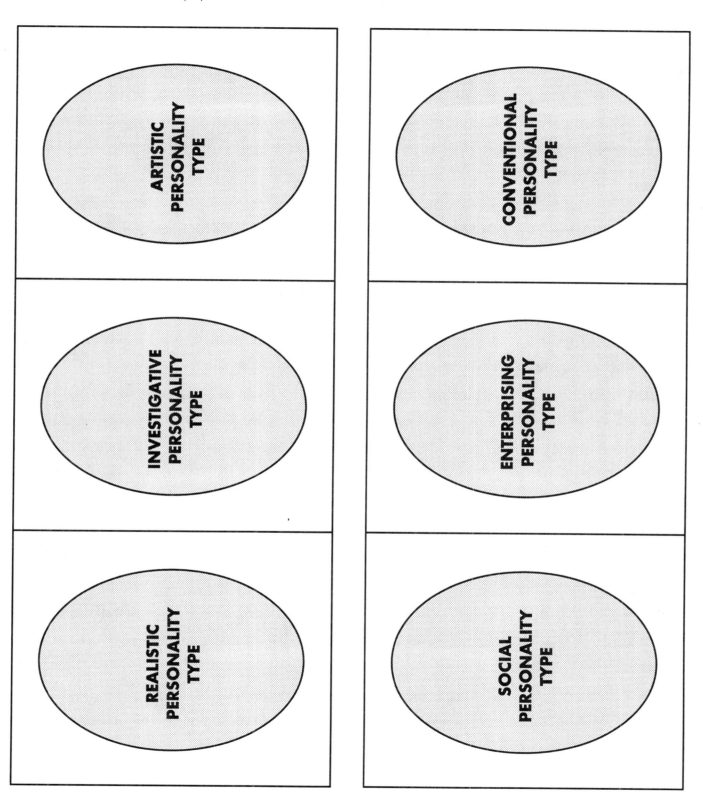

RIASEC BINGO

TOPIC

John Holland's Six Work Environments

LEARNING OBJECTIVE

Using a one-letter Holland code, participants will be able to match selected occupations to matching work environments.

NUMBER OF PARTICIPANTS

Any number

PLAYING TIME

20–25 minutes

REFERENCES

Gottfredson, G. D., and Holland, J. L. (1989). *Dictionary of Holland occupational codes*, 2nd ed. Odessa: Psychological Assessment Resources.

Holland, J. L. (1985). *Making vocational choices: A theory of vocational personalities and work environments*. Englewood Cliffs: Prentice-Hall.

REQUIRED MATERIALS

Pencils, RIASEC Bingo playing boards, and a small box or bag containing the Names of Selected Occupations printed on small slips of paper

TO PLAY

1. Review the key concepts of Holland's occupational congruence theory, including the six occupational environments.

2. Go over the learning objective for the game.

3. Distribute pencils and playing boards to all players. Inform players that the letters at the tops of the columns refer to Holland's six work environments: R for Realistic, I for Investigative, A for Artistic, S for Social, E for Enterprising, and C for Conventional.

4. Explain that the game is played similar to Bingo, except, when playing RIASEC Bingo, players write in the R1 space the name of the first Realistic Occupation drawn. They are to write in the R2 space the second Realistic occupation drawn, and so on. Participants win at RIASEC Bingo by getting four correct matches in a vertical (downward) direction or six correct matches in a horizontal (across) direction.

5. Begin play by drawing the name of an occupation from a container holding the Names of Selected Occupations.

6. Read the name of the occupation aloud twice.

7. Ask the players to write down the occupation in the first blank space in the appropriate column (R, I, A, S, E, or C) on their boards.

8. The facilitator should record the name of the occupation on a RIASEC Bingo playing board. This board will serve as the answer board for future reference (i.e., for checking the accuracy of players' boards when they call, "RIASEC").

9. Repeat steps 5–8 until a player gets four occupations down a column or six occupations across a single row and calls, "RIASEC."

10. Have the person who called "RIASEC" read her/his answers aloud while you call out the correctness of each answer. If all answers are correct, declare her/him the winner. If one of the answers is incorrect, resume play until someone wins.

11. Debrief players. Have players give their current occupations and see if the group can determine its first letter Holland code.

JOHN HOLLAND'S OCCUPATIONAL CONGRUENCE THEORY

John Holland, the noted career theorist, believes that people are attracted to work environments that match their personalities and backgrounds. He holds that individuals tend to identify with a specific occupational stereotype and choose occupations that satisfy their preferred interests and capabilities. Principal elements of the theory are as follows:

1. There are six kinds of work environments: realistic, investigative, artistic, social, enterprising, and conventional. Most occupations can be categorized as one of these six types.

   Samples of Realistic jobs include automobile mechanic, aircraft controller, surveyor, farmer, and electrician. They require mechanical abilities.

   Investigative jobs include biologist, chemist, physicist, anthropologist, geologist, and medical technologist. They call for mathematical and scientific skills.

   Artistic occupations include composer, musician, stage director, writer, interior decorator, and actor/actress. They require writing, musical, or artistic capabilities.

   Teacher, religious worker, counselor, clinical psychologist, psychiatric case worker, and speech therapist are Social occupations. They require good interpersonal skills.

   Samples of Enterprising jobs include salesperson, manager, business executive, television producer, sports promoter, and buyer. They call for strong leadership abilities.

   Bookkeeper, stenographer, financial analyst, banker, cost estimator, and tax expert are considered Conventional occupations. They demand clerical and arithmetic skills.

2. People search for occupations that will let them use their skills and abilities, express their attitudes and values, and take on agreeable roles.

3. Similarities among the six work environments and the degree of congruence between a person and an occupation (environment) can be depicted by a hexagonal model. The closer they appear in proximity to another on the hexagon, the more similar the occupations and the greater the congruence between personality and the work environment.

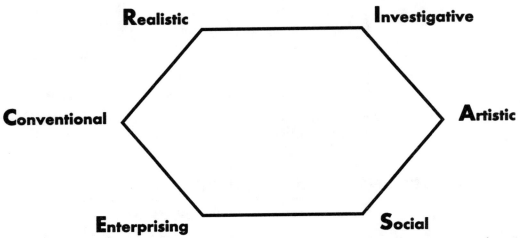

LIST OF SELECTED OCCUPATIONS

To prepare a set of RIASEC occupations draw slips, photocopy the following occupations. Cut out each occupation and place it into a small container. Occupations are listed according to their Holland type.

R	I	A
Farmer	Surgeon	Crossword puzzle maker
Blacksmith	Seismologist	Dancer
Garbage collector	Psychiatrist	Puppeteer
Bricklayer	Job analyst	Milliner
Dog groomer	Translator	Psychic/reader
House painter	Perfumer	Illustrator
Jockey	Criminalist	Actor
Bus driver	Taxidermist	Biographer

S	E	C
Teacher	Bellhop	Accountant
Police Chief	Motorcycle racer	Food checker
Clergy	Secretary of State	Broom maker
Hair stylist	Funeral director	Toy assembler
Dog catcher	Bouncer	Bibliographer
Home economist	Lawyer	Proofreader
Tutor	Manicurist	Timekeeper
Loan officer	Telephone solicitor	Usher

☆☆☆ RIASEC BINGO ☆☆☆

R	I	A	S	E	C
1 _____	1 _____	1 _____	1 _____	1 _____	1 _____
2 _____	2 _____	2 _____	2 _____	2 _____	2 _____
3 _____	3 _____	3 _____	3 _____	3 _____	3 _____
4 _____	4 _____	4 _____	4 _____	4 _____	4 _____

SECRETARY'S DREAM JOB

TOPIC   Dream Jobs

LEARNING
OBJECTIVE   Participants will be able to describe their dream jobs.

NUMBER OF
PARTICIPANTS Any number

PLAYING TIME 12-15 minutes

REFERENCE   None

REQUIRED
MATERIALS   Pencils and copies of Secretary's Dream Job

TO PLAY
1. Introduce players to the concept of dream jobs.
2. Divide participants into pairs.
3. Pass out game materials (pencils and copies of Secretary's Dream Job) to one member of each pair. Refer to her/him as the scribe. Explain that the scribes have been given a short story with missing words.
4. Inform scribes that they are to ask their partners to supply them with words to fill in the missing blanks without their partners ever having seen the story line. For instance, if the "name of a company" has been omitted, the scribe is to ask their partner to supply the name of a company. It can be a real or imagined company. The name of the company is then written in the blank space in the story. The scribe is to continue, requesting other words until all of the blank spaces are filled in.
5. Give players five minutes to fill in the missing words.
6. After five minutes, ask volunteers to read some of the more humorous stories. Scribes can now permit their partners to read the stories they helped write.
7. Have the group vote on the "best" story and declare that pair the winners.
8. Debrief players. Ask players to share their "real dream jobs." Discuss the appropriate part that dream jobs should play in job hunting.

Secretary's Dream Job

Janice, the new secretary, has landed the job of her dreams. To start off, her boss looks like _____ (famous man) with the personality of _____ (famous woman). She works in a luxurious office fully equipped with _____ (things) from _____ (number from 1 –12) to _____ (number from 1 –12) five days a week. Her equipment made by _____ (brand name) is top of the line. Janice's co-workers are great. They remind her of _____ (famous group of people). The boss has told her to order whatever supplies she needs. The supply budget is a generous _____ (amount of money). What more could a hard working professional want? Janice gets paid _____ (amount of money) per week plus free _____ (a need) and _____ (number) days paid vacation every year.

SUPER-O

TOPIC   Donald Super's Career Development Theory

**LEARNING
OBJECTIVE**   Participants will be able to associate various career development tasks with Super's five
career development stages.

**NUMBER OF
PARTICIPANTS**   Any number

PLAYING TIME   15–25 minutes

REFERENCE   Morrow, James. (1992). *Career life stages and career development tasks.* Unpublished
manuscript.

Super, D. (1990). *Career and life development.* San Francisco: Jossey-Bass Inc.

**REQUIRED
MATERIALS**   Super-O playing board and deck of Super-O Development Task Cards

TO PLAY

1. Introduce players to Super's five career development stages.

2. Go over the learning objective for the game.

3. Inform participants that they will be playing a game similar to Rack-O. It will require
   them to place five Super-O Career Development Task cards on their Super-O boards
   in the correct career development stage spaces (Growth, Exploration, Establishment,
   Maintenance, and Disengagement).

4. Divide the larger group into smaller groups of four or five players each.

5. Pass out a Super-O playing board to each player and one deck of Super-O Career
   Development Task Cards to each of the small groups.

6. Designate a dealer for each group and have her/him thoroughly shuffle the cards.

7. Ask dealers to deal five cards to each player in the respective groups. As each card
   is dealt, direct the player to place it face up on his or her board. The first card is to
   be placed face up in the shaded S rectangle (Growth space) on their boards. The
   next card goes face up on the U shaded rectangle (Exploration space), and so on.

8. When everyone has been dealt five cards, direct the dealer to place the remaining
   cards in the middle of the group to be used as a draw pile. Explain that the player to
   the left of dealer plays first. She/he is to draw a card from the draw pile. She/he may
   discard or exchange the drawn card with any other card on her/his board. The card
   taken from the board is placed face up in a discard pile next to the draw pile.

9. Have players continue playing in a clockwise direction around the group. Advise subsequent players that they may either draw a card from the draw pile or pick up the
   top card on the discard pile.

10. Tell players that the first one to get each of the five task cards in the correct career development stage spaces on her/his board is to call out, "Super-O."

11. Verify the answers of players who call "Super-O." Declare players with the correct placement of all five career development tasks the winners in their groups.

12. If answers are incorrect, the player is out of the game. Play continues until a player has five correct answers.

13. Debrief players. Ask players to identify which of Super's five career development stages that they believe they are in. Have them discuss some of the career development tasks they are currently working on.

DONALD SUPER'S CAREER DEVELOPMENT THEORY

The noted career development theorist, Donald Super, holds the following general tenets regarding the development of careers over a person's life span:

1. People differ in their abilities, interests, and personalities.

2. Each person is qualified for a number of occupations.

3. Each occupation requires characteristic patterns of abilities, interests, and personality traits (wide tolerance).

4. Vocational preferences and competencies (self-concept) change with time and experience, making choice and adjustment a continuous process.

5. Vocational choices and adjustments may be summed up in terms of life/career stages.

6. The nature of career patterns are determined by socioeconomic level, mental ability, personality, and opportunities.

7. Development through life/career stages can be guided by facilitating the maturation of abilities and interests, reality testing, and the development of self-concept.

8. The process of vocational development is essentially that of developing and implementing the self-concept. It is a compromise process between inherited characteristics, opportunities, and feedback on roles.

9. The process of compromise between individual and social factors and between self-concept and reality is one of role playing in the form of fantasy, part-time, or temporary jobs.

10. Work satisfaction depends on the extent to which an individual finds adequate outlets for interests, abilities, personality traits, and values. It depends on getting established in a type of work, work situations, and lifestyle in which a worker can play the kinds of roles she/he considers congenial and appropriate.

Figure 3.5. Donald Super's growth stages.

Stages and Substages	Ages	Career Development Tasks	Commentary
A. Growth Stage	Birth to age 14	Forming a picture of the kind of person one is (self-concept formation).	Self-concept develops through association and identification with key figures in family, school, and community and through exposure to and/or experiences with tasks, objects, and ideas.
		Developing an orientation to the world of work, including some understanding of the meaning of work and of the different ways in which it is possible to earn a living.	Knowledge of and attitudes toward work in general and occupations in particular are learned by exposure to and/or experiences with people, tasks, objects, and ideas
(Curiosity Substage)	Birth to age 3		Behavior is presumed to be motivated by needs and curiosity.
1. Fantasy substage	Ages 4 to 10		Behavior relevant to career development appears to be motivated primarily by fantasy in role playing.
2. Interest substage	Ages 11 to 12		Behavior relevant to career development appears to be motivated primarily by the individual's likes and dislikes.
3. Capacity substage	Ages 13 to 14		Behavior relevant to career development involves consideration of the individual's abilities and job requirements.
B. Exploration Stage	Ages 15 to 24		
1. Tentative substage	Ages 15 to 17	Crystallizing an occupational preference.	The individual begins to translate self-concept into general occupational terms. Possible appropriate fields and levels of work are identified.
2. Transition substage	Ages 18 to 21	Specifying an occupational preference.	Transition is made from school to work or from school to further education and/or training. Generalized choices are converted into a specific choice.
3. Trial (with little commitment) substage	Ages 22 to 24	Implementing an occupational preference.	A seemingly appropriate occupation having been selected or prepared for, a beginning job is found and tried out. Commitment to the occupation is still provisional and may be strengthened or weakened by experiences encountered on the job or in training. If weakened, the individual may change goals and repeat the process of crystallizing, specifying, and implementing an occupational preference.
C. Establishment Stage	Ages 25 to 44		Having found an appropriate field, effort is put forth to make a permanent place in it. For many individuals, these are the most productive and creative years.

Figure 3.5. Donald Super's growth stages (Continued).

Stages and Substages	Ages	Career Development Tasks	Commentary
1. Trial (with commitment) stage	Ages 25 to 30	Stabilization in the chosen occupation.	The individual settles down, supports self and contributes to family support, develops an appropriate lifestyle, makes use of abilities and training, and pursues meaningful interests.
2. Advancement substage	Ages 31 to 44	Consolidation in the chosen occupation.	After having settled down, individuals are commonly concerned with their place in an occupation or in an organization; security is the objective.
		Advancement in the chosen occupation.	In middle-class and upper-class circles, there is generally an expectation that individuals will get ahead financially and move to more challenging levels of responsibility and independence. Frustration often results when advancement is not forthcoming.
D. Maintenance stage	Ages 45 to 59	Holding on in the chosen occupation.	Having attained a secure and recognized position, the individual is expected to maintain it in the face of competition from others, technological change, health problems, and family demands. For some individuals, holding may deteriorate into stagnation.
		Updating the chosen occupation.	In some fields of work and for some individuals, just holding on is not enough; it may be important to keep abreast of new developments as fields change and as individual goals change in order to remain current.
		Innovating in the chosen occupation.	In some fields, such as high technology, individuals are expected to break new ground. Some individuals continue to feel the need to explore and to do something different or at least do things differently, even after they are well established.
E. Disengagement Stage	Age 60 on		As physical and/or mental powers decline, work activity changes and in due course ceases; the worker role is gradually supplanted by greater involvement in other life roles.
1. Deceleration substage	Ages 60 to 64	Selective reduction in pace and/or load of work.	Deceleration is common, especially among individuals who have some control over their work situations. Some begin to delegate part of their activities to younger persons and become more selective in what they themselves do.

Figure 3.5. Donald Super's growth stages (*Continued*).

Stages and Substages	Ages	Career Development Tasks	Commentary
		Planning for retirement.	Some individuals anticipate retirement and plan carefully for it; others gradually or suddenly become aware of the fact of impending retirement and plan less carefully, poorly, or not at all.
2. Retirement substage	Age 65 on	Retirement living.	Giving up a job or work for pay brings opportunities for individuals to increase their participation in other roles they fulfill in their home life, hobbies, civic activity, and sometimes study. Cessation of the worker role comes easily and pleasantly to some, to others with difficulty and disappointment, and to some only with death.

SOURCE: Published with permission of Jossey-Bass, Inc., 350 Sansome St., San Francisco, CA 94104, and Dr. James M. Morrow, 718 Magnolia Street, Mooresville, NC 28115.

CAREER DEVELOPMENT TASKS CARDS

To prepare a deck of Super-O Career Development Task Cards, make five photocopies on card stock paper and cut out the individual cards.

Forming a Picture of the Kind of Person One Is (Self-Concept Formation)

Developing an Orientation to the World of Work, Including Some Understanding of the Meaning of Work and the Different Ways in Which It Is Possible to Earn a Living

Crystallizing an Occupational Preference

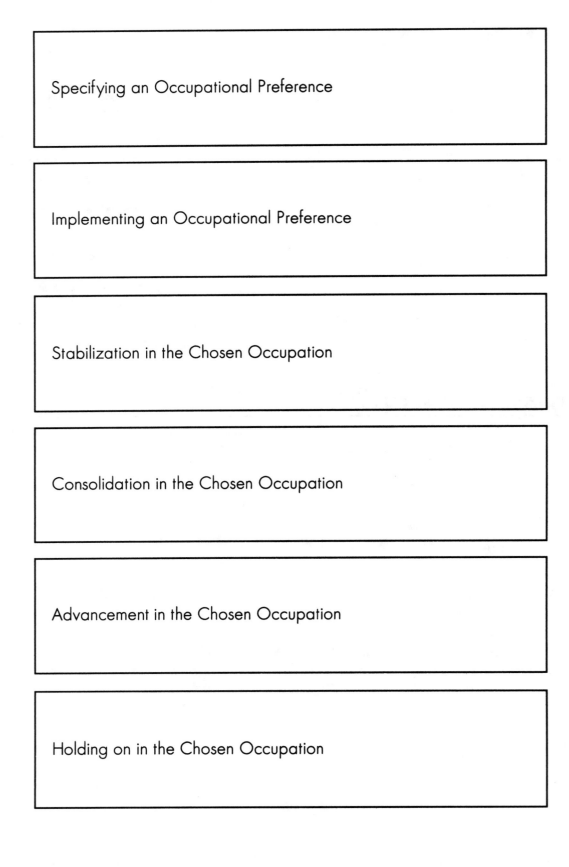

Specifying an Occupational Preference

Implementing an Occupational Preference

Stabilization in the Chosen Occupation

Consolidation in the Chosen Occupation

Advancement in the Chosen Occupation

Holding on in the Chosen Occupation

Updating the Chosen Occupation

Innovating in the Chosen Occupation

Selective Reduction in Pace and/or Load of Work

Planning for Retirement

Retirement Living

SUPER-O

GROWTH

S

EXPLORATION

U

ESTABLISHMENT

P

MAINTENANCE

E

DISENGAGEMENT

R

S

U

P

E

R

VALUES SWAP SHOP

TOPIC   Work Values

**LEARNING
OBJECTIVE**   Participants will be able to identify the characteristics of a work situation that hold the greatest importance for them.

**NUMBER OF
PARTICIPANTS**   7-21

PLAYING TIME   15-20 minutes

REFERENCE   Weiss, D. J., Dawis, R. V., England, G. W., and Lofquist, L. H. (1965). *Construct validation studies of the Minnesota Importance Questionnaire* (Minnesota Studies in Vocational Rehabilitation Monograph No. 18). Minneapolis: University of Minnesota, Work Adjustment Project Industrial Relations Center.

**REQUIRED
MATERIALS**   Pencils, Values Prioritizer Sheets, and deck of Values Swap Cards

TO PLAY

1. Introduce players to the concepts of work values and trade-offs.
2. Go over the learning objective for the game.
3. Pass out a pencil and a copy of the Values Prioritizer Sheets to each player.
4. Go over the directions at the top of the worksheet.
5. Give participants approximately two minutes to check the five values on the worksheet of greatest importance to them.
6. Hold up the deck of Values Swap Cards so that everyone can see them. Explain that the deck contains values cards, including the five values they have just checked on their Values Prioritizer Sheets.
7. Advise players that they are going to be randomly dealt five Values Swap Cards. They may be lucky enough to be dealt some of the same values they have just checked on their Values Prioritizer Sheets. Furthermore, they will have an opportunity to swap some of the cards they were dealt for cards they were not lucky enough to receive.
8. Inform participants that the goal of the game is to end up with as many of the five values cards they checked on their Values Prioritizer Sheets as possible.
9. Deal five Values Swap Cards to each player.
10. Inform players that when you call, "Swap," they are to begin swapping value cards. They can trade any number of their five cards for cards of their liking. After six minutes of swapping they will receive five points for each card matching the values checked on their Values Prioritizer Sheets. If they collect all five values cards checked on their Values Prioritizer Sheets, they will receive an additional 10 points.

11. Call, "Swap." Tell players to get out of their seats and start making trades.

12. Six minutes later call an end to the swap session and ask players to return to their seats.

13. Have players record five points on their Values Prioritizer Sheets (column 3) for each of their checked values for which they now have cards.

14. Have them add an additional 10 points if they have collected all the values cards checked on their Values Prioritizer Sheet.

15. Ask players to add up their scores. Declare the person(s) with the most points the winner(s).

16. Bestow on the winner(s) the title "Sultan of Swap."

17. Debrief players. Ask players to tell what they just learned about their own work values. Have them discuss the opportunities or lack of opportunities they had at their previous jobs to secure the things they most valued.

VALUES, REINFORCERS, AND WORK ADJUSTMENTS

One way of viewing work values is to think of them as expressed needs (i.e., attaching importance to things in the work environment that meet a person's needs). In the theory of Work Adjustment developed in 1964 by Dawis, England, and Lofquist, work is seen as an interaction between individuals and their work environment. The work environment sets certain behavioral requirements for individuals, and, in turn, individuals have certain needs they expect the work environment to fulfill. Work adjustment from the employer's perspective and job satisfaction from the worker's perspective are considered to be a continuous process by which individual workers and the work environment meet each other's requirements. If an acceptable adjustment and job satisfaction occur (i.e., acceptable trade-offs are negotiated), the workers perform satisfactorily and the work environment reinforces or meets workers' needs. Job satisfaction is maximized when an individual's values pattern (i.e., felt needs) closely corresponds to a similar pattern of reinforcers in the work environment.

Lofquist and Dawis identified 20 vocational needs (i.e., work values):

1. Ability utilization
2. Achievement
3. Activity
4. Advancement
5. Authority
6. Company policies and practices
7. Compensation
8. Co-workers
9. Creativity
10. Independence
11. Moral values
12. Recognition
13. Responsibility
14. Security
15. Social service
16. Social status
17. Supervision (human relations)
18. Supervision (technical)
19. Variety
20. Working conditions

The theorists believe most individuals hold these values or felt needs to varying degrees. They appear as items on both the Minnesota Satisfaction Questionnaire and the Minnesota Importance Questionnaire. The following Values Cards are abstracted from the Minnesota Importance Questionnaire.

To prepare a deck of Value Swap Cards, photocopy the following items using card stock paper and cut them out. For 7–10 players, use three sets of cards, and for 11–21 players use six sets of cards.

Making use of my abilities	Being able to do different things
Having the chance to try my own methods	Receiving high pay compared to the amount of work I do
Having an opportunity to "be somebody"	Having the freedom to use my own judgment
Having a feeling of accomplishment	Having pleasant working conditions

Being able to work alone	Receiving praise for doing a good job
Having a boss who is competent at working with subordinates	Being able to do things for people
Being able to keep busy	Having opportunities for advancement
Not being asked to do things against my conscience	Having co-workers that get along with one another
Having the chance to tell people what to do	Having steady employment

VALUES PRIORITIZER SHEET

Directions: Carefully read the list of values in column one. Consider how important these items are to you in terms of having a highly satisfying work situation. Place a checkmark (✓) in column 2 beside the five values of greatest importance to you at this time in your life and career. At the end of the card swap session, record 5 points in column 3 for each of the checked values for which you were able to secure a Values Swap Card. Award yourself 10 bonus points if you have secured all your selected values. Tally your score at the bottom of column three.

List of Work Values	✓	Points
1. Making use of my abilities	____	____
2. Being able to do different things	____	____
3. Having the chance to try my own methods	____	____
4. Receiving high pay compared to the amount of work I do	____	____
5. Having an opportunity to "be somebody"	____	____
6. Having the freedom to use my own judgment	____	____
7. Having a feeling of accomplishment	____	____
8. Having pleasant working conditions	____	____
9. Being able to work alone	____	____
10. Receiving praise for doing a good job	____	____
11. Having a boss who is competent at working with subordinates	____	____
12. Being able to do things for people	____	____
13. Being able to keep busy	____	____
14. Having opportunities for advancement	____	____
15. *Not* being asked to do things against my conscience	____	____
16. Having co-workers that get along with one another	____	____
17. Having the chance to tell people what to do	____	____
18. Having steady employment	____	____
Bonus points		____
Total number of points earned		_ _ _ _

SOURCE: Reproduced by permission of Vocational Psychology Research, University of Minnesota, N 620 Elliot Hall, Minneapolis, MN 55455.

Chapter Four
CAREER DYNAMICS GAMES

All occupations are not created equal. They vary greatly in a variety of dimensions. Furthermore, occupations do not remain static. Changes in technology, the law, and consumer demand can all have dramatic effects on career fields. An understanding of the dynamic nature of career fields is essential for anyone who desires to maintain a successful career.

The games in Chap. 4 examine occupations from several perspectives. For example, *Top Five (Novice Class)* and *Top Five (Pros Class)* look at selected occupations in terms of stressfullness, income, job security, physical strength requirements, perks provided, and working environment. *Getting No Respect* separates low- from high-status occupations. *Innies and Outies* scrutinizes career fields according to current demand. *Ladies Lineup (U.S. Occupations)* relates to the percentage of women in particular occupations, and *Titans of Turnover* focuses on longevity in different career fields.

Two of the games in Chap. 4 apply to the human resource development field (*HRD Acrossout* and *Where in the USA Is Jo(e) Trainer?*). *HRD Acrossout* relates to the specialized terminology used by trainers and *Where in the USA Is Jo(e) Trainer?* pertains to the work roles of trainers. These games can be used to introduce players to the emerging field of human resource development or to reinforce the importance of knowing the lingo and work roles inherent in any given occupation.

GETTING NO RESPECT

TOPIC   High- and Low-Status Occupations

LEARNING OBJECTIVE   Participants will be able to differentiate between high- and low-status occupations.

NUMBER OF PARTICIPANTS   6-12

PLAYING TIME   15–35 minutes depending on the number of players

REFERENCE   Nakao, K., and Treas, J. (1990). Computing 1989 occupational prestige scores (General social survey methodological report no. 70). Chicago: University of Chicago, National Opinion Research Center.

REQUIRED MATERIALS   Number tags, straight pins, and Occupation Pucks

TO PLAY
1. Introduce players to the concepts of status and respect.
2. Go over the learning objective for the game.
3. Divide participants into two teams with an equal number of members. Teams cannot exceed six players each.
4. Have the teams stand in straight lines, 10 feet apart, and facing each other.
5. Provide each player on the respective teams a number tag with a large number #1, #2, #3, #4, #5, or #6 printed on it. Each player on a team must have a number different from her/his teammates. However, there must be a player on the competing team with an identical number.
6. Provide players with straight pins, and ask that they pin the number tags to their blouses or shirts.
7. Explain that the two teams will be competing to pick up the most Occupation Pucks containing the names of "low-status occupations." In other words, the objective of the game is to be the team getting the "least respect."
8. Hold up an Occupation Puck. Advise players that you will be placing 24 different pucks (three at a time) along an imaginary parallel line exactly in the middle of the two teams (5 feet from the members of any team).
9. Inform players that, when you randomly call out a number from #1 to #6, the player on each team with that number is to rush forward, pick up as many pucks as they can, and return to their teams. After returning to their teams, the players are to read the names of the occupations on the bottoms of their Occupation Pucks. If it is a low-status occupation, their teams receive 1 point. If the occupation is high-status, they receive no point.
10. Place three pucks between the opposing teams.
11. Call out a number from #1 to #6.

12. Have players read the occupations on their pucks and award points accordingly.

13. Repeat steps 10 through 12 seven more times.

14. Tally each teams points. Declare the team with the most points the winner and the team with the "least respect."

15. Debrief players. Discuss with players what they believe causes occupations to differ in the social status and respect American society accords them. Have participants suggest occupations that they believe are given too much status by most Americans. Have players do the same for occupations they believe are bestowed too little status. Ask participants to what degree they believe status influences the occupations people choose.

OCCUPATION PUCKS

To make a set of 24 Occupation Pucks, use a felt-tip pen to write the names of the following occupations on the cork side of 24 cork coasters or on pieces of cardboard approximately 4 by 4 inches.

Figure 4.1. High-status occupations.

Rank	Occupation
1.	Physician-surgeon
2.	College president
3.	Astronaut
4.	High government official
5.	Lawyer
6.	Computer scientist
7.	College professor
8.	Physicist
9.	Chemist
10.	Chemical engineer
11.	Architect
12.	Biologist

SOURCE: Published with permission of the National Opinion Research Center, University of Chicago, 1155 E. 60th Street, Chicago, IL 60637.

Figure 4.2. Low-status occupations.

Rank	Occupation
1.	Panhandler
2.	Fortune teller
3.	Drug dealer
4.	Prostitute
5.	Envelope stuffer
6.	Dishwasher
7.	Shoeshiner
8.	Grocery bagger
9.	Street sweeper
10.	Migrant worker
11.	Carwash attendant
12.	Newspaper peddler

SOURCE: Published with permission of the National Opinion Research Center, University of Chicago, 1155 E. 60th Street, Chicago, IL 60637.

HRD ACROSSOUT

TOPIC Human Resource Development Terms

LEARNING OBJECTIVE Participants will be able to identify several terms associated with the work of human resource development specialists.

NUMBER OF PARTICIPANTS Any number

PLAYING TIME 15–20 minutes

REFERENCE Rothwell, W. J., and Scrdl, Henry J. (1992). *The ASTD reference guide to professional human resource development roles & competencies*, Vols. I & II, 2nd ed. Amherst, MA: HRD Press.

REQUIRED MATERIALS Pencils and copies of the HRD Acrossout worksheet

TO PLAY
1. Introduce players to the job of human resource developer.
2. Go over the learning objective for the game.
3. Divide participants into triads (groups of three players each).
4. Explain to participants that each group will have 12 minutes to solve an HRD crossout puzzle containing HRD-related terms.
5. Pass out game materials (pencils and HRD Acrossout).
6. Go over the directions to the HRD Acrossout.
7. Tell players to begin.
8. After 12 minutes call, "Stop."
9. Give answers to the puzzle, while having each group check their own work.
10. Declare the group(s) with the correct saying at the bottom of the puzzle the winner(s).
11. Debrief players. Discuss the importance of "knowing the language" or current "buzz words" in a particular field. Ask players to list five to ten buzz words in their own fields that every job hunter should know.

Directions: Use a letter from each box across (10-letter word) and each box down (7-letter word) to form HRD-related words (seven 10-letter & ten 7-letter words). Cross out each letter as you use it. When the puzzle has been completed, one letter remaining in each box will spell out a saying reading from left to right across each line.

	1	2	3	4	5	6	7	8	9	10
1	V / T T	H / C O	E / C D	H / E A	T / U W	M / D I	O / A A	P / N N	R / A P	E / M L
2	R / S S	A / O P	E / E U	D / C R	I / R C	A / E E	D / L N	E / L I	R / V S	T / E E
3	L / A C	O / O R	O / P V	M / R U	E / I D	N / S I	N / T A	F / A A	O / T I	E / N E
4	I / L T	E / D E	E / C A	C / H T	N / T T	R / I O	L / L A	O / C N	G / T M	T / S Y
5	M / P N	A / E E	O / N L	P / A A	I / L G	G / E E	M / Y W	I / N E	O / N T	O / T H
6	A / I E	R / N W	O / I S	T / T D	R / E N	U / V N	S / C A	E / R T	O / T I	R / R E
7	T / R E	V / S Y	A / O P	L / E F	G / U S	S / A K	I / T T	I / L R	L / O E	S / S N

Saying

_____ _____ _____ _____ _____ ____

_____ _____ ____ _____ _____ _____ _____ .

INNIES AND OUTIES

TOPIC

Occupations That Are Becoming More in Demand (Innies) and Those That Are Becoming Less in Demand (Outies)

LEARNING OBJECTIVE

Participants will be able to differentiate between occupations that are becoming more and less in demand.

NUMBER OF PARTICIPANTS

Any number

PLAYING TIME

10–12 minutes

REFERENCE

Russell, M., Wiggins, P., and Johnson, S. (April, March–April). Today's hot fields: what's in/out. *Career Opportunities News.*

REQUIRED MATERIALS

Pencils and Innies and Outies Worksheet

TO PLAY

1. Introduce players to the concept of occupational "outlook." Define "innies" and "outies" in terms of occupations forecasted to be in greater and lesser demand in the 1990s.

2. Go over the learning objective for the game.

3. Tell players that they are about to play a little game which will test their ability to identify jobs that are "on their way in" and "on their way out."

4. Inform participants that they will be given an Innies and Outies Worksheet, which will list 48 different occupations. Twenty-one of the occupations are innies and 27 are outies.

5. Pass out the materials for the game (pencils and Innies and Outies Worksheets).

6. Explain that they have three minutes to cross out (draw a line through) the 27 outies listed on their worksheets.

7. Allow three minutes for participants to complete the worksheet.

8. Give players the numbers of the occupations that they should have crossed out.

9. Have participants add up the number of occupations they correctly placed a line through.

10. Have participants add up the number of occupations they incorrectly placed a line through.

11. Direct players to subtract the number of incorrectly crossed-out occupations from the number of correctly crossed-out occupations. The resulting number is their score. Declare the person with the highest score the group's "top occupational forecaster."

12. Debrief players. Go over some of the social, economic, and demographic changes that can result in a particular occupation becoming less in demand. Discuss the proper use of occupational forecasts in career planning.

Directions: Draw a line through the following occupations that are outies (i.e., becoming less in demand in our ever-changing economy).

1. Advertising	25. Home furnishing
2. Agriculture	26. Home remodeling
3. Air transportation	27. Insurance
4. Automobiles	28. Jewelry
5. Banking	29. Law
6. Biotechnology	30. Manufacturing
7. Business systems	31. Medicine
8. Cable TV	32. Military services
9. Career counseling	33. Mortgage refinancing
10. Catering	34. Personal computers
11. Coal mining	35. Pharmaceuticals
12. Computer networking	36. Real estate
13. Consumer products	37. Restaurants
14. Defense industry	38. Savings and loan
15. Department stores	39. Securities
16. Discount merchandising	40. Security
17. Environmental services	41. Software
18. Federal government	42. Sports marketing
19. Food chains	43. State and local governments
20. Health benefits	44. Steel
21. Health care	45. Teaching
22. Health maintenance organizations	46. Telephone companies
23. Health services	47. Timber
24. Home construction	48. Waste management

SOURCE: Published with permission of *Career Opportunities News*, P.O. Box 190, Garrett Park, MD 20896.

LADIES LINEUP (U.S. OCCUPATIONS)

TOPIC Percentage of American Women in Selected Occupations

LEARNING OBJECTIVE Participants will be able to identify U.S. occupations with the highest percentage of women in them.

NUMBER OF PARTICIPANTS Any number

PLAYING TIME 10–15 minutes

REFERENCE *Employment and earnings* (January, 1993). U.S. Department of Labor, Bureau of Labor Statistics.

REQUIRED MATERIALS Pencils and Ladies Lineup (U.S. Occupations)

TO PLAY

1. Introduce players to the concept of female- versus male-dominated occupations.
2. Explain the learning objective behind the puzzle about to be passed out.
3. Supply each participant with a pencil and a copy of the Ladies Lineup (U.S. Occupations).
4. Go over the directions of the puzzle. Ask participants *not* to begin until you call, "Lineup." (*Note:* See answers to puzzle in Appendix B for an illustration of the correct way to draw puzzle lines.)
5. Inform players that the participant(s) with the most correct answers will be named the winner(s).
6. Advise players that they have five minutes to complete the puzzle.
7. Call, "Lineup."
8. Five minutes later call, "Time."
9. Provide participants the correct answers while they check the accuracy of their own puzzles.
10. Recognize the player(s) with the most correct answers as the winner(s).
11. Debrief players. Discuss the possible reasons why some occupations have so many while others have so few women in them. Ask players to list the potential advantages and disadvantages of entering occupations dominated by members of one gender, race, or nationality.

Directions: Draw a line extending from the name of an occupation through the percentage that correctly indicates the current percentage of women working in that occupation.

Percentage of Women
in 10 Occupations

Dental hygenists	9	9.0%
Editors and reporters	9	9.0%
Firefighters	9	8.6%
Household child care workers	9	7.3%
Painters, sculptors, craft artists, and artist printmakers	9	7.1%
Prekindergarten and kindergarten teachers	5	0.4%
Real estate sales	5	0.3%
Receptionists	4	9.7%
Secretaries	0	7.0%
United States Senators	0	2.4%

SOURCE: Published with permissions of *The Atlanta Journal* and *The Atlanta Constitution*, P.O. Box 4689, Atlanta, GA 30302.

TITANS OF TURNOVER

TOPIC   Longevity in Selected Occupations

LEARNING OBJECTIVE   Participants will be able to tell whether longevity is low, medium, or high in selected occupational fields.

NUMBER OF PARTICIPANTS   10–20

PLAYING TIME   17–25 minutes

REFERENCE   Dahlstrom & Company. (1994). *Surviving a layoff.* Holliston, MA: author.

REQUIRED MATERIALS   Occupations Cards and Occupational Longevity Chart

TO PLAY

1. Introduce players to the concept of occupational longevity.

2. Go over the learning objective for the game.

3. Tell players that are about to compete in a game to determine how good they are at guessing how long individuals typically work in selected occupational fields.

4. Explain that they will be handed a card with the name of an occupation printed on it. They will then have to determine whether the average person stays in this occupation 1–5 years (few number of years), 6–10 years (medium number of years), or more than 10 years (a high number of years).

5. Advise participants that when you call, "Turnover," they are to go to the right side of the room if they think members of the occupation appearing on their card stay for a few number of years. If they think they stay for a medium number of years, they are to go to the left side of the room. If they believe members of the occupation remain in the occupation for a high number of years, they are to stand in the back of the room.

6. Inform players if they are correct they will be given another Occupations Card and may continue playing the game. If they guess wrong, they will be out of the game and will have to take their seats.

7. Tell players that the game continues until there is only one person remaining in the game or until the facilitator runs out of Occupations Cards.

8. Pass out one Occupations Card to each player.

9. Call, "Turnover."

10. Give the average stay for the occupations passed out for this round.

11. Tell players who went to the wrong part of the room (i.e., did not correctly guess the average length of stay in the occupation appearing on their Occupations Card) to be seated.

12. Repeat steps 8 through 11 until only one player remains in the game or until there are no more Occupations Cards.

13. Declare the last player or players remaining in the game "Titan(s) of Turnover."

14. Debrief players. Ask participants to speculate on why people remain in occupations for widely varying amounts of time. Discuss how longevity in an occupation might affect those looking for jobs in that particular field.

Figure 4.3. Occupational longevity chart.

Occupations in Which Individuals Remain Only a Few Number of Years

F	Advertising	F	Janitors and cleaners
F	Artists and performers	F	Kitchen workers
F	Bakers	F	Legal assistants
F	Bank tellers	F	Machine operators
F	Bartenders	F	Maids and housemen
F	Cashiers	F	Office clerks
F	Child care workers	F	Packaging and filling machine operators
F	Computer operators	F	Personnel, trainers
F	Computer programmers	F	Physical therapists
F	Construction laborers	F	Receptionists
F	Economists	F	Roofers
F	Freight, stock, and material handlers	F	Sewing machine operators
F	Garage and service station workers	F	Short-order cook
F	Guards	F	Taxi drivers and chauffeurs
F	Health record technicians	F	Truck drivers, light
F	Hotel clerks	F	Typists
F	Insurance adjusters and investigators	F	Waiters and waitresses

Occupations in Which Individuals Remain a Medium Number of Years

M	Accountant and auditors	M	Hairdressers and cosmetologists
M	Actors and directors	M	Heat and air conditioning mechanics
M	Administrative managers and supervisors	M	Lawyers
M	Architects	M	Librarians
M	Authors	M	Licensed practical nurses
M	Automobile mechanics	M	Mail carriers, postal service
M	Billing clerks	M	Meter readers
M	Bookkeepers and auditors	M	Nursing aides and orderlies
M	Brick masons and stonemasons	M	Painters, construction, and maintenance
M	Bus drivers	M	Photographers
M	Butchers and meat cutters	M	Physicians' assistants
M	Buyers (except farm)	M	Plumbers, pipefitters, and steamfitters
M	Carpenters	M	Police officers, sheriffs, and bailiffs
M	Chemical engineers	M	Psychologists
M	Computer system analysts	M	Real estate sales
M	Concrete finishers	M	Registered nurses
M	Correctional officers	M	Secretaries
M	Counselors	M	Sheet metal workers
M	Dental hygienists	M	Speech therapists
M	Drafters and mechanical drawers	M	Stenographers
M	Editors and reporters	M	Teachers (postsecondary)
M	Electrical and electronic engineers	M	Telephone operators
M	Electrical and electronic technicians	M	Timber cutters and loggers
M	Engineers	M	Truck drivers, heavy
M	Financial managers	M	Upholsterers
M	Firefighters		

Occupations in Which Individuals Remain a High Number of Years

H	Airplane Pilots	H	Heavy equipment mechanics
H	Barbers	H	Machinists
H	Chemists	H	Pharmacists
H	Civil engineers	H	Radiologic technicians
H	Clergy	H	Tailors
H	Construction inspectors	H	Teachers (elementary and high school)
H	Crane operators	H	Tool and die makers
H	Doctors, dentists, veterinarians	H	Truck and bus mechanics
H	Farmers		

To make a set of Occupations Cards, photocopy the following items and cut them out.

Accountants and auditors	Actors and directors	Administrative managers and supervisors
Advertising	Airplane pilots	Architects
Artists and performers	Authors	Automobile mechanics
Bakers	Bank tellers	Barbers
Bartenders	Billing clerks	Bookkeepers and auditors
Brick masons and stonemasons	Bus drivers	Butchers and meat cutters

Buyers (except farm)	Carpenters	Cashiers
Chemical engineers	Chemists	Child care workers
Civil engineers	Clergy	Computer operators
Computer programmers	Computer system analysts	Concrete finishers
Construction inspectors	Construction laborers	Correctional officers
Counselors	Crane operators	Dental hygienists

Doctors, dentists, veterinarians	Drafters and mechanical drawers	Economists
Editors and reporters	Electrical and electronic engineers	Electrical and electronic technicians
Engineers	Farmers	Financial managers
Firefighters	Freight, stock, and material handlers	Garage and service station workers
Guards	Hairdressers and cosmetologists	Health record technicians
Heat and air conditioning mechanics	Heavy equipment mechanics	Hotel clerks

Insurance adjusters and investigators	Janitors and cleaners	Kitchen workers
Lawyers	Legal assistants	Librarians
Licensed practical nurses	Machine operators	Machinists
Maids and housemen	Mail carriers, postal service	Meter readers
Nursing aides and orderlies	Office clerks	Packaging and filling machine operators
Painters, construction, and maintenance	Personnel, trainers	Pharmacists

Photographers	Physical therapists	Physicians' assistants
Plumbers, pipefitters, and steamfitters	Police officers, sheriffs, and bailiffs	Psychologists
Radiologic technicians	Real estate sales	Receptionists
Registered nurses	Roofers	Sewing machine operators
Secretaries	Sheet metal workers	Short-order cooks
Speech therapists	Stenographers	Tailors

Taxi drivers and chauffeurs	Teachers (elementary and high school)	Teachers (postsecondary)
Telephone operators	Timber cutters and loggers	Tool and die makers
Truck drivers, heavy	Truck drivers, light	Truck and bus mechanics
Typists	Upholsterers	Waiters and waitresses

TOP FIVE (NOVICE CLASS)

TOPIC
The Top Five Occupations in Selected Categories

LEARNING OBJECTIVE
Participants will be able to identify the top occupations in stressfulness, income, and job security.

NUMBER OF PARTICIPANTS
Any number

PLAYING TIME
7-10 minutes

REFERENCE
Krantz, L., ed. (1988). *The jobs rated almanac.* New York: World Almanac.

REQUIRED MATERIALS
Pencils, list of Top Five for Novice Occupations, and Top Five (Novice Class) playing board

TO PLAY
1. Introduce players to the concepts of job stress, income level, and job security.
2. Pass out game materials to each player [pencils, list of Top Five for Novice Occupations, and Top Five (Novice Class) playing board].
3. Explain that they have five minutes to rewrite the list of occupations on the playing board in rank order.
4. Say, "Go."
5. Five minutes later call, "Stop."
6. Give players the correct answers, with each participant checking her/his own answers.
7. Declare the individual(s) with the most correct answers the winner(s).
8. Debrief players. Discuss the aspects of jobs or occupations that make them more or less stressful, that are high- or low-paying, or that vary in their job security. Have players cite observed relationships between high-paying occupations and stress and between high-paying occupations and job security.

TOP FIVE FOR NOVICE OCCUPATIONS

Most Stressful	Highest Income	Best Job Security
Surgeon	Race car driver (Indy class)	Bank officer
Football player	Basketball player (NBA)	Hospital administrator
Firefighter	Football player (NFL)	Civil engineer
Race car driver (Indy class)	Surgeon	Technical/copy writer
Astronaut	Baseball player (major league)	Industrial engineer

TOP FIVE (NOVICE CLASS) PLAYING BOARD

Directions: In rank order, rewrite your list of occupations in the boxes below.

Most Stressful	Highest Income	Best Job Security
1	1	1
2	2	2
		Civil Engineer
3	3	3
Astronaut		
4	4	4
	Football Player NFL	
5	5	5

126

TOP FIVE (PROS CLASS)

TOPIC

The Top Five Occupations in Terms of Physical Strength Requirements, Having the Most Perks, and Having the Best Working Environments

LEARNING OBJECTIVE

Participants will be able to give the top-ranking occupations in the areas of physical strength required, having the most perks, and having the best working environments.

NUMBER OF PARTICIPANTS

Any number

PLAYING TIME

12-15 minutes

REFERENCE

Krantz, L., ed. (1988). *The jobs rated almanac.* New York: World Almanac.

REQUIRED MATERIALS

Pencils, list of Top Five for the Pros Occupations, and Top Five (Pro Class) playing board.

TO PLAY

1. Introduce players to the concepts of physical strength, perks, and work environment.

2. Pass out game materials to each player [pencils, list of Top Five for the Pros Occupations, and Top Five (Pro Class) playing board].

3. Explain that they have seven minutes to rewrite the list of occupations on the playing board in rank order.

4. Say, "Go."

5. Seven minutes later call, "Stop."

6. Give players the correct answers, with each participant checking her/his own answers. Have players award themselves 1 point for having an occupation in the right column and another point for having an occupation in the correct box.

7. Declare the individual(s) with the most correct answers the winner(s).

8. Debrief players. Discuss the aspects of jobs or occupations that make them require greater strength, allow for more perks, or provide a more favorable working environment. Have players cite possible relationships between a more favorable work environment and requirements of greater strength and a more favorable work environment and more perks.

TOP FIVE FOR THE PROS OCCUPATIONS

Actuary	Dairy farmer	Roustabout
Attorney	Firefighter	Seaman
Basketball coach	Historian	Senator/congressperson
Clergyman	Hotel manager	Statistician
Computer systems analyst	Mathematician	Undertaker

TOP FIVE (PRO CLASS) PLAYING BOARD

Directions: In rank order, rewrite your list of occupations in the boxes below.

Requiring Greatest Strength	Has the Most Perks	Best Environment to Work in
1	1	1
		Mathematician
2	2	2
3	3	3
Undertaker		
4	4	4
5	5	5
	Senator/congressperson	

UNEMPLOYMENT LINE

TOPIC   Occupations with the Highest and Lowest Unemployment Rates

**LEARNING
OBJECTIVE**   Participants will be able to sort out occupations with low unemployment rates from those
                     with high unemployment rates.

**NUMBER OF
PARTICIPANTS**   Up to 17 players with one set of unemployment cards or up to 35 players with two sets of
                     unemployment cards

PLAYING TIME   15-20 minutes depending on the number of players

REFERENCE   *Current Population Survey*. (1992). Washington, DC: U.S. Department of Labor, Depart-
                     ment of Labor Statistics.

**REQUIRED
MATERIALS**   Occupation Cards, Occupation Employment Rate Sheets, bulletin board or large table,
                     and thumb tacks

TO PLAY   **1.** Introduce players to the concept of unemployment rates among various occupations.

                     2. Go over the learning objective for the game.

                     3. Tell participants that they are going to play a brief little game called *Unemployment
                     Line.*

                     4. Explain to players that they will be asked to select an occupation from among several
                     other career fields.

                     5. Inform them that the goal of the game is to pick out an occupation with a low unem-
                     ployment rate and thereby stay out of the unemployment line.

                     6. Advise players that they have only 60 seconds to go to the back of the room and re-
                     move an occupation from the bulletin board and return to their seats. Otherwise, they
                     must stand in the unemployment line. (Prior to the game the facilitator needs to tack
                     the Occupation Cards in alphabetical order on a bulletin board in the back of the
                     room. If no bulletin board is available, the cards can be placed on a large table face
                     up.)

                     7. Tell players to get an occupation from the bulletin board. Remind them that they must
                     be back in their seats within 60 seconds.

                     8. After 60 seconds call, "Time." Ask players still out of their seats to form an unemploy-
                     ment line in the front of the room. Collect their occupation cards and retack them to
                     the bulletin board.

                     9. In a clockwise direction around the room, have each player reveal the occupation
                     she/he selected. If the occupation is on the list of occupations with the highest un-
                     employment rates (Fig. 4.3), ask that player to go stand in the unemployment line.

10. Have all of the players who are still seated (i.e., individuals who chose occupations with low unemployment rates) to once again go to the back of the room and select an occupation.

11. Repeat steps 8 and 9.

12. Declare all of the players who managed to escape the unemployment line both times the winners.

13. Debrief players. Discuss what determines whether an occupation has a high or low unemployment rate. Ask participants on which list (high or low unemployment) they would place their own occupations. Ask players who place their career fields on the highest unemployment list if they would still choose this occupation regardless of its high unemployment rate. Have them explain why.

Figure 4.4. High unemployment rate sheets in selected occupations.

Occupation	Percentage of Workers Unemployed
Grader and sorter of agricultural products	34.0
Structural metal worker	30.3
Concrete and terrazzo finisher	28.0
Construction helper	25.2
Construction laborer	22.9
Drywall installer	21.1
Production helper in industrial occupation	19.9
Grader or sorter in nonagricultural industry	18.4
Insulation worker	18.2
Brick mason or stonemason	17.7
Roofer	16.3
Pressing machine operator	16.2
Vehicle washer or equipment cleaner	15.3
Carpenter	14.5
Garage or service station worker	14.2
Painter (construction or maintenance)	14.1
Packaging or filling machine operator	13.8
Laborer in nonconstruction industry	13.7
Actor or director	13.5
Hand packer or packager	13.4

Figure 4.5. Low unemployment rate sheets in selected occupations.

Occupation	Percentage of Workers Unemployed
Speech therapist	0.1
Respiratory therapist	0.1
Stenographer	0.1
Farmer	0.3
Clergy person	0.4
Physician	0.5
Police supervisor	0.5
Dental hygienist	0.5
Dentist	0.6
Radiological technician	0.7
Pharmacist	0.8
Funeral director	0.9
Dental lab/medical appliance technician	0.9
Registered nurse	1.1
Lawyer	1.2

To prepare a set of occupation cards, photocopy the following items on card stock paper and cut out the individual cards.

Grader and sorter of agricultural products	Structural metal worker
Concrete and terrazzo finisher	Construction helper
Construction laborer	Drywall installer
Production helper in industrial occupation	Grader or sorter in nonagricultural industry

Insulation worker

Brick mason or stonemason

Roofer

Pressing machine operator

Vehicle washer or equipment cleaner

Carpenter

Garage or service station worker

Painter (construction or maintenance)

Packaging or filling machine operator	Laborer in nonconstruction industry
Actor or director	Hand packer or packager
Speech therapist	Respiratory therapist
Stenographer	Farmer

Clergy person	Physician
Police supervisor	Dental hygienist
Dentist	Radiological technician
Pharmacist	Funeral director

Dental lab/medical appliance technician

Registered nurse

Lawyer

WHERE IN THE USA IS JO(E) TRAINER?

TOPIC

Training Roles and Competencies

LEARNING OBJECTIVE

Participants will be able to associate human resource development outputs and/or competencies with selected human resource developer roles.

NUMBER OF PARTICIPANTS

Any number

PLAYING TIME

15–45 minutes depending on the number of cases solved

REFERENCE

McLagan, P. (1989). The models. *In Models for HRD Practice,* Vols. 1–4. Alexandria, VA: American Society for Training and Development.

REQUIRED MATERIALS

Pencils, Where in the USA Is Jo(e) Trainer? Playing Board, and Where in the USA Is Jo(e) Trainer Clue Cards

TO PLAY

1. Introduce players to the concepts of work roles, work outputs, and competencies.

2. Inform players that human resource developers play such work roles as researcher, marketer, organization change agent, needs analyst, program designer, HRD materials developer, instructor/facilitator, individual career development advisor, administrator, evaluator, and HRD manager.

3. Explain that the object of the game is to solve a mystery regarding a trainer. To solve the mystery, their group of detectives must identify Jo(e)'s job (work role), her/his employing organization, and the city in which she/he works.

4. Advise players that they will be given up to five clue cards (one every minute) for each case they work on. If they solve the case within the first minute, they receive 50 points. If they solve it within two minutes, they receive 40 points, and so on until, if they solve it within the maximum five minutes allowed to solve a mystery, they receive 10 points.

5. Tell participants that they must get all three items (the job, the company, and the city) correct to solve the mystery.

6. Divide the larger group into smaller groups of three to five members each.

7. Pass out game materials (pencils, one playing board per group, and clue card #1 for the first case). Tell participants to yell, "Solution" when they think they have solved the mystery.

8. Advise players they must give their answer aloud. If they are correct, they will receive the appropriate number of points and play moves on to next case.

9. Warn players that, if any group's solution is incorrect, they are out of the game for that mystery. Play continues until there is a winner or until the entire five minutes allowed to solve a case elapses.

10. After each minute passes, hand groups another clue card.

11. Congratulate groups as they solve the respective mysteries.

12. At the end of the last round played, add up the total number of points each team has accumulated. Declare the group with the most points "master human resource development detectives."

13. Debrief players. Discuss the job titles and roles of various human resource development positions. Talk about some of the competencies that might be needed to play these roles.

WHERE IN THE USA IS JO(E) TRAINER? PLAYING BOARD

ANSWER CARD

	CITY	COMPANY	HRD JOB
1			
2			
3			
4			
5			

CLUE CARD #1

	CITY	COMPANY	HRD JOB
C A S E 1	This city has some 30 foreign language newspapers.	This company produces wearing apparel.	This person is responsible for the learning environment.

CLUE CARD #2

	CITY	COMPANY	HRD JOB
C A S E 1	This city has the museum ship, the Balclutha.	This is a family-run company. It has only had one CEO who was not a family member. He held the job one year.	This person provides feedback to learners.

CLUE CARD #3

	CITY	COMPANY	HRD JOB
C A S E 1	This city is on one of the world's greatest natural harbors.	The company headquarters facility is described as having "the trappings of a worker's paradise."	This person facilitates Media Based Learning Events.

CLUE CARD #4

	CITY	COMPANY	HRD JOB
C A S E 1	While here, a tourist may want to take a cable car to the top of Nob Hill.	Unions have never been opposed by this company.	Some group discussions are facilitated by this person.

CLUE CARD #5

	CITY	COMPANY	HRD JOB
C A S E 1	Tony Bennett left his heart here, perhaps on the Golden Gate Bridge.	The name of this company is often used synonymously for any brand of blue jeans.	The main job of this person is to present the material to be learned.

CLUE CARD #1

CASE 2

CITY	COMPANY	HRD JOB
This city's China Town covers a tiny nine square blocks.	This company has a close-knit family atmosphere.	This position requires cost-benefit analysis skill.

CLUE CARD #2

CASE 2

CITY	COMPANY	HRD JOB
Fraunces Tavern, built in 1719 is one of the few remaining restored colonial buildings in this city.	This company encourages employees to look for new challenges by moving around in the company.	This position requires understanding of organizational behavior.

CLUE CARD #3

CASE 2

CITY	COMPANY	HRD JOB
Frank Lloyd Wright's *Spiral* is at the Guggenheim Museum here.	This company is sometimes viewed as a "preppy institution."	This person takes large amounts of information, sorts it, and organizes it into a useful form.

CLUE CARD #4

CASE 2

CITY	COMPANY	HRD JOB
Greenwich Village was this city's first residential suburb, started in the late 1730s.	This company is the largest magazine publisher in the nation.	This person provides feedback to other team members and interested parties.

CLUE CARD #5

CASE 2

CITY	COMPANY	HRD JOB
Many people come here to take in plays on and off Broadway.	Book ventures include such topics as the *Old West* and *Psychic Phenomena*.	This person assesses the impact of an intervention on individuals and organizational effectiveness.

CLUE CARD #1

CASE 3

	CITY	COMPANY	HRD JOB
	This city has the largest traditional Japanese garden in the United States, Shaw's Botanical Garden.	This company sells more of its type of beverage than anyone else in the world.	This person must understand the way adults learn.

CLUE CARD #2

CASE 3

	CITY	COMPANY	HRD JOB
	This city is known for its German traditions.	In 1982, Jesse Jackson threatened to boycott this company in an effort to promote minority economic development.	This person must be able to identify learning objectives and put them in sequential order.

CLUE CARD #3

CASE 3

	CITY	COMPANY	HRD JOB
	This city is located on the Mississippi.	This company has been in the process of changing from an authoritarian family-run business to a professionally managed company.	This person finds creative ways of transferring what is learned in the classroom back to the work site.

CLUE CARD #4

CASE 3

	CITY	COMPANY	HRD JOB
	Busch Memorial Stadium is here, providing entertainment for baseball fans.	Three of this company's headquarters complexes are historical landmarks.	This person constructs the blueprint for a training program.

CLUE CARD #5

CASE 3

	CITY	COMPANY	HRD JOB
	Here we find the Jefferson National Expansion Memorial, Gateway to the West.	Clydesdale horses and Ed McMahon are familiar figures in this company's advertisements.	This person identifies objectives to be met and appropriate interventions to meet these objectives.

CLUE CARD #1

	CITY	COMPANY	HRD JOB
C A S E 4	This city is know for its Greek revival architecture.	In the health care field itself, this company pays its employees to keep fit.	This person is responsible for training managers and supervisors to conduct formal training at their sites.

CLUE CARD #2

	CITY	COMPANY	HRD JOB
C A S E 4	This city is a state capital.	This company furnishes training through its audiovisual department.	This person evaluates staff training programs.

CLUE CARD #3

	CITY	COMPANY	HRD JOB
C A S E 4	Vanderbilt University has its mailing address in this city.	Employees can set aside 10 percent of their salaries to purchase stock in this company at a 15 percent discount.	The person is familiar with the terms "formative" and "summative."

CLUE CARD #4

	CITY	COMPANY	HRD JOB
C A S E 4	Andrew Jackson called the Hermitage "home" near here.	Emphasis is on business management expertise rather than the other functions associated with this company.	This person plans and schedules work for their unit for optimum efficiency.

CLUE CARD #5

	CITY	COMPANY	HRD JOB
C A S E 4	This is the home of the "Grand Ole Opry" and Opryland USA.	This company is the largest for-profit hospital in the world.	Running the HRD department is this person's responsibility.

CLUE CARD #1

	CITY	COMPANY	HRD JOB
C A S E **5**	This city is part of an 11-county standard metropolitan statistical area of 8360 square miles.	This company produces high-tech products, yet has a down-home image.	This job requires knowledge of adult development theories.

CLUE CARD #2

	CITY	COMPANY	HRD JOB
C A S E **5**	In physical size, this city has the largest airport in the United States.	All stores, both franchised and company-owned, are considered profit centers, and bonuses are a way of life.	This person works with individuals rather than with groups.

CLUE CARD #3

	CITY	COMPANY	HRD JOB
C A S E **5**	This city is close to Arlington Stadium, home of the Rangers of baseball fame.	This company matches between 40 and 80 percent of employees' contribution to company stock purchases.	Individuals are helped to identify their personal competencies, values, and goals by this person.

CLUE CARD #4

	CITY	COMPANY	HRD JOB
C A S E **5**	One may go to rodeos at the Cowtown Coliseum here.	An eight-foot bronze statue of the founder of this company stands on the grounds of the county courthouse.	From this person, individuals learn how to develop a plan for their life's work.

CLUE CARD #5

	CITY	COMPANY	HRD JOB
C A S E **5**	With Dallas, this city is the Gateway to the North.	Though they sell many different electronic items, only one is mentioned in the name of this company's stores.	People in career transitions may get support and assistance from this person.

Chapter Five
CAREER CLIMATE GAMES

There is an internal and an external dimension to careers. The *internal dimension* includes that which is inside an individual's psyche. It comprises a person's occupational interests, abilities, skills, values, self-concept, and personality traits. The *external dimension* includes such things as jobs, employing organizations, career fields, economic cycles, and societal norms. Collectively these and other external elements make up *career climate*. An understanding of current career climate conditions enables workers to make more informed career choices and adjustments.

Chapter 5 contains 10 games to supplement instruction aimed at helping learners become aware of the current career climate. Five games pertain to selected business and/or work trends. *Everybody Merge* and *Honey, They've Shrunk the Company* address recent mergers and downsizings. *Heads Up 2000* and *Ladies Lineup (World)* relate to employment trends. *Playing the Career Odds* looks at the frequency at which selected work events occur.

Three games in Chap. 5 focus on major corporate competitors. *Logo Roundup* tests players' general awareness of U.S. businesses, and *Company Capers* exposes participants to leading companies in selected manufacturing and service industries. The final two games, *Notes and Quotes* and *Translation, Please,* deal with American beliefs about work that have made their way into song lyrics and old adages.

COMPANY CAPERS (MANUFACTURING)

TOPIC   Leading Companies in Selected Manufacturing Industries

LEARNING
OBJECTIVE   Participants will be able to identify various companies within selected manufacturing industries.

NUMBER OF
PARTICIPANTS   Any number

PLAYING TIME   10–35 minutes depending on how many rounds played

REFERENCE   Moskowitz, M., Levering, R., and Katz, M., eds. (1990). *Everybody's business: A field guide of the 400 leading companies in America.* New York: Doubleday Currency.

REQUIRED
MATERIALS   Pencils and Capers Boards 1–5

TO PLAY   1. Discuss why it is important from a career perspective to know something about leading companies in selected industries.

2. Go over the learning objective for the game.

3. Explain to players that they are now going to test their knowledge of American companies by means of a game similar to *Tic-tac-toe.*

4. Ask players what industry group they would first like to test their knowledge of (autos, computers, health and beauty, petroleum, or personal vices).

5. Pass out pencils and copies of the Caper Board dealing with the industry that the participants have chosen.

6. Explain that the object of the game is to get three correct answers in a row (such as three in a row horizontally, vertically, or diagonally) or to get four correct answers, one in each corner of the board.

7. Give players two minutes to fill in their answers.

8. Give the correct answers, having participants check their own responses.

9. Repeat the process for up to five rounds. After the last round, determine which player(s) won the most rounds. Declare them the winner(s) and most knowledgeable player(s) regarding American manufacturers.

10. Debrief players. Discuss which leading companies became leaders only within the past 10 years. Ask participants to speculate on what made these companies leaders in their industry groups. As a group, conjecture as to which companies might not be leaders 10 years from now and cite why.

Directions: First read each of the following nine questions. Write the names of companies in only three squares, in either a horizontal, a vertical, or a diagonal row. As an alternative, you may choose to write the names of four companies in the corner squares.

1. What automobile company making five brands of cars is also second in the country in mortgage banking?	2. What company, which calls Dearborn Michigan home, sold their model Ts in 1914 for $440 each and paid their workers an unheard of $5 per day?	3. What U.S. automaker, rescued by Iacocca, owns Lamborghini and a small interest in Maserati?
4. What rural backwater Japanese car company broke into the business by using people recruited from GM operations in Japan?	5. What car company, whose founder was the first Japanese auto executive inducted into the American Automobile Hall of Fame, makes Accords in Ohio and exports them to Japan?	6. What automaker started in the United States by selling their cars under the Chrysler name, and then joined forces with them to build an auto plant in Illinois?
7. What auto company, a creation of Adolph Hitler, and the number one automaker in Europe, is experiencing a dwindling market in the United States?	8. What Japanese auto company's chairman said in 1980 that the problems of U.S. automakers were of their own making because nobody wants to work?	9. In 1989, what German luxury automaker introduced 12- and 24-month warrantees on their used cars sold here by their U.S. dealers?

Directions: First read each of the following nine questions. Write the names of companies in only three squares, in either a horizontal, a vertical, or a diagonal row. As an alternative, you may choose to write the names of four companies in the corner squares.

1. What Dayton, Ohio company makes the machines used for years to ring up retail sales?	2. What company is not only number one in mainframe computers, but also in charitable contributions?	3. What company in the early years had rock and roll music in the halls and meeting rooms named after the seven Dwarfs and the deadly sins?
4. What software company was started by a 19-year-old Harvard dropout who ultimately became the country's youngest billionaire?	5. What company, known as the "Father of Silicon Valley," introduced a handheld calculator in 1972, making the slide rule obsolete?	6. What company was created by a Chinese immigrant who acquired a Ph.D. in physics from Harvard?
7. Instead of making "better" IBM-type computers, what company now makes its own, using a consensus type of management to solve problems?	8. What much smaller company produced its VAX mainframe system to compete with IBM's more expensive and complex systems?	9. The founder of what company, referred to as the virus-plagued giant by some, has been criticized for paying more attention to social causes rather than the bottom line?

Directions: First read each of the following nine questions. Write the names of companies in only three squares, in either a horizontal, a vertical, or a diagonal row. As an alternative, you may choose to write the names of four companies in the corner squares.

1. What world's largest consumer goods company gives you the aroma of Liz Taylor's "Passion" and a "Pepsodent Smile?" _____	2. What company can cure a hangover with a "plop, plop, fizz, fizz," but cannot market the one product it's famous for, aspirin, under its own name in the United States? _____	3. What company, which brought Proctor & Gamble into the cosmetic business, has made the skin cream in the blue jar since 1917? _____
4. What number one shaving goods and toothbrush maker agreed in 1989 to remove a carcinogen from the formula of their Liquid Paper product? _____	5. What company merged with Bristol Meyers and plans to invest hundreds of millions of dollars in research to develop more drugs like its heart drug, Capoten? _____	6. What company makes Motrin to cure the ache in your head and Rogaine to put hair on it? _____
7. What company started selling toothpaste in jars in 1877, ribbon dental cream in 1908, and in 1985 drew criticism for allowing its Hong Kong acquisition to market a toothpaste named "Darkie"? _____	8. Though the leading maker of equipment used to analyze blood, what healthcare company is also the leader in infant formulas? _____	9. What cosmetic company's products, found in upscale department stores, might you shop for while wearing "white linen"? _____

Directions: First read each of the following nine questions. Write the names of companies in only three squares, in either a horizontal, a vertical, or a diagonal row. As an alternative, you may choose to write the names of four companies in the corner squares.

1. What company, once known for job security and prestige, had a major reduction in workforce in the 1980s, which may have contributed to this country's largest oil spill and disorganized clean-up efforts?	2. What foreign-held U.S. oil company is the former Standard Oil of Ohio and has replaced such brand names as Gulf, Mobil, and Sohio in some areas of the country with their own logo?	3. What company makes this nation's leading motor oil, owns 80 percent of the Jiffy Lube chain, and was first known as Zapata Oil founded by Hugh Liedtke and George Bush?
4. What oil company's media ad said that, "You can trust your car to the man who wears the star"?	5. What Anglo-Dutch oil company, based in Houston, Texas, is the top contender with Exxon for the title of "world's largest oil company"?	6. What company, which was once called Socony-Vacuum and which used a flying red horse as its logo, now offers to come to your home or place of work to change the oil in your car?
7. What oil company, owners of Ortho lawn products and a winery, was once Standard Oil of California and bought and dismantled Gulf Oil?	8. In 1987, the Council on Economic Priorities gave their first Corporate Conscience Award to what midwestern oil company based in Chicago?	9. What oil company, founded in 1903 as Anchor Oil, now bears the name of its founder and a famous U.S. highway?

Directions: First read each of the following nine questions. Write the names of companies in only three squares, in either a horizontal, a vertical, or a diagonal row. As an alternative, you may choose to write the names of four companies in the corner squares.

1. What company might allow you to ride through Winston-Salem, North Carolina, on a "Ritzy" camel while eating the middle of your Oreos first?	2. What company makes Roman Meal Bread, Eagle Snacks, and runs theme parks in addition to brewing the King of Beers?	3. What number one winemaker, started by Ernest & Julio, hired the fictional Frank and Ed to do commercials for their wine coolers?
4. In what company might the ever loyal Marlboro man eat an Oscar Meyer Weiner, covered with Kraft cheese, washed down with a Miller beer, and have Jello pudding for dessert?	5. What number one distiller of hard liquor, with such brands as V.O., Chivas Regal, and Meyers Rum, also makes Tropicana juices to mix them with?	6. What company, the nation's largest casino operator and slot machine maker, is also number one in health clubs?
7. What Rocky Mountain brew, not found east of the Mississippi before 1980, is now sold in Japan and Canada?	8. What company makes Pall Mall cigarettes and Jim Beam whiskey, but doesn't supply the "wild, wild women" of old folk ballad fame?	9. What Lacrosse, Wisconsin brewer of Old Style Beer, was sold in 1987 to Australian Alan Bond?

COMPANY CAPERS (SERVICE)

TOPIC   Leading Companies in Selected Service Industries

LEARNING OBJECTIVE   Participants will be able to identify various companies within selected service industries.

NUMBER OF PARTICIPANTS   Any number

PLAYING TIME   10-35 minutes depending on how many rounds played

REFERENCE   Moskowitz, M., Levering, R., and Katz, M., eds. (1990). *Everybody's business: A field guide of the 400 leading companies in America.* New York: Doubleday Currency.

REQUIRED MATERIALS   Pencils and Capers Boards 6-10

TO PLAY

1. Discuss why it is important from a career perspective to know something about leading companies in selected industries.

2. Go over the learning objective for the game.

3. Explain to players that they are going to test their knowledge of American companies by means of a game similar to *Tic-tac-toe.*

4. Ask players to select a service industry in which they would like to test their knowledge (conglomerates, grocers, hotels and restaurants, publishing, or travel and transport).

5. Pass out pencils and copies of the Caper Board dealing with the industry the participants have chosen.

6. Explain that the object of the game is to get three correct answers in a row (three in a row horizontally, vertically, or diagonally) or get four correct answers, one in each corner of the board.

7. Give players two minutes to fill in their answers

8. Provide the correct answers, having participants check their own responses.

9. Repeat the process for up to five rounds. After the last round, determine which player(s) won the most rounds. Declare them the winner(s) and most knowledgeable player(s) regarding American service industries.

10. Debrief players. Discuss which leading companies became leaders only within the past 10 years. Ask participants to speculate on what made these companies leaders in their industry groups. As a group, conjecture as to which companies might not be leaders 10 years from now and cite why.

COMPANY CAPERS BOARD #6: CONGLOMERATES

Directions: First read each of the following nine questions. Write the names of companies in only three squares, in either a horizontal, a vertical, or a diagonal row. As an alternative, you may choose to write the names of four companies in the corner squares.

1. What company, which owns such things as financial services companies and a TV network, promises "to bring good things to light"? _____	2. What company, originally started to mine corundum, stuck to its principles with its most famous product "scotch tape"? _____	3. What company, no longer driving buses, is now more concerned with catering airline food to nice smelling passengers? _____
4. What former telecommunications company has dumped its phone business for such things as antilock brakes, hotels, and insurance? _____	5. Though still retaining its original gas pipelines, what company also owns the world's largest private shipyard at Newport News, Virginia and has a name that sounds like it's from the volunteer state? _____	6. Hanson Industries has among its holdings Faberware cookware, Ground Round restaurants, and what famous brand of whirlpool baths? _____
7. What company, once known for its microwave oven, now concentrates on military electronics? _____	8. Charles Thompson, Simon Ramo, and Dean Woodridge got together to form which prime contractor in the "Star Wars" program? _____	9. Which company includes under its "roof" Carrier Air Conditioners and Otis Elevators? _____

COMPANY CAPERS BOARD #7: ON THE GROCER'S SHELVES

Directions: First read each of the following nine questions. Write the names of companies in only three squares, in either a horizontal, a vertical, or a diagonal row. As an alternative, you may choose to write the names of four companies in the corner squares.

1. What Atlanta-based soft drink company's first product was invented by a pharmacist who claimed it would cure various maladies caused by overindulgence? _____	2. What company controls over 70 percent of the baby food market, claiming "babies are our business—our only business"? _____	3. What Arkansas chicken company is not only number one in the United States, but was the first nationally advertised chicken brand in Japan? _____
4. What number one chocolate and candy company makes E.T.'s favorite snack although they have no products from outer space? _____	5. What company, owners of the Olive Garden and Red Lobster restaurants, is the number one maker of flour and cake mixes? _____	6. What former Girl Scout cookie maker still knows "the right thing to do"? _____
7. What farm supply co-op is the number one supplier of quality butter? _____	8. What well liked frozen food maker might wear Bali underwear while using Fuller Brush products? _____	9. An ice box manufacturer, fruit merchant, and chemist founded what company that was first to sell a name brand product coast-to-coast? _____

COMPANY CAPERS BOARD #8: HOTELS AND RESTAURANTS

Directions: First read each of the following nine questions. Write the names of companies in only three squares, in either a horizontal, a vertical, or a diagonal row. As an alternative, you may choose to write the names of four companies in the corner squares.

1. In what upscale hotel room would you find not only a Gideon's Bible, but also a Book of Mormon and a biography of the founder, Joseph Smith?	2. What motel under a distinctive green sign is number three and has the most rooms to rent?	3. What international chain, which sounds like it could have been founded by a superlative cowboy, is a nonprofit association of independently owned and operated facilities?
4. What company owns both the Waldorf Astoria in New York and the Palmer House in Chicago, but derives its greatest income from its "casino hotels"?	5. What upscale hotel chain, under the fancy "S" sign and subsidiary of ITT, was the first hotel chain listed on the New York Stock Exchange in 1949?	6. Started by two brothers in college at the time, but now owned by Pepsico, what number one pizza restaurant "delivers"?
7. What number one fast food chain opened its largest store to date in 1990 in Moscow's Pushkin Square?	8. What fast food chain owes its success to the colonel's secret recipe?	9. What company, started by Dave Thomas, asked in the 1980s, "Where's the beef?"?

155

Directions: First read each of the following nine questions. Write the names of companies in only three squares, in either a horizontal, a vertical, or a diagonal row. As an alternative, you may choose to write the names of four companies in the corner squares.

1. What company not only owns two of the top ten U.S. newspapers, one in Chicago and one in New York, but also purchased the Chicago Cubs in 1981 and lit up Wrigley Field?	2. What media giant, though retaining the original founder's name, is controlled by nonfamily and owns TV and radio stations, book publishers, and such magazines as *Esquire* and *Cosmopolitan*?	3. What book publisher, under former leader Bennett Cerf, won the most famous censorship case in the history of the United States (James Joyce's *Ulysses*)?
4. What company has the world's most widely read magazine, maybe because its condensed stories take less time to read?	5. To what newspaper company did Virginia write concerning the existence of Santa Claus, because if it was printed in this paper it must be so?	6. What number one book publisher in the United States also owns Prentice-Hall, Ginn, and Silver Burdett textbook publishers?
7. What company, publisher of *The Wall Street Journal*, has a strong influence on stock market action?	8. What book company, whose mission since 1888 has been to supply information about industries, publishes *Business Week* magazine?	9. What newspaper, noted for its investigative reporting of Watergate, owns *Newsweek* magazine?

COMPANY CAPERS BOARD #10: TRAVEL AND TRANSPORT

Directions: First read each of the following nine questions. Write the names of companies in only three squares, in either a horizontal, a vertical, or a diagonal row. As an alternative, you may choose to write the names of four companies in the corner squares.

1. What "golden spike" railroad opened up the West, has 23,000 miles of track in 19 states, and hauls coal from company-owned mines in Wyoming?	2. What airline, recognizable by the logo of its initials and wings, in its early years employed Charles Lindbergh and was first to have a plane built to its own specifications?	3. What package delivery service claims to run "the tightest ship in the shipping industry"?
4. What passenger rail service is owned and subsidized by the federal government?	5. What trucking company, whose name describes the surface beneath its tires, was first started to ship tires made in Akron, Ohio to consumer auto plants?	6. What "puddle jumper" airline in the early days of its existence devised a method of dropping off a container of mail and picking up another without landing?
7. What number one overnight package service was first conceived by a young Yale college student in a term paper for which he received a C?	8. What airlines, an amalgamation of several small ones, was the first to hire a stewardess, Ellen Church, in 1930?	9. What railroad lost one of the biggest ever race bias suits in 1983 and a class action suit brought by female employees in 1986?

EVERYBODY MERGE

TOPIC   Recent Mergers of American Companies

LEARNING OBJECTIVE   Participants will be able to give the names and years in which selected American companies merged.

NUMBER OF PARTICIPANTS   Any even number 4–60

PLAYING TIME   10–15 minutes depending on the size of the group

REFERENCES   Hanson, R., ed. (1992). *Moody's Industrial Manual 1992*. New York: Moody's Investor Service, Inc.

Hanson, R., ed. (1993). *Moody's Industrial News Reports*. New York: Moody's Investor Service, Inc.

Stevens, R., ed. (1992). *Moody's Transportation Manual*. New York: Moody's Investor Service, Inc.

REQUIRED MATERIALS   Pencils, Merger Chart, and set of Merger Cards

TO PLAY

1. Introduce players to the concepts of mergers and acquisitions.
2. Go over the learning objective for the game.
3. Explain that they are about to be handed a card with the name of a company printed on it. Another person in the room will be given a card with the name of a company that has recently merged with their company.
4. Inform participants that they are to find the other person who has the card bearing the name of the company that has merged with their firm.
5. Tell players that they will have 5–10 minutes (5 minutes for groups with 16 or less members and 10 minutes for groups over 16 members) to find the correct company. They can ask any question of any person in the room to help them find the company that merged with their organization.
6. Advise players that, after they have located the person with the correct company card, they are to write the year their two companies merged on the backs of their cards. They are not to ask others in the room for assistance in coming up with the merger year.
7. Pass out pencils to each of the players.
8. Shuffle a stack of Merger Cards in front of the players. Make certain the stack has the correct number of matching sets of cards in it. Have a participant come forward and cut the deck.

9. Go around the room, having each participant draw one card from the top of the stack.

10. Give players the appropriate amount of time (5 or 10 minutes) to locate their merged companies and determine the year they merged.

11. Call, "Time."

12. Read the answers aloud from the Merger Chart. Have pairs raise their hands if they have located the correct company. Congratulate these players and award them 5 points.

13. Ask for pairs who guessed the correct year their companies merged to raise their hands. Congratulate them for coming up with the correct date in addition to the correct company. Award them 5 more points and declare them "major merger moguls."

14. Debrief players. Discuss some of the reasons why there has been so many mergers in recent years. Ask participants to list some of the ways mergers impact the careers of individuals employed by the merging companies.

MERGER CARDS

To prepare a deck of Merger Cards, make a photocopy of the following items using card stock paper. Cut out individual cards.

Texaco	Getty Oil Co.
RJ Reynolds	Nabisco Brands, Inc.
Phillip Morris Companies, Inc.	General Foods Corp.
General Motors Corp.	Hughes Aircraft Co.
Turner Broadcasting System, Inc.	MGM/UA

HJ Heinz Co.	Pet Foods
Time, Inc.	Warner Communications
Sony Corp.	Columbia Pictures Entertainment
Chrysler Corp.	Thrifty Rent-A-Car
Consolidated Freightways	Emery Air Freight Corp.
Dr. Pepper Co.	I.B.C. Root Beer
Hershey Foods Corp.	Ronzoni Foods Corp.
Pennzoil	Jiffy Lube
Pepsi Foods Intl.	Hostess Frito-Lay
Proctor & Gamble Co.	Revlon, Inc.'s Max Factor

Sara Lee Corp.	Playtex Apparel, Inc. Co.
Shoney's, Inc.	Big Boy Restaurants
Walt Disney Co.	Miramax Film Corp.
Great Atlantic & Pacific Tea Company	Big Star Supermarkets
Shell Oil Co.	Super America Service Stations

MERGER CHART

Year	Acquirer	Company Acquired
1984	Texaco	Getty Oil Co.
1985	RJ Reynolds	Nabisco Brands, Inc
1985	Phillip Morris Companies, Inc.	General Foods Corp.
1985	General Motors Corp.	Hughes Aircraft Co.
1986	Turner Broadcasting System, Inc.	MGM/UA
1988	HJ Heinz Co.	Pet Foods
1989	Time, Inc.	Warner Communications
1989	Sony Corp.	Columbia Pictures Entertainment
1989	Chrysler Corp.	Thrifty Rent-A-Car
1989	Consolidated Freightways	Emery Air Freight Corp.
1990	Dr. Pepper Co.	I.B.C. Root Beer
1990	Hershey Foods Corp.	Ronzoni Foods Corp.
1991	Pennzoil	Jiffy Lube
1991	Pepsi Foods Intl.	Hostess Frito-Lay
1991	Proctor & Gamble Co.	Revlon, Inc.'s Max Factor
1992	Sara Lee Corp.	Playtex Apparel, Inc. Co.
1992	Shoney's, Inc.	Big Boy Restaurants
1993	Walt Disney Co.	Miramax Film Corp.
1993	Great Atlantic & Pacific Tea Company	Big Star Supermarkets
1993	Shell Oil Co.	Super America Service Stations

HEADS UP 2000

TOPIC The Changing American Workforce

LEARNING OBJECTIVE Participants will be able to determine whether statements about the emerging American workforce are true or false.

NUMBER OF PARTICIPANTS Any number

PLAYING TIME 10–15 minutes

REFERENCE Boyett, J., and Conn, H. (1991). *Workplace 2000: The revolution reshaping American business.* New York: Dutton.

REQUIRED MATERIALS Heads Up 2000 Worksheet and 10 pennies for each player

TO PLAY

1. Introduce players to the concept of a changing workforce.

2. Pass out a Heads Up 2000 Worksheet and 10 pennies to each player.

3. Explain that the worksheet contains 10 statements about the current or future U.S. workforce.

4. Tell players they have five minutes to read through the statements.

5. Advise participants that they are to place a penny heads up in the T or F column if they believe a statement is true and that they are to place a penny tails up if they think a statement is false. Let participants know that at the end of the game they get to keep all the correctly placed pennies.

6. Give players five minutes to place their pennies on their worksheets.

7. At the end of five minutes, give participants the right answers while they check their own worksheets.

8. Collect all incorrectly placed pennies.

9. Debrief players. Go over some of the statements that players answered incorrectly. Discuss why they thought the statement might be true or false. Ask them to identify the most significant changes that have already occurred or are likely to occur in the workforce by the year 2000. Have players speculate on how upcoming changes in the workforce might impact on their own careers.

Directions: Place a penny heads up in the T or F column if the statement is true. Place a penny tails up in the same column if the statement is false.

T or F	PROJECTION
	1. The "Basic Skills Gap" between what business needs and the qualifications of the entry-level workers available to business is widening.
	2. Demographics tell us that a much greater proportion of future labor force entrants will be women, blacks, Hispanics, and immigrants.
	3. White males will account for 50 percent of new entrants to the labor force during the balance of the 20th century.
	4. Three out of four American corporations provide some form of basic skills training for employees.
	5. According to the U.S. Bureau of Census, approximately 38 percent of all American adults have completed four years of college.
	6. Ten to 20 percent of dislocated workers are functionally illiterate.
	7. Workers will change jobs five to six times during their normal work lives.
	8. A total of 500,000 workers are permanently displaced each year and will require assistance to re-enter the work force.
	9. Employers already spend an estimated $210 billion annually on formal and informal training—almost as much as America spends on formal education in our schools.
	10. Only 7 percent of all new jobs from 1988 to 1995 will have been in the high-technology areas.

HONEY, THEY'VE SHRUNK THE COMPANY

TOPIC Downsizing of American Companies

LEARNING OBJECTIVE Participants will be able to give the percentages by which selected U.S. companies have downsized during recent years.

NUMBER OF PARTICIPANTS Even number of players ranging from 8 to 16

PLAYING TIME 20-30 minutes depending on the number of players

REFERENCES Appleton, E. L. (1992, June 15). The Datamation 100 (company profile). *Datamation*, pp. 46-49.

Brousell, D. R. (1992, June 15). The Datamation 100 (company profile). *Datamation*, p. 42.

Davis, D. B. (1992, June 15). The Datamation 100 (company profile). *Datamation*, p. 148.

Holman, R. L. (1993, June 30). German railroads to slash jobs. *The Wall Street Journal*, p. 11.

Kerr, S. (1992, June 15). The Datamation 100 (company profile). *Datamation*, p. 55.

Kerr, S. (1992, June 15). The Datamation 100 (company profile). *Datamation*, p. 141.

Lam Research Corp 'redeploys,' staff cut. (1992, April 13). *Electronic News*, p. 19.

Lindholm, E. (1992, June 15). The Datamation 100 (company profile). *Datamation*, pp. 77-80.

Margolis, N. (1992, August 31). Humana cuts staff, rolls out IS services firm. (Information services). *Computerworld*, p. 97.

McCusker, T. (1992, June 15). The Datamation 100 (company profile). *Datamation*, p. 147.

McManus, J. (1991, April 1). CBS cuts back. *Mediaweek*, p. 1.

Moad, J. (1992, June 15). The Datamation 100 (company profile). *Datamation*, pp. 37-38.

Mullaney, A. D. (1989, Summer). Downsizing: How one hospital responded to decreasing demand. *Health Care Management Review*, p. 41.

Nulty, P. (1991, December 2). The less-is-more strategy. *Fortune*, pp. 102-106.

The wages of peace. (1992, August 24). *Time*, p. 14.

Volocci, A. L. (1992, January 27). United Technologies Restructures in bid to boost profitability, competitiveness. *Aviation Week and Space Technology*, p. 35.

Wagel, W. H. (1989, November). Inplacement at ALL (Aid Association for Lutherans) (retraining employees during downsizing). *Personnel*, p. 8.

White, J. B. (1992, December 4). GM names 8 more plants to be shut; latest plan cuts 14,000 jobs in stepped-up effort to regain profitability. *The Wall Street Journal*, p. 3.

Transparency of Downsize-O-Meter, overhead projector, one 3-by-5-inch index card, and Downsizings Chart

TO PLAY

1. Introduce players to the concepts of downsizing.

2. Go over the learning objective for the game.

3. Divide participants into two opposing teams.

4. Explain that they will be competing in a game requiring them to guess the percentages of downsizing that selected companies have undergone in recent years. A team will score 10 points if it is within 5 percentage points of the actual amount of downsizing and its estimate doesn't exceed the amount of the downsizing.

5. Advise players that members from each team will come forward one at a time to guess the amount of a particular downsizing. When all the players have taken a turn, the game is over. The team with the highest score wins.

6. Place a transparency of the Downsize-O-Meter on an overhead projector. Explain that you will be giving a company's name and the year of its downsizing. As you slowly slide an index card down the Downsize-O-Meter and approach the percentage that a player believes to be the amount of the company's downsizing, they are to call out "Honey, they've shrunk the company." At this point you will stop moving the index card. The place where the card stops will indicate a player's estimate.

7. Demonstrate step 6 by means of an example.

8. Begin the game by asking a player from one of the opposing teams to come forward. Give the company name and the year it downsized (see Fig. 5.1). Slide an index card down the Downsize-O-Meter transparency until she/he calls, "Honey, they've shrunk the company." If the card stops within 5 percentage points of the actual downsizing and doesn't exceed the amount of the downsizing, award that player's team 10 points.

9. Select a player from the opposing team and repeat step 8.

10. After every player has taken a turn, add up the number of points for each team.

11. Declare the team with the most points the winners.

12. Debrief players. Discuss some of the reasons why there have been so many downsizings of major companies in recent times. Ask participants to elaborate on how downsizings in their local communities have affected people's careers.

Figure 5.1. Downsizings chart.

Year	Company	Past Number of Employees	New Number of Employees	Percentage of Reduction
1991	Xerox	120,000	100,000	16
1992	Unisys Corp.	67,000	57,000	15
1991	Teradata	1600	1425	11
1988	Bundesbahn (Western German rail enterprise)	223,000	171,710	23
1991	TRW	16,327	14,695	10
1991	3 COM Corp.	1949	1676	14
1992	Lam Research Corp.	915	865	5
1991	Prime Computer, Inc.	7273	6973	11
1992	Data General	8334	7334	12
1992	Humana, Inc.	10,000	9600	4
1991	MAI Systems Corp.	3400	2300	14
1991	McDonnell Douglas	113,000	99,000	12
1991	IBM	363,396	334,396	8
1989	Ohio Valley Health Services and Education Corp.	2600	2000	23
1980	Quantex Corp.	94	62	34
1992	United Technologies	193,000	179,000	7
1989	Aid Association for Lutherans	1400	1150	18
1993	General Motors	200,000	186,000	7

DOWNSIZE-O-METER

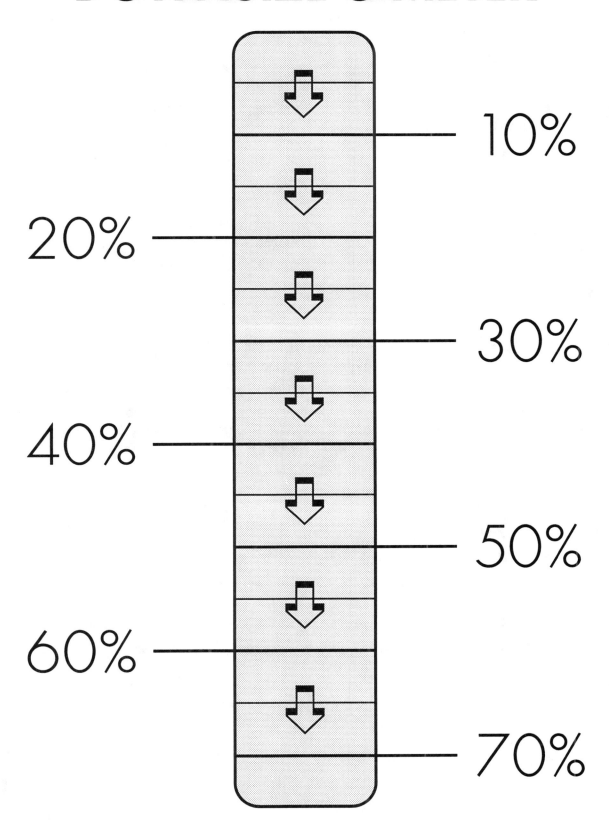

10%

20%

30%

40%

50%

60%

70%

LADIES LINEUP (WORLD)

TOPIC   Worldwide Employment Trends for Women

LEARNING OBJECTIVE   Participants will be able to compare women's salaries and work hours in the United States to those in selected countries.

NUMBER OF PARTICIPANTS   Any number

PLAYING TIME   12-18 minutes

REFERENCE   Mollison, Andrew. (June 2, 1992). Around world, more are earning wages, but jobs are often low paying, part time. *Atlanta Journal/Constitution,* pp. B, 1-2.

REQUIRED MATERIALS   Pencils and Ladies Lineup (World) Puzzle

TO PLAY

1. Introduce players to the concept of wage disparity.
2. Explain the learning objective for the puzzle about to be handed out.
3. Supply each participant a pencil and a copy of the Ladies Lineup (World) Puzzle.
4. Go over the directions at the top of the puzzle. Ask participants *not* to begin until you call, "Lineup." (*Note:* See answers to puzzle in Appendix B for an illustration of the correct way to draw the puzzle lines.)
5. Inform players that the participant with the most correct answers will be named the winner.
6. Advise players that they have six minutes to complete both lineup puzzles.
7. Call, "Lineup."
8. Six minutes later call, "Time."
9. Provide participants the correct answers, with them checking the accuracy of their own work.
10. Recognize the player(s) with the most correct answers as the winner(s).
11. Debrief players. Discuss the possible reasons why women's salaries (as percentages of men's earnings) in several other countries are higher than in the United States. Ask if they think there is any relationship between women's salaries in a country and the percentage of women who work part-time outside the home.

LADIES LINEUP (WORLD) PUZZLE

Directions: Draw a line extending from the name of a country through the percentage that correctly indicates the percentage of men's wages earned by women in that country.

Weekly Wages as Percentage of Men's Earnings

Australia	9	1%
Belgium	8	8%
Denmark	8	2%
France	8	0%
Germany	7	9%
Iceland	7	7%
Netherlands	7	5%
New Zealand	7	4%
United States	7	0%

Percentage of Employed Women Working Part-Time

Australia	6	2%
Britain	4	8%
Denmark	4	4%
Germany	4	1.5%
Japan	4	0.5%
Netherlands	4	0%
New Zealand	3	5%
Norway	3	2%
Sweden	3	1%
United States	2	5%

SOURCE: Published with permission of *The Atlanta Journal* and *The Atlanta Constitution*, P.O. Box 4689, Atlanta, GA 30302.

LOGO ROUNDUP

TOPIC   Company Logos

**LEARNING
OBJECTIVE**   Participants will be able to recognize the logos of selected companies.

**NUMBER OF
PARTICIPANTS**   Any number

PLAYING TIME   5 minutes

REFERENCE   Moskowitz, M., Levering, R., and Katz, M., eds. (1990). *Everybody's business: A field
                       guide of the 400 leading companies in America.* New York: Doubleday Currency.

**REQUIRED
MATERIALS**   Pencils and Logo Roundup Puzzles for each player

TO PLAY
1. Define "logo" and discuss the purpose a company logo serves.
2. Go over the learning objective for the game.
3. Ask participants to read the directions at the top of the Logo Roundup Puzzle.
4. Explain that they have one minute to match company names with the 15 logos appearing on the puzzle.
5. Give learners one minute to write down the letters of as many companies as they can.
6. After one minute call, "Time."
7. Give the right answers to players as they check their own puzzles.
8. Congratulate those individuals with the most correct answers and declare them "logo lizards."
9. Debrief players. Discuss with the class the logos they found to be the most recognizable. Speculate on some probable reasons for this greater recognition. Consider some of the career advantages of working for companies with household names and symbols.

Directions: This page contains the names of 10 companies and their respective logos. In one minute, see how many logos you can associate with their corresponding organizations. Record the letter of the correct company below its logo.

A   Alcoa
B   Amtrak
C   Apple Computer
D   Bell Systems
E   Black and Decker
F   Burlington Industries
G   Burlington Northern
H   Chase

I   Chrysler
J   Hilton
K   Nabisco Brands, Inc.
L   National Cash Register
M   Ralston Purina
N   Reebok
O   Sterling Drug

SOURCE: Published with permission of:
   Aluminum Company of America, 1501 Alcoa Building, Pittsburgh, PA 15219.
   Amtrak National Railroad Passenger Corporation, 400 North Capitol Street, NW, Washington, DC 20001.
   BellSouth, 1155 Peachtree Street, NE, Atlanta, GA 30309-3610.
   Black & Decker Corporation, 701 East Joppa Road, Towson, MD 21204.
   Burlington Industries, Inc. 3330 West Friendly Avenue, Greensboro, NC 27420.
   Chrysler Corporation, 12000 Chrysler Drive, Highland Park, MI 48288-1919.
   Hilton Hotels Corporation, P.O. Box 5567, 9336 Civic Center Drive, Beverly Hills, CA 90209.
   Ralston Purina Company, Checkerboard Square, St. Louis, MO 63134.
   Sterling Winthrop, Inc., 90 Park Avenue, New York, NY 10016.
   The Chase Manhattan Bank, 1 Chase Manhattan Plaza, New York, NY 10081.

NOTES AND QUOTES

TOPIC   Feelings About Work Put to Music

**LEARNING
OBJECTIVE**   Participants will be able to recall some of the more popular songs about work.

**NUMBER OF
PARTICIPANTS**   Any number divided into groups of three members each

PLAYING TIME   7–12 minutes

REFERENCE   Lomax, John A., and Lomax, Alan, eds. (1972). *American ballads and folk songs,* 23rd ed. New York: MacMillan Co.

Whitman, Wanda W., ed. (1969). *Songs that changed the world.* New York: Crown Publishing.

**REQUIRED
MATERIALS**   Pencils and Notes and Quotes quiz

TO PLAY

1. Introduce participants to the notion that art (such as the music of the times) reflects cultural norms and attitudes.

2. Go over the learning objective of the game.

3. Inform participants that they will be divided into groups of three and will have five minutes to put their heads together and identify various song titles. All of the songs are about work.

4. Pass out the Notes and Quotes quiz. Go over the directions.

5. Divide the large group into small groups of three members each.

6. Tell the groups they have five minutes to identify as many of the song titles as possible.

7. Five minutes later call, "Stop."

8. Give players the correct answers while they check their own responses.

9. Declare the group(s) with the most correct answers the winner(s).

10. Debrief players. Have players identify the song or songs they believe most accurately express their feelings about work. Ask participants, "If you were to write a new song expressing your feelings about work, what might be its title?"

Directions: Circle the letter of the song that contains the lyrics in quotes.

1. "I ain't workin' here no more"
   a. Washerwoman Blues
   b. Take This Job and Shove It
   c. I'm Gonna Get Me a Government Job

2. "Barely getting by, there's no taking and no giving"
   a. Momma's Got a High Payin' Job
   b. I'm a Poor Workin' Dog
   c. 9 To 5

3. "The white line is the lifeline to the nation"
   a. Daddy's Hauling Semi
   b. Wolf Creek Pass
   c. Movin' On

4. "Doan you heah the whistle blowin"
   a. I've Been Workin' on the Railroad
   b. It's Quitting Time
   c. Workers' Morning Parade

5. "I am a lineman for the county"
   a. Football Playing Fool
   b. Wichita Lineman
   c. Hear You on the Wires

6. "St. Peter don't you call me, 'cause I can't go"
   a. Sixteen Tons
   b. Coal Miner's Daughter
   c. The Bargeman's Lament

7. "Hello America, let me thank you for your time"
   a. Uncle John, the Congressman
   b. Advertising jingle for "Timex" watches
   c. Forty Hour Week

8. "Should be sitting in an airconditioned office in a swivel chair"
   a. Diggin' Up Bones
   b. I'm a Bloomin' Genius
   c. Workin' at the Carwash Blues

9. "I've got a mule, her name is Sal"
   a. Milkman's Song
   b. Farmer Brown's Critters
   c. Erie Canal

10. "In eighteen hundred and forty-wan, I put me cord'roy breeches on"
    a. Paddy Works on the Erie
    b. Slavin' in the Mills
    c. Panning for Gold

11. "When there's too much to do, don't let it bother you"
    a. Sing a Song
    b. Whistle While You Work
    c. On Cloud Nine

12. "After thirty years, they finally understand"
    a. Momma Was a Working Man
    b. Working Girls
    c. Red Tape

PLAYING THE CAREER ODDS

TOPIC The Frequency of Selected Work Events

LEARNING OBJECTIVE Participants will be able to state the frequency in which selected work events occur.

NUMBER OF PARTICIPANTS Any number

PLAYING TIME 15-25 minutes depending on the number of players

REFERENCE Shook, M. D. and Shook, R. L. (1991). *The book of odds*. New York: Plume.

REQUIRED MATERIALS Pencils, play money (see Appendix B), and Playing the Odds Worksheet

TO PLAY
1. Discuss with players the concept of frequency in terms of percentages.
2. Go over the learning objective for the game.
3. Pass out a pencil, Playing the Odds Worksheet, and $100 of play money to each player.
4. Explain that they will have the opportunity to bet on the frequency in which 10 selected work events occur. Inform players that they have $100 to wager. Each correct answer pays off $2 for each $1 wagered.
5. Go over the directions to Playing the Odds Worksheet.
6. Have participants fill out the wager portion of their playing sheet.
7. Give players five minutes to complete the events portion of their playing sheet.
8. At the end of five minutes, provide the correct answers while players check their own responses. To be counted as correct, answers must be within 10 percentage points of the correct answer.
9. Have players tally and register their winnings (correct answers receive one dollar for each dollar wagered). Hand participants play money equal to this amount.
10. Determine who has the most money. Declare this person the winner and the "Jimmy the Greek of Career Odds."
11. Debrief players. Discuss how a person's perceived likelihood or expectations for a career event occurring (such as finding a new job, getting a raise or promotion, getting laid off) affect her/his behavior. Ask players to tell if they normally over- or underestimate the likelihood of "good" career events occurring for them.

Directions: You have $100 to wager on how accurately you can guess the frequency (percentage) in which the following events occur in the American workplace. Record your wagers in column 1 for each event. In column 2, write the percentages (i.e., how many times out of 100 cases) you believe the event occurs. Register your winnings in column 3.

$$$ WAGERED	ODDS ON WORK EVENT OCCURRING	$$$ RETURN
$	1. _____ % of American companies with less than 100 workers.	$
$	2. _____ % of American workers who are satisfied with their jobs.	$
$	3. _____ % of U.S. workers who are paid by the hour.	$
$	4. _____ % of employees who say their boss is generally fair.	$
$	5. _____ % of American workers who want their boss's job.	$
$	6. _____ % of employees fired because of incompetence.	$
$	7. _____ % of small business owners who hold a degree.	$
$	8. _____ % of American clergy who are women.	$
$	9. _____ % of American workers who moonlight.	$
$	10. _____ % of the nation's workers who walk to work.	$
$ _____ **TOTAL WAGERED**		$ _____ **TOTAL EARNED**

TRANSLATION, PLEASE

TOPIC Common American Sayings About Work

LEARNING OBJECTIVE Participants will be able to recognize some common sayings about work.

NUMBER OF PARTICIPANTS Any number

PLAYING TIME 7–12 minutes

REFERENCE Brown, R. L. (1970). *A book of proverbs*. New York: Taplinger Publishing Co.

Lewis, F. W. (1957). *One man's philosophy*. New York: American Book-Stratford Press.

REQUIRED MATERIALS Pencils and Translation, Please worksheet.

TO PLAY
1. Introduce players to the concept of adages.
2. Go over the learning objective for the game.
3. Explain that they are going to be involved in a contest to see how many sayings about work they can recognize. They will be competing in teams of three or four members each.
4. Divide the group into small groups of three or four members each.
5. Pass out pencils and copies of the Translation, Please worksheet to all players.
6. Go over the directions at the top of the worksheet.
7. Advise participants that they have five minutes to translate as many of the sayings as they can.
8. After five minutes call, "Stop."
9. Provide players the answers as they check their own worksheets.
10. Determine which group(s) made the most correct translations and declare them winners.
11. Debrief players. Discuss what the sayings tell us about American's attitudes toward work.

Directions: Listed below are 10 sayings about work often heard in American society. However, they have been paraphrased using "highbrow English." Your task is to translate the sayings into the everyday language in which they are most often spoken. Record your translation on the lines below each paraphrased saying.

1. Much labor with no recreation causes John to be a boring lad.

_____

2. A female's toil goes on forever.

_____

3. Strenuous labor has always failed to slay a mortal.

_____

4. Most recently employed, let go before all others.

_____

5. A female sheep must remit fees.

_____

6. Individuals seem to elevate to a personal plateau of ability dysfunction.

_____

7. It's sufficiently near to satisfy the needs of the ruling body's labor.

_____

8. Lack of apiary dwellers, lack of flower nectar; lack of toil, lack of cash.

_____

9. Toil overcooked is sufficient compensation.

_____

10. The man labors as a canine.

_____

Chapter Six
CAREER PROMOTION GAMES

Career promotion refers to the process of locating and taking advantage of employment opportunities within one's chosen occupation. In good economic times and in poor economic times, individuals with superb career promotion capabilities are able to secure excellent positions.

Two of the games in Chap. 6, *Political Horse Cents* and *U.S. Boss's Pageant,* look at some of the broad aspects of career promotion. *Political Horse Cents* familiarizes players with various political scripts available to them, and *U.S. Boss's Pageant* helps them to identify career promotion styles they rely on most frequently. *Baldertrash* presents the facts on the effectiveness of various job hunting methods.

A majority of the games in the Chap. 6 focus on specific career promotion skills. *Catch a Trend* helps participants to look for career opportunities among social trends, and *My Notable Network* helps players to look for opportunities among social acquaintances. The game *Leads* pertains to the practical skill of securing tangible job leads. *Resumé Race* offers some rules for resumé preparation, and *Jobpardy* covers the intricacies of selling yourself during a job interview. While *Jobpardy* helps players to prepare for frequently asked interview questions, *Interviews à la Internationale* goes a step further by preparing learners to better interact with persons in the European business community.

BALDERTRASH

TOPIC   The Ways People Get Jobs

**LEARNING
OBJECTIVE**   Participants will be able to identify the most effective ways of getting a job.

**NUMBER OF
PARTICIPANTS**   Any number

PLAYING TIME   15-20 minutes

REFERENCE   Bureau of the Census. (Winter, 1976). Use and effectiveness of job search methods. *Occupational Outlook Quarterly.* Washington, DC: U.S. Government Printing Office, United States Department of Labor.

Bolles, R. (1990). *What color is your parachute? A practical manual for job hunters and career changers.* Berkley, CA: Ten Speed Press.

**REQUIRED
MATERIALS**   Pencils, a set of Job Hunting Methods Cards, and a piece of scratch paper on which to keep score

TO PLAY
1. Introduce players to the various ways people attempt to find jobs.
2. Go over the learning objective for the game.
3. Divide the group into pairs.
4. Pass out a pencil, piece of scratch paper, and a deck of Job Hunting Methods Cards to each pair of participants.
5. Ask the oldest member of each pair to shuffle and deal nine cards to each person.
6. Direct players to pick up the cards and look at them. Explain that each card has two statements about how often people find jobs using a particular job search method. One statement is true and the other is false.
7. Inform players that they will be taking turns reading the statements on the cards to one another. They may read either the true or false version of the statement.
8. Explain that, after one partner reads a statement, the other member of the pair must judge whether the statement is true or false. She/he says, "True" if the statement is true, or "Baldertrash" if it is false. The player reading the statement must next show the card to her/his opponent as proof of the correct answer.
9. Tell players that the reader of a statement scores a point each time an opponent incorrectly guesses the truthfulness of the statement. Participants can score points only during their turns to read a statement from a Job Hunting Methods Card. Since each player is dealt nine cards at the beginning of the game, it is possible for a player to score up to 9 points.

10. Tell players to begin play with the nondealing member of the group reading the first statement. Players then take turns reading statements, alternating back and forth between each other.

11. When the groups are finished reading all of their cards, have them add up their scores.

12. Ask players who earned the most points in their pairs to raise their hands. Declare them winners and natural born "prevaricators."

13. Debrief players. Ask players to identify the job hunting methods they have typically relied on during past job searches. Discuss what research has found to be the most and least effective job hunting methods.

JOB HUNTING METHODS CARDS

To make a deck of Job Hunting Methods Cards, photocopy the following items using card stock paper and cut out each card.

TRUE	FALSE
Forty-eight out of every 100 job hunters find jobs by applying directly to employers.	Twenty-eight out of every 100 job hunters find jobs by applying directly to employers.

FALSE	TRUE
Two out of every 100 job hunters find jobs by asking friends about jobs where they work.	Twenty-two out of every 100 job hunters find jobs by asking friends about jobs where they work.

TRUE	FALSE
Twenty-four out of every 100 job hunters find jobs by answering local newspaper ads.	Four out of every 100 job hunters find jobs by answering local newspaper ads.

FALSE		**TRUE**
Two out of every 100 job hunters find jobs by asking friends about jobs elsewhere.		Twelve out of every 100 job hunters find jobs by asking friends about jobs elsewhere.

TRUE		**FALSE**
Fourteen out of every 100 job hunters find jobs by using state employment services.		Forty-four out of every 100 job hunters find jobs by using state employment services.

FALSE		**TRUE**
Sixty-nine out of every 100 job hunters find jobs by asking relatives about jobs where they work.		Nineteen out of every 100 job hunters find jobs by asking relatives about jobs where they work.

TRUE		**FALSE**
Seven out of every 100 job hunters find jobs by asking relatives about jobs elsewhere.		Forty-seven out of every 100 job hunters find jobs by asking relatives about jobs elsewhere.

FALSE		**TRUE**
Four out of every 100 job hunters find jobs by using private employment agencies.		Twenty-four out of every 100 job hunters find jobs by using private employment agencies.

TRUE		FALSE
Thirteen out of every 100 job hunters find jobs by taking civil service examinations.		Thirty-three out of every 100 job hunters find jobs by taking civil service examinations.

FALSE		TRUE
Fifty-two out of every 100 job hunters find jobs by using school placement offices.		Twelve out of every 100 job hunters find jobs by using school placement offices.

TRUE		FALSE
Ten out of every 100 job hunters find jobs by answering nonlocal newspaper ads.		Thirty out of every 100 job hunters find jobs by answering nonlocal newspaper ads.

FALSE		TRUE
Twenty-four out of every 100 job hunters find jobs by asking a teacher or professor about jobs.		Twelve out of every 100 job hunters find jobs by asking a teacher or professor about jobs.

TRUE		FALSE
Twenty-two out of every 100 job hunters find jobs through union halls.		Forty-four out of every 100 job hunters find jobs through union halls.

FALSE		TRUE
Three out of every 100 job hunters find jobs by using local organizations.		Thirteen out of every 100 job hunters find jobs by using local organizations.

TRUE		FALSE
Seven out of every 100 job hunters find jobs by answering ads in professional journals.		Twenty-seven out of every 100 job hunters find jobs by answering ads in professional journals.

FALSE		TRUE
Thirty-one out of every 100 job hunters find jobs by placing ads in local papers.		Thirteen out of every 100 job hunters find jobs by placing ads in local papers.

FALSE		TRUE
Eighteen out of every 100 job hunters find jobs by going to where employers pick up people.		Eight out of every 100 job hunters find jobs by going to where employers pick up people.

TRUE		FALSE
Forty out of every 100 job hunters find jobs by miscellaneous approaches.		Four out of every 100 job hunters find jobs by miscellaneous approaches.

CATCH A TREND

TOPIC Societal Trends on Which Careerists Can Capitalize

LEARNING OBJECTIVE Participants will be able to identify several trends that they can capitalize on careerwise.

NUMBER OF PARTICIPANTS Any even number up to 40 players

PLAYING TIME 20-30 minutes depending on the number of players

REFERENCE None

REQUIRED MATERIALS Trend Balloons, a nonfolding chair, and a pencil

TO PLAY

1. Introduce players to the concept of capitalizing on social, economic, and political trends as a means to build one's career.

2. Go over the learning objective for the game.

3. Divide players into two teams with an equal number of players on each.

4. Explain that the team catching the most trends will be considered the winning team.

5. Call on one player from each team to come to the center of the room, where a chair has been placed. Have the two participants stand back to back at right angles to the chair.

6. Climb onto the chair with a Trend Balloon in hand. Explain that the balloon contains a slip of paper naming a societal trend for careerists in the 1990s.

7. Advise the two contestants that you are going to hold a Trend Balloon above their heads and drop it. Their goal is to be the one who "catches the trend" before it touches the floor. They are not to move until you call, "Catch."

8. When everyone understands what to do, hold the Trend Balloon above the heads of the two contestants and drop it. Call, "Catch" at the precise moment the balloon leaves your hand.

9. Reward 1 point to the team of the player who catches the Trend Balloon before it reaches the floor. Ask the player to pop the balloon with the pencil and read the trend aloud. If neither player catches the balloon, no points are awarded.

10. Repeat steps 8 and 9 until everyone on both teams has had a chance at catching a trend. Declare the team with the most points "champion trend catchers."

11. Debrief players. Ask participants to identify trends that they find particularly appealing from a career perspective. Discuss ways players might be able to capitalize on such trends.

To make a set of Trend Balloons, photocopy the following trends for careerists. Then cut each out, stuff it into a balloon, blow the balloon up, and tie the neck of the balloon securely so that no air will escape.

More women are seeking and being elected to public office.

Women are now allowed to serve in combat positions in the armed forces.

More women are etching out careers in professional sports.

Women's health issues are receiving more attention in the 1990s.

Striking a balance between work and home life is becoming a top priority for today's careerists.

An accelerated pace of change is causing greater uncertainty in the business community.

Companies of the 1990s are leaner, more streamlined organizations.

The workforce of the 1990s is a diverse group of employees from various cultural backgrounds.

More of the work of organizations is being accomplished through self-directed work teams.

Rank and file workers now make decisions formerly made by middle managers.

Many married couples are postponing parenthood until they've established their careers.

More young workers in their twenties are living at home with Mom and Dad until they can get established financially.

Increased competition is causing businesses to give greater attention to customer service.

Foreign competition has made American manufacturers more quality-conscious.

Advances in technology have made training and retraining a fact of life for most American workers.

The Americans with Disabilities Act is opening up employment opportunities for the physically and mentally challenged.

Greater enforcement of the EEOC's "Guidelines on Sexual Harassment in the Workplace" is providing more women equal opportunities.

The drive for increased productivity is expanding the application of cutting edge technologies.

An aging U.S. citizenry is becoming preoccupied with nutrition and fitness concerns.

A widely perceived increase in violent crime has spurred a rapidly growing security industry.

INTERVIEWS À LA INTERNATIONALE

TOPIC   Business Practices in Selected European Countries

LEARNING OBJECTIVE   Participants will be able to cite European business practices that every international job hunter should know.

NUMBER OF PARTICIPANTS   Any multiple of 5

PLAYING TIME   20–25 minutes per round

REFERENCE   Braganti, N. L., and Devine, E. (1992). *European customs and manners: How to make friends and do business in Europe.* New York: Meadowbrook.

REQUIRED MATERIALS   Pencils and Interview Question Sheets

TO PLAY

1. Introduce or review with players the concept of cultural diversity. Discuss the importance of being able to work with co-workers and clients of diverse cultural backgrounds.

2. Discuss the learning objective for the game. Tell participants that, by playing the roles of job interviewers and job applicants, they are about to find out some of the ways European business practices differ from American business practices.

3. Divide participants into groups of five members each. Designate three members of each group "interviewers" and two members "applicants." Have participants select a European country from among 12 options (Denmark, France, Germany, Great Britain, Greece, Italy, The Netherlands, Poland, Spain, Sweden, Switzerland, and Turkey). Pass out the Interview Question Sheets for the selected country to each interviewer. Do *not* pass out the Interview Question Sheets to applicants.

4. Explain that the applicants have applied for a European management position in a large American manufacturing firm (Yankee Incorporated) with a major division in Europe. Applicants have been invited to a screening interview. If they do well, they will be invited back for another interview.

5. Tell players that during the first five minutes of the game, each group will interview one of its two applicants while the other applicant waits in a designated waiting area (out of earshot of the interviews). After five minutes have passed, the two applicants will exchange places.

6. Advise interviewers that they are to record the applicants' answers on the Interview Question Sheets during the screening interviews (columns 2 and 3). Correct answers to the interview questions will be given after the interviews have been conducted and recorded in column 4.

7. Explain that the goal for interviewers is to choose the applicant who answered the most questions correctly. The goal for the applicant is to be invited back for a second interview.

8. Give interviewers five minutes to interview the first applicant.

9. Give interviewers five minutes to interview the second applicant.

10. Provide interviewers five minutes to decide which applicant will be invited back for a second interview. Ask that they record their choice at the bottom of the Interview Questions Sheet.

11. Give the correct answers to interview questions. Ask interviewers to record at the bottoms of columns 2 and 3 on the Interview Questions Sheets the number of correct answers given by each applicant.

12. Ask all groups who invited back the applicant who answered the most interview questions correctly to now stand. Declare them "winning international human resource managers."

13. Ask all applicants who were invited back for a second interview to stand. Declare these individuals "international business stars."

14. Repeat this process for additional rounds of play.

15. Debrief players. Compare and contrast European business practices with those in the United States. Discuss the practices players found most surprising. Ask them to identify the practices they might have the most difficulty adjusting to.

Question	Applicant #1's Answer	Applicant #2's Answer	Correct Answer
1. You are in Denmark attempting to negotiate a collaboration on a research project with representatives from a Danish company. You emphasize that your company is an old and respected firm in the United States, which is very impressive to the Danes.	☐ True ☐ False	☐ True ☐ False	☐ True ☐ False
2. Time is short and your schedule and that of your Danish counterpart is hectic. You feel pressured to close the deal so you suggest a weekend business session to wrap things up. Your Danish contacts are really impressed with your drive.	☐ True ☐ False	☐ True ☐ False	☐ True ☐ False
3. You are a woman going to Denmark to represent your company in some very important negotiations. You are not worried about your abilities, but rather that you won't be taken seriously. Danes would rather deal with men.	☐ True ☐ False	☐ True ☐ False	☐ True ☐ False
4. You are going to Denmark to close an important multi-million dollar deal for your company. You have your secretary make reservations for you at the finest hotel in the city you're going to because the expense is justified by the image you need to project.	☐ True ☐ False	☐ True ☐ False	☐ True ☐ False
5. On a trip to Denmark, you conduct your business with members of middle management. However, you are prepared to wait for the final decisions on the deal to be made by a few people at the top.	☐ True ☐ False	☐ True ☐ False	☐ True ☐ False
6. You are planning ahead for a business trip to a large manufacturing company in Denmark. You come up with the idea of going in July and taking the family along as a vacation. This is a great money saving idea.	☐ True ☐ False	☐ True ☐ False	☐ True ☐ False
7. You are going to have to spend a lot of time in Denmark closing a deal for parts your company needs. Extra time is necessary because of the slow, ponderous way the Danes do business.	☐ True ☐ False	☐ True ☐ False	☐ True ☐ False
8. The Danish business people you have been dealing with have seemed open and honest, but rather abrupt in your conversations with them. This is probably because they do not feel comfortable with you or sure of your honesty.	☐ True ☐ False	☐ True ☐ False	☐ True ☐ False
9. You are in Denmark on a business trip and wish to invite your business contacts to lunch. You are intrigued by the basement cafes and suggest going to one of these. This suggestion will meet with great approval.	☐ True ☐ False	☐ True ☐ False	☐ True ☐ False
10. You are planning a trip to Denmark to collaborate with your counterpart in a Danish company in developing a new product. You want to take a gift to this person and decide on a lovely pictorial history book of your city. This is a good choice.	☐ True ☐ False	☐ True ☐ False	☐ True ☐ False
Total number of correct answers given by each applicant	_____ Number correct	_____ Number correct	

Applicant to be invited back _____

Question	Applicant #1's Answer	Applicant #2's Answer	Correct Answer
1. After a phone conversation with a French businessman, you send him a follow-up letter written in English rather than French. Since his English was perfect, your letter should cause no problems at his end.	☐ True ☐ False	☐ True ☐ False	☐ True ☐ False
2. You are dealing with a French company that has been reorganized by American consultants. Though there is evidence of American influence, company policies will remain rigid.	☐ True ☐ False	☐ True ☐ False	☐ True ☐ False
3. As an American woman dealing with a group of French businessmen, you are worried that their flirtatious manner indicates that they only see you as a female and not as a businesswoman. You are best advised to ignore their flirting and act very businesslike.	☐ True ☐ False	☐ True ☐ False	☐ True ☐ False
4. Your company needs to do business with an old family company in France. It is probably best to send one of the highest-ranking people from your company.	☐ True ☐ False	☐ True ☐ False	☐ True ☐ False
5. You are attempting to get an advertising contract from a French company who will be selling their product on the American market. You are afraid that you will be offered wine at your meeting with their representatives and you don't drink. They will be offended if you turn down the drink.	☐ True ☐ False	☐ True ☐ False	☐ True ☐ False
6. At a meeting with a team of French businesspeople, you recap your last meeting with them with the help of precise notes you took at that time. The businesspeople are very impressed with your efficiency.	☐ True ☐ False	☐ True ☐ False	☐ True ☐ False
7. In negotiations with a French business executive, you run up against a roadblock to concluding the deal. You feel that the problem stems from stubbornness on the part of the other person and tell her/him so. The French love a good argument in business.	☐ True ☐ False	☐ True ☐ False	☐ True ☐ False
8. At a business dinner with some French executives in a Paris restaurant, you are at a loss as to what to order. Your hosts are flattered when you ask for their suggestions rather than trying to bluff your way through.	☐ True ☐ False	☐ True ☐ False	☐ True ☐ False
9. You are negotiating a contract with a French company. Though the French insist that the contract be a precise legal document, you cannot be certain that they will stick to it.	☐ True ☐ False	☐ True ☐ False	☐ True ☐ False
10. You are attending a meeting with a group of French upper-management people at their company. You may tend to direct many of your persuasive comments to the person at the middle of the group, who is most likely to be the most influential.	☐ True ☐ False	☐ True ☐ False	☐ True ☐ False
Total number of correct answers given by each applicant	_____ Number correct	_____ Number correct	

Applicant to be invited back _____

Question	Applicant #1's Answer	Applicant #2's Answer	Correct Answer
1. Your company wants to expand its market for several of its products to Germany. You are assigned the task of doing the market research. The first place you should contact for assistance is the Federal Statistics Office in Wiesbaden.	☐ True ☐ False	☐ True ☐ False	☐ True ☐ False
2. You need a fairly quick response to your business letter to a German firm. You should address the letter to the specific person who signed a previous letter to your company to receive the most prompt response.	☐ True ☐ False	☐ True ☐ False	☐ True ☐ False
3. Your company has a huge overstock of a product that was test marketed in the United States and didn't go over well. You need to get rid of the stuff and see in Germany a progressive country with an interest in American goods. You should negotiate with a German company for a one-shot deal.	☐ True ☐ False	☐ True ☐ False	☐ True ☐ False
4. You are a female vice president in your company who is consulting with your male counterpart in a German company. Though you are extremely efficient and knowledgeable, the German executive may expect you to confer with your male boss before coming to an agreement.	☐ True ☐ False	☐ True ☐ False	☐ True ☐ False
5. Your boss tells you that the businesspeople whom you will be dealing with on your trip to a German firm all speak English. You decide to learn a few Germans words anyway. The Germans will likely be flattered.	☐ True ☐ False	☐ True ☐ False	☐ True ☐ False
6. You are hard at work writing a contract you negotiated with a German company and discover a problem. You phone the executive in Germany only to find that he has gone home for the day. It's permissible to phone the person at home.	☐ True ☐ False	☐ True ☐ False	☐ True ☐ False
7. You enter the office of a German executive and are invited to sit down. The distance between your chair and the person's desk seems too large to have a friendly conversation so you pull the chair up closer to the desk. Germans like to establish a camaraderie with their co-workers.	☐ True ☐ False	☐ True ☐ False	☐ True ☐ False
8. As a representative of your company, you are attending a German business meeting. A comment made by one of the group reminds you of a funny joke that would probably lighten up the serious atmosphere, but it would not be good practice to tell the joke at this time.	☐ True ☐ False	☐ True ☐ False	☐ True ☐ False
9. You are introducing your company's new product to a group of German businesspeople in their corporate offices. Your product comes in different colors and styles and you have brought several samples. This is helpful to the group.	☐ True ☐ False	☐ True ☐ False	☐ True ☐ False
10. You have just made a presentation to a group of German businesspeople. The presentation took about 25 minutes with only a few questions from the group. You can take this as a positive sign.	☐ True ☐ False	☐ True ☐ False	☐ True ☐ False
Total number of correct answers given by each applicant	_____ Number correct	_____ Number correct	

Applicant to be invited back _____

Question	Applicant #1's Answer	Applicant #2's Answer	Correct Answer
1. Early in your dealings with a British executive, she/he starts calling you by your first name; so you reciprocate. This is proper British etiquette.	☐ True ☐ False	☐ True ☐ False	☐ True ☐ False
2. You have been asked to address a group of stockholders in a British Company that you will be doing business with. You are to be allotted 30 minutes for your portion of the meeting. You will need to prepare a talk of exactly 30 minutes.	☐ True ☐ False	☐ True ☐ False	☐ True ☐ False
3. It is 9:00 P.M. and you have just arrived in Great Britain. Tomorrow you will be meeting with a group of businesspeople at their company, but you have a few questions. It is permissible to call one of your contacts at home up until 10:00 P.M.	☐ True ☐ False	☐ True ☐ False	☐ True ☐ False
4. You have just agreed to a last-minute deal with a representative from a British company. She/he feels that a handshake is all that is necessary to seal the deal since time is so short. You are afraid that the person will be offended and back out of the deal if you don't agree; so you should go along with her/him.	☐ True ☐ False	☐ True ☐ False	☐ True ☐ False
5. You've waited for an answer for three weeks since you met with some British businesspeople about selling your company's services to them. You have heard that British business dealings are a little slower than U.S. dealings; so you should not be unduly worried.	☐ True ☐ False	☐ True ☐ False	☐ True ☐ False
6. You are working with a tradesperson in Great Britain and need her/his product very quickly. The tradesperson tells you that the required shipment will be made "pretty soon." You can expect the shipment to be made in a couple of days.	☐ True ☐ False	☐ True ☐ False	☐ True ☐ False
7. A business associate in Great Britain invites you to lunch. She/he takes you to a pub instead of a restaurant. This is because the British are frugal and pubs are cheaper.	☐ True ☐ False	☐ True ☐ False	☐ True ☐ False
8. You are in Great Britain to sell your company's products to a distribution company there. You choose a moderately priced hotel close to the company rather than an elaborate hotel known to cater to businesspeople. This will indicate that you are sensible to the British.	☐ True ☐ False	☐ True ☐ False	☐ True ☐ False
9. You are going to Great Britain to meet with some people who may be interested in investing in your business. You have never met the people, but would like to take along a gift to impress them. This would be a good business move.	☐ True ☐ False	☐ True ☐ False	☐ True ☐ False
10. After a meeting with your counterpart in a British firm, you feel that the other person had appeared a bit scattered. It is probably wise to write a follow-up letter to the person recounting what you discussed and agreed upon.	☐ True ☐ False	☐ True ☐ False	☐ True ☐ False
Total number of correct answers given by each applicant	_____ Number correct	_____ Number correct	

Applicant to be invited back _____

Question	Applicant #1's Answer	Applicant #2's Answer	Correct Answer
1. You have been meeting with an executive from a client firm in Greece. You shake hands firmly with the person as you leave just as you did when you arrived. This is common courtesy.	☐ True ☐ False	☐ True ☐ False	☐ True ☐ False
2. You will soon be going to Greece to complete some very important negotiations for your company. In preparation for the trip, you study a bit of Greek history. This may score some points with those you will be dealing with.	☐ True ☐ False	☐ True ☐ False	☐ True ☐ False
3. You are in Greece to discuss trade agreements. Representatives from the Greek company were in the United States a few weeks ago and were late to nearly every meeting. You may assume that this is also expected of you.	☐ True ☐ False	☐ True ☐ False	☐ True ☐ False
4. You have been negotiating with a group of Greek businesspeople for over four hours. Faced with these formidable opponents, you are about to say that you are done talking and they can either take or leave your offer. The Greeks will respect your resolution.	☐ True ☐ False	☐ True ☐ False	☐ True ☐ False
5. On a business trip, your plane lands in Athens and you are picked up by your business contact, who not only takes you to your hotel, but also takes you to all your meals and sees to all your comforts. Hospitality is common practice for Greek businesspeople.	☐ True ☐ False	☐ True ☐ False	☐ True ☐ False
6. You are in a restaurant in Greece with people from a company that does business with yours. In conversation, you ask how business is for them. They reply that it is horrible. This could indicate that a deal may be more difficult to make.	☐ True ☐ False	☐ True ☐ False	☐ True ☐ False
7. You are meeting with Greek executives. Instead of getting down to business, they are discussing a stupid action taken by Parliament the day before. Politics are a passion with many Greeks and take precedence over other things.	☐ True ☐ False	☐ True ☐ False	☐ True ☐ False
8. During a business lunch with several Greek businesspeople, a very loud and enthusiastic argument breaks out among the group. Almost everyone in the group joins in. Free expression is promoted by the Greeks.	☐ True ☐ False	☐ True ☐ False	☐ True ☐ False
9. You have been consulting with a Greek firm for several months. You are astounded by the number of family members working for the company. Many of the Greek businesses are family-owned.	☐ True ☐ False	☐ True ☐ False	☐ True ☐ False
10. You are a single woman whose brains and hard work have helped you climb the corporate ladder. You are going to Greece with a team from your company to negotiate a multimillion-dollar deal with a large shipping firm. You know that women are accepted in Greek businesses and you can be expected to be treated as an equal by the men.	☐ True ☐ False	☐ True ☐ False	☐ True ☐ False
Total number of correct answers given by each applicant	_____ Number correct	_____ Number correct	

Applicant to be invited back _____

Question	Applicant #1's Answer	Applicant #2's Answer	Correct Answer
1. Having recently been assigned to work on a project with an Italian company, you pick up the phone to call your business contact there. A co-worker quickly tells you that it is better to send a letter as a first contact. The co-worker is correct.	☐ True ☐ False	☐ True ☐ False	☐ True ☐ False
2. At a Friday afternoon meeting in an office of an Italian company, you and an Italian business representative come to an agreement on a deal. The Italian wishes to draw up the contract for approval. You can expect it to be completed by Monday morning.	☐ True ☐ False	☐ True ☐ False	☐ True ☐ False
3. You are negotiating an important sale with Italian businesspeople. You have maintained a laid-back stance in the negotiations, appearing almost unconcerned. This could damage your position in the eyes of the Italians.	☐ True ☐ False	☐ True ☐ False	☐ True ☐ False
4. You realize that, because there are not often women in top levels of business, you as a female need to look and act professional. You chose your clothing carefully for an upcoming meeting with top executives of an Italian auto company. To be taken seriously, you will have to make it clear that you are not a secretary to male executives attending the meeting with you.	☐ True ☐ False	☐ True ☐ False	☐ True ☐ False
5. While in Italy wrapping up the last details of a contract between your firm and an Italian company, an upper-level executive with whom you have been working asks you to a party where you will meet many of his associates from other firms. This will be a good chance for you to pass out your business cards and drum up more business for your company.	☐ True ☐ False	☐ True ☐ False	☐ True ☐ False
6. As you are being introduced to several people in an Italian corporation, you are struck by their formality. First names are not used in the introduction; so you may assume that this is proper business etiquette.	☐ True ☐ False	☐ True ☐ False	☐ True ☐ False
7. On arrival in Italy, you wish to confirm arrangements with your business contact. You should make only a quick call to her/his office to check on the schedule.	☐ True ☐ False	☐ True ☐ False	☐ True ☐ False
8. Negotiations between your U.S. company and an Italian firm have been slow. The Italian businesspeople speak fairly good English, but things could be speeded up if important papers were translated to Italian.	☐ True ☐ False	☐ True ☐ False	☐ True ☐ False
9. You are an American woman taking your Italian business contacts to lunch in Florence. At the end of the meal, an Italian man insists on paying the check, even though you argue with him. Italians will not allow a visiting guest to pay.	☐ True ☐ False	☐ True ☐ False	☐ True ☐ False
10. You are inviting your Italian business contact to dinner on your last night in Rome. You should ask the person which of her/his colleagues should also be invited.	☐ True ☐ False	☐ True ☐ False	☐ True ☐ False
Total number of correct answers given by each applicant	_____ Number correct	_____ Number correct	

Applicant to be invited back _____

Question	Applicant #1's Answer	Applicant #2's Answer	Correct Answer
1. You are hosting a team of Dutch businesspeople in the meeting room at your hotel. Offering refreshments is not proper in this circumstance.	☐ True ☐ False	☐ True ☐ False	☐ True ☐ False
2. You are an American businessman arriving for an appointment at a Dutch company. You are met in a reception room and offered a cigar by an attendant. You should tip the attendant.	☐ True ☐ False	☐ True ☐ False	☐ True ☐ False
3. A Dutch businessperson, who is preparing a purchase agreement for your boss's signature, says that it will be ready by the end of the week. You can safely assume that it will be at least a two- or three-week wait.	☐ True ☐ False	☐ True ☐ False	☐ True ☐ False
4. In making a presentation to a group of Dutch businesspeople, you are using lots of facts and figures with charts and graphs to reinforce your statements. This makes a positive impression on the Dutch.	☐ True ☐ False	☐ True ☐ False	☐ True ☐ False
5. You are among a delegation of businesspeople going to the Netherlands to learn Dutch business practices firsthand. The Dutch firm hosts a companywide reception in honor of your team's visit. This is highly unusual in Dutch business.	☐ True ☐ False	☐ True ☐ False	☐ True ☐ False
6. On a sales trip to the Netherlands, you will be hosting people from several Dutch corporations to dinner at your hotel. In this instance it is important to select a top-class hotel.	☐ True ☐ False	☐ True ☐ False	☐ True ☐ False
7. You are arranging for your business trip to the Netherlands next month. In your letter to your business contact, you invite him/her to dinner on a specific evening. The Dutch like to be organized and appreciate the advance notice.	☐ True ☐ False	☐ True ☐ False	☐ True ☐ False
8. You are traveling to the Netherlands to meet with representatives from a Dutch company that your firm would like to do business with. On the plane, you again go over your notes on the Dutch market and your competition there. It is extremely important to be familiar with the Dutch business climate.	☐ True ☐ False	☐ True ☐ False	☐ True ☐ False
9. You are preparing to negotiate with people from a Dutch company. You should plan to start out with a higher cost for your products so that you can lower them after lengthy bargaining.	☐ True ☐ False	☐ True ☐ False	☐ True ☐ False
10. Your contact in a Dutch corporation is a female vice president. You are surprised because in your work in a couple of other European countries this was not the case. In fact, in the Netherlands, women have the same chance to succeed as men.	☐ True ☐ False	☐ True ☐ False	☐ True ☐ False
Total number of correct answers given by each applicant	_____ Number correct	_____ Number correct	

Applicant to be invited back _____

Question	Applicant #1's Answer	Applicant #2's Answer	Correct Answer
1. You are writing to a contact in a Polish company to set up a meeting. You know that English is the second language there, but you should have your letter translated to Polish anyway to make a good first impression.	☐ True ☐ False	☐ True ☐ False	☐ True ☐ False
2. You are planning your trip to Poland to present your firm's products to some Polish businesspeople. The information you have received from your hotel there indicates that they have both copy and fax machines. Now you won't have to take up luggage space with copies of all your papers.	☐ True ☐ False	☐ True ☐ False	☐ True ☐ False
3. On your business trip to Warsaw, you think that perhaps reading a local English-language newspaper will give you an accurate picture of the Polish business climate. The *Warsaw Voice* would be a good choice.	☐ True ☐ False	☐ True ☐ False	☐ True ☐ False
4. For your presentation to the sales staff of a Polish company, you have prepared elaborate visual materials. The expense of these graphics is justifiable.	☐ True ☐ False	☐ True ☐ False	☐ True ☐ False
5. You are one of two women included in a delegation your company has sent to do business with a Polish corporation. The other woman is very aggressive in her business behavior. You would do well to follow her lead.	☐ True ☐ False	☐ True ☐ False	☐ True ☐ False
6. You will be meeting with people from a Polish company in Warsaw in two weeks. The appointment was made and confirmed three weeks ago. You should follow up with reminder notes, however.	☐ True ☐ False	☐ True ☐ False	☐ True ☐ False
7. You have met with several people at different levels in a Polish company in an attempt to negotiate a contract. You can assume that all of those people will participate in the final decision.	☐ True ☐ False	☐ True ☐ False	☐ True ☐ False
8. You will be negotiating with a group from a Polish company. Most of the group speaks only basic English. It is your duty to bring an interpreter with you.	☐ True ☐ False	☐ True ☐ False	☐ True ☐ False
9. The Polish firm you have been dealing with is very anxious to do business with your company. In fact, representatives of the company have promised to have things ready at their end more quickly than in reality they can. You need to make allowances for their zealousness.	☐ True ☐ False	☐ True ☐ False	☐ True ☐ False
10. You have worked with persons at several levels on your business trip to a Polish firm. However, when you invite businesspeople to dinner at your hotel, it is proper to invite only those of equal status to you.	☐ True ☐ False	☐ True ☐ False	☐ True ☐ False
Total number of correct answers given by each applicant	_____ Number correct	_____ Number correct	

Applicant to be invited back _____

Question	Applicant #1's Answer	Applicant #2's Answer	Correct Answer
1. Your company wants to do business in Spain. Last summer you met and became friendly with a Spanish businessman and his family on a trip to Disneyland. You have his address, and writing to ask him for help in making business contacts in Spain could open doors for you.	☐ True ☐ False	☐ True ☐ False	☐ True ☐ False
2. You are dealing with an executive of equal status to you in a Spanish company. You should make an effort to be very friendly with her/his office staff in an effort to win your counterpart's regard.	☐ True ☐ False	☐ True ☐ False	☐ True ☐ False
3. You are a female executive doing business with your male counterpart in a Spanish firm. You should dress with conservative elegance and treat him with the same friendly banter that you use on your male co-workers.	☐ True ☐ False	☐ True ☐ False	☐ True ☐ False
4. At your first sales meeting with a prominent Spanish company, you are asked more about your background, education, and interests than your product. This is the Spanish way of making you feel at ease.	☐ True ☐ False	☐ True ☐ False	☐ True ☐ False
5. You are presenting your company's services to a group of Spanish businesspeople. You should explain each point clearly and thoroughly because the Spanish will not likely wish to embarrass themselves by asking for clarification.	☐ True ☐ False	☐ True ☐ False	☐ True ☐ False
6. You are part of a team from your company who will be in Spain to negotiate a deal with an important corporation there. The Spanish are good bargainers; so you must carefully prepare for cost and other concessions.	☐ True ☐ False	☐ True ☐ False	☐ True ☐ False
7. You are in an important meeting with a high-ranking Spanish executive. He will have told his secretary to hold all calls until you are finished no matter who is calling.	☐ True ☐ False	☐ True ☐ False	☐ True ☐ False
8. In your collaboration with a group of marketing people for a Spanish company, you find you don't like their approach to promoting your company's products in their country. You should tell them straight out how you feel and insist they change their tactics.	☐ True ☐ False	☐ True ☐ False	☐ True ☐ False
9. In your work as a foreign liaison for the U.S. government, you are in Spain to hammer out the details of a trade agreement. You have been meeting with a group of middle-ranking government officials and have come to an agreement. However, the final decision rests with top officials in that branch of government.	☐ True ☐ False	☐ True ☐ False	☐ True ☐ False
10. You were on time for a meeting with a vice president of a Spanish company, which has for years done business with your employer. The executive is now 20 minutes late. You should expect this and wait uncomplainingly.	☐ True ☐ False	☐ True ☐ False	☐ True ☐ False
Total number of correct answers given by each applicant	Number correct	Number correct	

Applicant to be invited back _____

INTERVIEW QUESTION SHEET FOR SWEDEN

Question	Applicant #1's Answer	Applicant #2's Answer	Correct Answer
1. Next month you will be going to Sweden to open up negotiations with a firm there to buy your company's services. In preparation, you have read several books on Swedish culture and history. Knowing the name of the Swedish king will be helpful.	☐ True ☐ False	☐ True ☐ False	☐ True ☐ False
2. During a presentation at a Swedish firm, you have several handouts to distribute. It is correct to have enough copies for each person present.	☐ True ☐ False	☐ True ☐ False	☐ True ☐ False
3. Your company makes handheld electronic games, and you are in Sweden trying to interest a company in buying them for distribution there. The Swedes would enjoy seeing and playing with a good selection of your games.	☐ True ☐ False	☐ True ☐ False	☐ True ☐ False
4. You will be negotiating a multimillion-dollar deal with a large Swedish corporation. The business climate has become so fast-paced that you'll only need to make one or two trips.	☐ True ☐ False	☐ True ☐ False	☐ True ☐ False
5. You wish to host a dinner for several of the Swedish businesspeople you've worked with on this trip. Contracts will be signed on the afternoon of the day of your planned dinner. Since you and the Swedes are still connected in a business sense, it is not proper to invite spouses to the dinner.	☐ True ☐ False	☐ True ☐ False	☐ True ☐ False
6. You have negotiated with representatives of a Swedish company for the past week. You have finally reached agreement this afternoon. You can relax a bit now as a contract will likely be forthcoming.	☐ True ☐ False	☐ True ☐ False	☐ True ☐ False
7. As a top-notch salesperson for an American firm, you will be going to Sweden to approach several companies about buying your products. It will be necessary to carry letters of introduction to gain an audience at your intended companies.	☐ True ☐ False	☐ True ☐ False	☐ True ☐ False
8. You are in Sweden to meet with a person from a Swedish company interested in purchasing some industrial machinery from your firm. Your contact may not be a member of top management, but an agreement is reached to buy the machinery from you. Decisions are made at lower levels in Sweden than they are in the United States.	☐ True ☐ False	☐ True ☐ False	☐ True ☐ False
9. In your initial meeting with your Swedish business contact, you are amazed at her/his knowledge of your corporation's business practices. As a rule, the Swedes are very knowledgeable about international politics and business.	☐ True ☐ False	☐ True ☐ False	☐ True ☐ False
10. For the past three days you have been in Stockholm negotiating with two businesspeople from different departments of a Swedish corporation. You wish to take them to lunch, and it is proper to also invite their immediate superiors.	☐ True ☐ False	☐ True ☐ False	☐ True ☐ False
Total number of correct answers given by each applicant	_____ Number correct	_____ Number correct	

Applicant to be invited back _____

INTERVIEW QUESTION SHEET FOR SWITZERLAND

Question	Applicant #1's Answer	Applicant #2's Answer	Correct Answer
1. One of the people who dealt with a couple of Swiss firms that are customers of your company has resigned, and you have been promoted to her/his job. A course in French or German will be necessary for this position.	☐ True ☐ False	☐ True ☐ False	☐ True ☐ False
2. Your contact in a Swiss corporation is a woman. She is extremely knowledgeable and seems to be doing very well in her career, but is not in top management. This is probably because she does not possess an advanced degree.	☐ True ☐ False	☐ True ☐ False	☐ True ☐ False
3. You have a 10:00 A.M. meeting with an executive at a Swiss firm. You overslept and are ten minutes late for your scheduled one-hour appointment. It is possible that you may be docked another 10 minutes resulting in only a 40-minute meeting.	☐ True ☐ False	☐ True ☐ False	☐ True ☐ False
4. In your sales pitch to representatives of a Swiss company, you have maintained a low-key approach. High-pressure tactics do not work well on the conservative Swiss businesspeople.	☐ True ☐ False	☐ True ☐ False	☐ True ☐ False
5. You arrive at a Swiss company for a meeting and announce your name to the receptionist. However, when you meet with your contact, you give her/him your business card.	☐ True ☐ False	☐ True ☐ False	☐ True ☐ False
6. You will be presenting a program on your company's services to a group of Swiss businesspeople in Geneva. It doesn't matter how lengthy your talk is as long as you cover every detail of your services.	☐ True ☐ False	☐ True ☐ False	☐ True ☐ False
7. You have been assigned by your employer, an old and respected U.S. firm, to work on opening up contacts in the Swiss business community. Your business card, printed with the founding date of your company, your corporate title, and your academic degrees, is impressive to the Swiss.	☐ True ☐ False	☐ True ☐ False	☐ True ☐ False
8. You are preparing for negotiations with people from a Swiss firm. The Swiss businesspeople will likely know what the competition is offering; so you would do well to focus on every aspect of your product.	☐ True ☐ False	☐ True ☐ False	☐ True ☐ False
9. You wish to take the Swiss people you've been negotiating with out to lunch. It's acceptable to also ask the boss's secretary, who may be a source of inside information.	☐ True ☐ False	☐ True ☐ False	☐ True ☐ False
10. You are preparing cost figures to present to a team of Swiss business executives. You will need to check on any fees on your products that may be levied through the European business community.	☐ True ☐ False	☐ True ☐ False	☐ True ☐ False
Total number of correct answers given by each applicant	_____ Number correct	_____ Number correct	

Applicant to be invited back _____

Question	Applicant #1's Answer	Applicant #2's Answer	Correct Answer
1. Your employer assigns you to the task of opening up contacts with a Turkish company. If you don't have a personal referral, contacting the U.S. embassy in Turkey is the next best move.	☐ True ☐ False	☐ True ☐ False	☐ True ☐ False
2. You are a female vice president in an American corporation who is going to Turkey to negotiate an important contract. You may not be well received, since Turkish women are rarely in top positions.	☐ True ☐ False	☐ True ☐ False	☐ True ☐ False
3. Prior to your business meeting at a Turkish firm, there will probably be a period of chit-chat. If you are meeting with a Turkish man, a good move would be to ask him about his sons.	☐ True ☐ False	☐ True ☐ False	☐ True ☐ False
4. You arrive at a Turkish company for a business meeting and are offered tea. Since you detest tea, it is acceptable to decline.	☐ True ☐ False	☐ True ☐ False	☐ True ☐ False
5. It's been a long arduous day of negotiations between you and a group of Turkish businesspeople. You have invited them to dinner at your hotel. Since you are the host, it is permissible to order your favorite cocktail while waiting for your meal.	☐ True ☐ False	☐ True ☐ False	☐ True ☐ False
6. You are visiting a Turkish manufacturing company and are given a tour of one of their factories. You should shake hands with the workers when you arrive and again when you leave.	☐ True ☐ False	☐ True ☐ False	☐ True ☐ False
7. You are engaged in trade talks with members of a Turkish corporation. Your habits of looking into the eyes of the person you're speaking to and talking with sincerity will emphasize your honesty with the Turks.	☐ True ☐ False	☐ True ☐ False	☐ True ☐ False
8. You will be staying in Turkey while meeting with representatives of several Turkish firms. You'll make a good impression by staying at a good, moderately priced hotel.	☐ True ☐ False	☐ True ☐ False	☐ True ☐ False
9. You will be visiting a Turkish company as a representative of your American employer. It is protocol to give your business card only to those people with whom you will be working directly.	☐ True ☐ False	☐ True ☐ False	☐ True ☐ False
10. You are making a proposal to a team of Turkish businesspeople, including the head of the corporation. You should give copies of the proposal to the top person, who will distribute them to the others.	☐ True ☐ False	☐ True ☐ False	☐ True ☐ False
Total number of correct answers given by each applicant	Number correct	Number correct	

Applicant to be invited back _____

JOBPARDY

TOPIC Job Interview Questions

LEARNING OBJECTIVE Participants will be able to give appropriate answers to frequently asked interview questions.

NUMBER OF PARTICIPANTS 3 Jobpardy players, a scorekeeper, and any number of supporters divided into three groups

PLAYING TIME 25-35 minutes

REFERENCES Jackson, T. (1992). *The perfect job search.* New York: Doubleday.

Gerberg, R. J. (1980). *The professional job changing system, world's fastest way to get a better job.* Parsippany, NJ: Performance Dynamics, Inc.

Madley, H.A. (1992). *Sweaty palms.* Berkley, CA: Ten Speed Press.

REQUIRED MATERIALS List of Jobpardy Answers, Jobpardy board, a transparency of the Jobpardy Scoreboard, a transparency marker, an overhead projector, three folding chairs, and one die

TO PLAY

1. Introduce players to the concept of job interviews.
2. Go over the learning objective for the game.
3. Explain to the group that they are going to play a game of Jobpardy, which is similar to *Jeopardy.* Three members of the audience will be contestants, one will keep score, and the rest will be supporters.
4. Randomly divide participants into three groups of equal size.
5. Have each of the three groups select a Jobpardy contestant to represent their group.
6. Ask the three contestants to come forward.
7. Go over the rules of the game. Inform contestants that, when it is their turn, they are to ask for a question of a specific value (such as $100, $200, $300, $400, or $500) from one of the six categories (Illegal Questions, Job Skills, Last Job, Potpourri, Salary, or Values). If they give the correct answer in the form of a question, they receive the dollar amount specified for that particular question. The contestant with the most money at the end of the game, along with her/his supporting team members in the audience, will be considered the winners of the game.
8. Advise players that the player rolling the highest number on a die chooses the first question. Subsequent questions will be selected by the contestant who answered the last question correctly. Unlike in the television game of *Jeopardy,* all contestants must be seated. The first contestant to stand completely upright gets a chance at answering the question first. Persons who stand before the question is completely asked are

disqualified from answering the question. If an answer is declared "incorrect," other contestants may immediately stand, be called on, and attempt to answer it.

9. Place an overhead transparency of the Jobpardy Scoreboard on an overhead projector so that both the contestants and the audience can see it.

10. Select a scorekeeper from the audience. Ask her/him to take a place at the overhead projector. Direct the scorekeeper to write the first names of contestants in the cells for which they give a correct answer and an X in cells for which no correct answer is provided. Contestants are not penalized for incorrect answers.

11. Role the die to determine who goes first and begin the game.

12. When all the questions have been asked, tally the scores of each of the three contestants. Declare the contestant with the most money and their supporting team members in the audience "Jobpardy champions."

13. Debrief players. Discuss alternative answers to some of the interview questions asked during the game. Have players share their opinions on what they believe to be the most difficult interview questions to answer.

EFFECTIVE INTERVIEWS

The high points of every job search are the job interviews. This is when the time and effort spent on preparation, research, contact building, and referral interviews shows tangible results. However, everything done in a job campaign can be lost if individuals cannot convert interviews into job offers. This is why it is so very important that job hunters acquire superb interviewing skills.

As job hunters approach their first interview, they should remember that their goal is to be asked back for a second interview. Offers of jobs worth having are rarely made during the first interview. The initial interview is an opportunity to find out more about the interviewer, the company, and the job. It is a time to establish rapport.

For making job interviews more effective, consider some of the rules for good interview control appearing in Fig. 6.1.

Figure 6.1. Rules for interview control.

In most interview situations, attempt to do the following:	In most interview situations, attempt to avoid doing the following:
■ Dress successfully (on the conservative side).	■ Applications forms, if possible.
■ Control the interview.	■ Being interviewed by substitutes.
■ Speak clearly.	■ Being early.
■ Use soft sell.	■ Being kept waiting.
■ Be truthful.	■ Apologizing for liabilities.
■ Be calm.	■ Flaunting your resumé.
■ Be professional.	■ Hard liquor.
■ Turn liabilities into strengths.	■ Being a threat to the interviewer.
■ Image yourself.	■ Acting curious or bored.
■ Emphasize the most important things.	■ Discussing controversial subjects.
■ Be ready for periods of silence.	■ Promising miracles.
■ Protect your present employer.	■ Being a braggart or name dropper.
■ Use flattery.	■ Giving references in advance of a job offer.
■ Project good health.	■ Being pressured.
■ Be a good listener.	■ Offering samples of work.
■ Question the interviewer.	■ Letting the interview drag.
■ Arrive on time.	■ Hanging around after the interview is over.
■ Deal with the objectives and needs of both you and the interviewer.	■ Wearing a coat into the office.
■ Be sincere.	■ Putting your papers on the interviewer's desk.
■ Act interested.	■ Smoking unless a cigarette or cigar is offered.
■ Make the appointment for early in the day.	■ Stressing your need for a job.
■ Be prepared.	■ Asking for a job.
■ Be polite and pleasant, smile!	■ Monday and Friday appointments.
■ Let the interviewer feel "in control."	■ More than two appointments in the same day.
■ Look the interviewer in the eye.	■ Interrupting the interviewer.
■ Stress contributions you can make.	■ Giving a salary statement in advance of a job offer.
■ Use the interviewer's name during the interview.	■ Negotiating salary in advance of a firm job offer.
■ Get an explanation or clarification of the position.	■ Accepting a job offer on the spot.
■ End the interview on a friendly note.	■ Hasty first impressions.

JOBPARDY

LAST JOB	SALARY $$$$	VALUES	ILLEGAL ?S	JOB SKILLS	POTPOURRI
IT DIDN'T LAST LONG ENOUGH—I WAS LAID OFF. **$500**	IF EVERYONE ELSE TAKES SIMILAR CUTS. **$500**	WORK SHOULD BE FUN BUT PEOPLE NEED THEIR OWN SOCIAL LIVES. **$500**	OUR FAMILY IS COMPLETE. **$500**	I HOPE TO MAKE A CONTRIBUTION RIGHT AWAY. **$500**	AS LONG AS I AM CHALLENGED AND CAN MAKE A CONTRIBUTION. **$500**
IT WAS A GREAT COMPANY—I HAD NO SERIOUS COMPLAINTS. **$400**	I WOULD PREFER TO DISCUSS SALARY AFTER A JOB OFFER. **$400**	I ENJOY WORKING ALONE AND WITH A TEAM. **$400**	10 PERCENT CHEROKEE. **$400**	I'VE HAD A FEW DISAPPOINT-MENTS BUT NO FAILURES. **$400**	I WOULD DISCUSS MY CONCERNS WITH MY BOSS. **$400**
I THINK I ENJOYED THE CHALLENGE MOST OF ALL. **$300**	SALARY PLUS COMMISSION. **$300**	I FEEL THAT WOMEN MAKE EXCELLENT MANAGERS. **$300**	MY EARTHLY POSSESSIONS AMOUNT TO $150,000. **$300**	I SOMETIMES EXPECT TOO MUCH OF MYSELF. **$300**	I ONLY MISSED ONE DAY OF WORK DUE TO ILLNESS LAST YEAR. **$300**
HE WAS A GREAT SUPERVISOR. WE GOT ALONG VERY WELL. **$200**	I AM ADEQUATELY COMPENSATED FOR MY WORK. **$200**	Q _____ IS WHATEVER THE CUSTOMER SAYS IT IS. **$200**	I AM DIVORCED. **$200**	I AM AN EXCELLENT PROBLEM SOLVER. **$200**	I HOPE TO MAKE SUPERVISOR IN THREE YEARS. **$200**
I WAS LAID OFF. **$100**	THE JOB, BUT THE MONEY IS ALSO IMPORTANT. **$100**	YES. A LITTLE PRESSURE MOTIVATES ME. **$100**	65 YEARS OLD. **$100**	I INVENTED THE POST-IT NOTE PADS. **$100**	I CAN HELP THE COMPANY ACHIEVE ITS GOALS. **$100**

JOBPARDY SCOREBOARD

LAST JOB	SALARY $$$$	VALUES	ILLEGAL ?S	JOB SKILLS	POTPOURRI
$500	$500	$500	$500	$500	$500
$400	$400	$400	$400	$400	$400
$300	$300	$300	$300	$300	$300
$200	$200	$200	$200	$200	$200
$100	$100	$100	$100	$100	$100

These are answers to the questions appearing on the *Jobpardy* board. The questions are to be read aloud by the game host/facilitator, when selected by a Jobpardy contestant. The facilitator should accept any answer similar to the following:

Illegal Questions

$100	How old are you?
$200	Are you married?
$300	What is your net worth?
$400	Aren't you part Indian?
$500	Do you plan to have any more children?

Job Skills

$100	What is your most outstanding accomplishment?
$200	What are you best at?
$300	What is your greatest weakness?
$400	What is your biggest failure?
$500	How long will it take you to make a contribution?

Last Job

$100	Why did you leave your former employer?
$200	How did you get along with your former boss?
$300	What did you like most about your previous job?
$400	What did you most dislike about your former employer?
$500	What did you dislike most about your previous job?

Potpourri

$100	Why should we hire you?
$200	What is your short-range career goal?
$300	Are you in good health?
$400	What would you do if you had a work-related problem?
$500	How long do you expect to work here?

Salary

$100	Which is more important, the job or the money?
$200	Are you satisfied with your current salary?
$300	Do you prefer to work on commission or straight salary?
$400	If we offer you the job, what salary would you expect?
$500	If business gets slow in the future, would you be willing to take a temporary pay cut?

Values

$100	Can you work under pressure?
$200	How do you define quality?
$300	Do you think that women make good managers?
$400	Do you prefer to work on your own or as part of a team?
$500	Should people mix business with pleasure?

LEADS

TOPIC   Job Leads

**LEARNING
OBJECTIVE**   Participants will be able to identify various ways of securing job leads.

**NUMBER OF
PARTICIPANTS**   Any number in groups of 4-6 players each

PLAYING TIME   30-45 minutes

REFERENCES   Parker Brothers Inc. (1986). *Clue*. Deerfield, IL.

                   Germann, Richard, and Arnold, Peter. (1980). *Bernard Haldane Associates' job and career building*. New York: Harper & Row.

**REQUIRED
MATERIALS**   Leads Game Board, set of Leads Game Cards, a deck of Occupational Ignoramus Cards, one die, six player markers (see App. B for ideas), pencils, a pad of Leads Scoresheets, and one Hidden Job Mystery File (small #6¾ envelope)

TO PLAY

1. Introduce players to the concepts of job leads and the hidden job market.

2. Go over the learning objective for the game.

3. Explain that they are about to play a game called *Leads*. It is similar to the game *Clue*. However, in *Leads* the goal is to solve a job vacancy mystery (i.e., identify the job, the employing organization, and how the job is being advertised) rather than to solve a murder mystery.

4. Divide the group into smaller groups of four to six players each.

5. Have groups reassemble themselves around tables.

6. Provide each group a *Leads* game.

7. Have each group place their game board on the table so that all members can see it. Explain that the board contains a grid, with eight organizations around its periphery and one organization in the middle.

8. Ask groups to create a Hidden Job Mystery File. Direct them to place the nine organization cards, six job cards, and six advertisement cards into separate piles and to shuffle each pile thoroughly. Have the oldest player in each group blindly draw one card from each of the piles and place the three cards into a small envelope (#6¾). This Hidden Job Mystery File now contains the mystery that each individual will attempt to be the first to solve.

9. Have everyone place her/his marker in one of the organization spaces on the Leads Board.

10. Ask a dealer to deal all of the Leads Playing Cards (i.e., except for those in the Hidden Job Mystery File) to the players in their group.

11. Ask an individual in each group to shuffle and place the deck of Occupational Ignoramus Cards near their board. The cards should be placed with the question side of the cards facing upward and the answer facing downward.

12. Determine who will play first by having each player in the various groups roll a die. The person rolling the highest number is to play first. Advise participants that play advances around each group in a clockwise direction.

13. Have the person who won the right to play first begin the game by rolling a die. If a one, two, or three is rolled, the player's game marker remains on the board in the same organization space and the play goes to the next player. If a player rolls a four, five, or six she/he may (but doesn't have to) move the marker to another organization (such as City Hall, Chocolate Factory, Health Club, Mercy General Hospital, County Technical College, Municipal Airport, Louis' Beauty Salon, Bob's New Car Sales, or Tony's Pizza) and draw an Occupational Ignoramus Card. A player who chooses to move the marker to another organization and correctly answers the question on the Occupational Ignoramus Card may offer a "suggestion" to the solution of the hidden job mystery.

14. Explain that, to make a "suggestion," a player suggests the job, the employing organization, and how the job is being advertised. The person to the immediate left of the suggester attempts to prove the player wrong by showing her/him (no one else) one of the three cards just named in the suggestion. If the player to the immediate left can't prove the suggestion wrong, other players in turn are afforded opportunities to do so. Through the making of suggestions and the process of elimination, players move closer and closer to the solution of the hidden job mystery.

15. Explain that play continues around the board with individuals rolling a die, moving their markers to different organizations, drawing and answering Occupational Ignoramus Cards, and making suggestions to the solution of the hidden job mystery until a player feels ready to actually solve the mystery. All formal solutions to the mystery are made in the form of "accusations."

16. Inform players that making an accusation is similar to making a suggestion, with three notable differences. When making accusations: (1) the accuser must have her/his marker in the organization where the supposed job opening exists, (2) the accuser and only the accuser gets to check the Hidden Job Mystery File to determine if she/he is correct, and (3) if the accusation is correct, the player shows her/his opponents the cards from the Hidden Job Mystery File and becomes the winner of the game. If the accusation is not correct, the player is out of the game. Play continues among the remaining players until a correct accusation is made.

17. Walk around the room, helping each group as needed. Groups who finish quickly may attempt to play a second game.

18. When all the groups have solved at least one hidden job mystery, ask the winners in their respective groups to stand. Declare them winners and bestow on them the title of "Master Job Detective."

19. Debrief players. Discuss various ways of securing job leads. Identify ways of penetrating what is sometimes referred to as the "hidden job market."

LEADS GAME BOARD

To make copies of Leads Game Board, enlarge and photocopy the follow item on large sheets of colored paper. Glue the paper to large sheets of poster board.

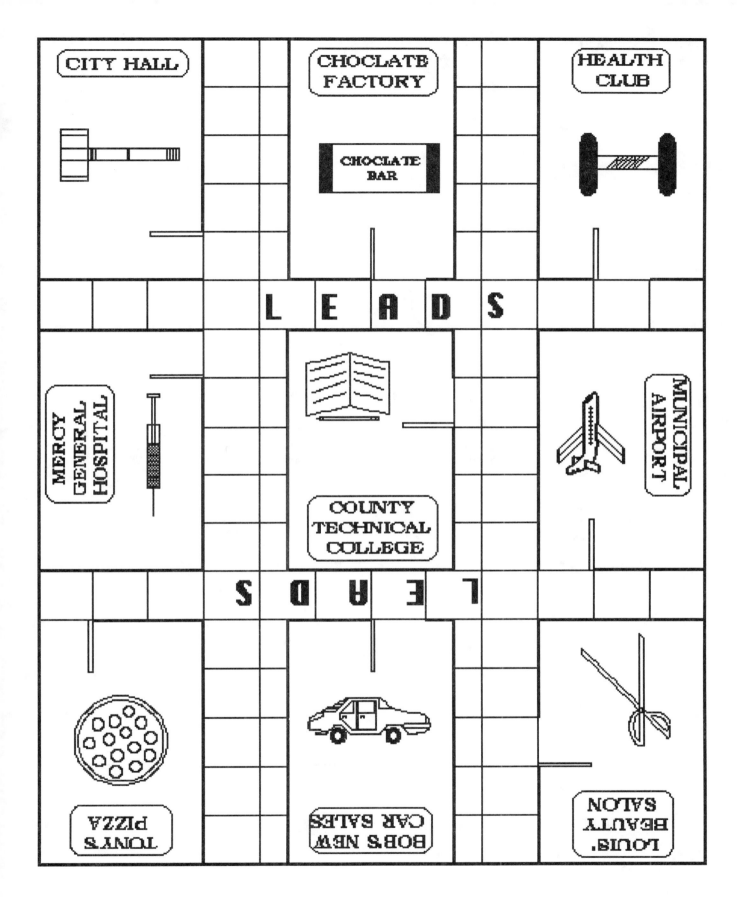

To make a set of Leads Game Cards, photocopy the follow items, using card stock paper, and cut them out.

CITY HALL	**CHOCOLATE FACTORY**	**HEALTH CLUB**
MERCY GENERAL HOSPITAL	**COUNTY TECHNICAL COLLEGE**	**MUNICIPAL AIRPORT**
TONY'S PIZZA	**BOB'S NEW CAR SALES**	**LOUIS' BEAUTY SALON**

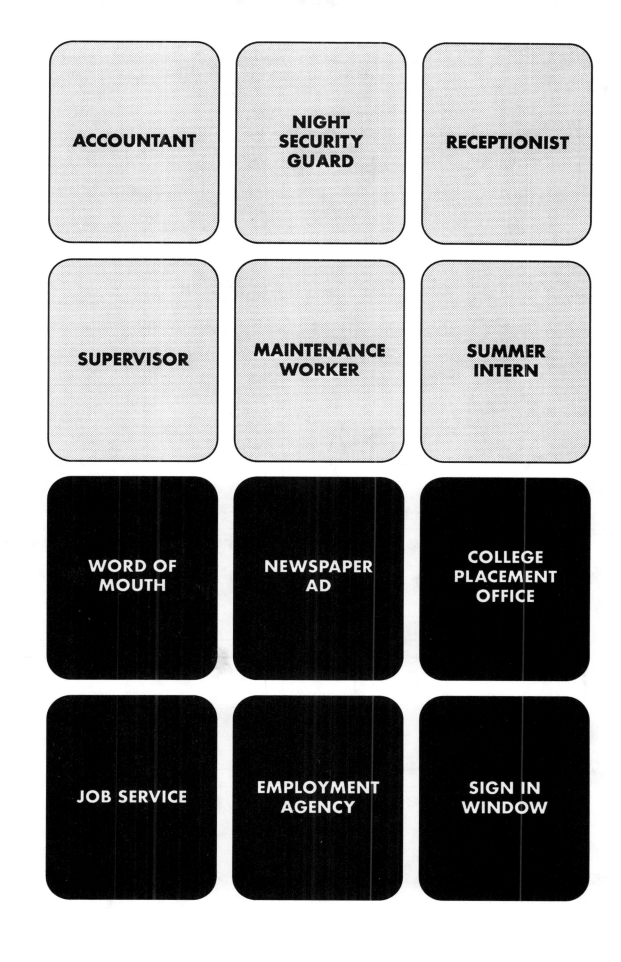

ACCOUNTANT

NIGHT SECURITY GUARD

RECEPTIONIST

SUPERVISOR

MAINTENANCE WORKER

SUMMER INTERN

WORD OF MOUTH

NEWSPAPER AD

COLLEGE PLACEMENT OFFICE

JOB SERVICE

EMPLOYMENT AGENCY

SIGN IN WINDOW

To make a deck of Occupational Ignoramus Cards, photocopy the follow items using card stock paper and cut them out. Write the answer to each question on the reverse side of the card (see answers in Appendix A).

True or False Successful careers just happen.	**True or False** Most of the job offerings today require a four-year college degree.	**True or False** Individuals learn much about how to manage their career from the mistakes they make.
True or False If you are frustrated at work, you should quit your job immediately.	**True or False** The earlier a person selects a career the better.	**True or False** The only way to find a job is to find a job vacancy.
True or False The job market dictates what career a person should choose.	**True or False** You must have good contacts to get a really good job.	**True or False** Tests are able to tell you what career you should enter.
True or False A person is hired because she/he is the best candidate.	**True or False** Women are better in careers traditionally held by women.	**True or False** If you are over 40 years of age it is much more difficult to get a job.
True or False To get ahead in a career, you should learn to be very aggressive.	**True or False** Changing careers is costly and very risky.	**True or False** A good resumé is written in the chronological style listing all past positions and employers.
True or False By virtue of their abilities, most individuals are suited for a variety of jobs.	**True or False** Employment agencies work for job seekers.	**True or False** In addition to the income it provides, a job affects a person's life in many other ways.

True or False

Personnel departments do most of the hiring.

True or False

During her/his lifetime, a person is likely to work at several different occupations.

True or False

The sole purpose of an interview is to get a job offer.

True or False

Apprentices are paid as they learn a trade.

True or False

When asked to do so, you should present a salary to a prospective employer.

True or False

Besides taking a job in a field, there are many ways of finding out if a person might enjoy working in an occupation.

True or False

The unemployment rate for individuals holding college degrees is typically lower than that of high school dropouts.

True or False

The best way to begin planning for a career is to find out more about your career interests (i.e., what types of tasks you most enjoy doing).

True or False

Most people find job openings through word of mouth.

True or False

If a person is highly interested in several occupations, she/he should research each of the options before making a choice.

True or False

Approximately 5 percent of current workers find out about their jobs through newspaper ads.

True or False

If a person chooses an occupation with which she/he is unhappy, she/he can switch to another career if she/he so desires.

True or False

Approximately the same percentage of workers find out about jobs through college placement offices as those who find out about jobs through employment agencies.

True or False

In choosing an occupation to enter, one should always take into consideration the number of projected openings for that field (i.e., its outlook).

True or False

Nearly one-fourth of all workers find out about jobs through direct contact with employers.

True or False

In most occupational fields, women earn less than men doing the same work.

True or False

Sending a large number of unsolicited resumés to prospective employers is a poor way to get a job interview.

True or False

After a job interview, it is advisable to mail the interviewer a thank-you note.

To make a pad of Leads Scoresheets, photocopy the follow items using card stock paper and cut them out.

LEADS
Job Vacancy

Accountant	☐
Maintenance worker	☐
Night security guard	☐
Receptionist	☐
Summer intern	☐
Supervisor	☐

Employing Organization

Bob's New Car Sales	☐
Chocolate Factory	☐
City Hall	☐
County Technical College	☐
Health Club	☐
Louis' Beauty Salon	☐
Mercy General Hospital	☐
Municipal Airport	☐
Tony's Pizza	☐

Method of Advertising

College placement office	☐
Employment agency	☐
Job service	☐
Newspaper ad	☐
Sign in window	☐
Word of mouth	☐

LEADS
Job Vacancy

Accountant	☐
Maintenance worker	☐
Night security guard	☐
Receptionist	☐
Summer intern	☐
Supervisor	☐

Employing Organization

Bob's New Car Sales	☐
Chocolate Factory	☐
City Hall	☐
County Technical College	☐
Health Club	☐
Louis' Beauty Salon	☐
Mercy General Hospital	☐
Municipal Airport	☐
Tony's Pizza	☐

Method of Advertising

College placement office	☐
Employment agency	☐
Job service	☐
Newspaper ad	☐
Sign in window	☐
Word of mouth	☐

MY NOTABLE NETWORK

TOPIC	Networking
LEARNING OBJECTIVE	Participants will be able to identify different categories of people in their networks.
NUMBER OF PARTICIPANTS	At least 20 people who already know many others in the group
PLAYING TIME	7–12 minutes
REFERENCE	None
REQUIRED MATERIALS	Pencils and My Notable Network worksheet

TO PLAY

1. Introduce players to the concept of networking.
2. Discuss how networks can be used to help people find jobs.
3. Go over the learning objective for the game.
4. Pass out pencils and copies of My Notable Network.
5. Tell participants that they are about to enter into a networking competition.
6. Explain that they have five minutes to go around the room and get as many individuals as possible to sign their networking worksheet. However, all signatures must be written in the appropriate spaces on their worksheet. For example, the space labeled "People Who Owe Me a Big Favor" must only be signed by people in the room who owe the networker a big favor.
7. Advise players that they are to collect only two signatures for each category and that an individual's signature may appear in only one category.
8. Begin the game by calling, "Network."
9. After five minutes call, "Stop."
10. Declare the person(s) with the greatest number of signatures the winner(s).
11. Debrief players. Discuss some of the special needs people have during a job search (such as informational needs, financial needs, psychological needs, emotional needs). Ask players to list specific ways various individuals appearing on their network chart might be helpful during a job search.

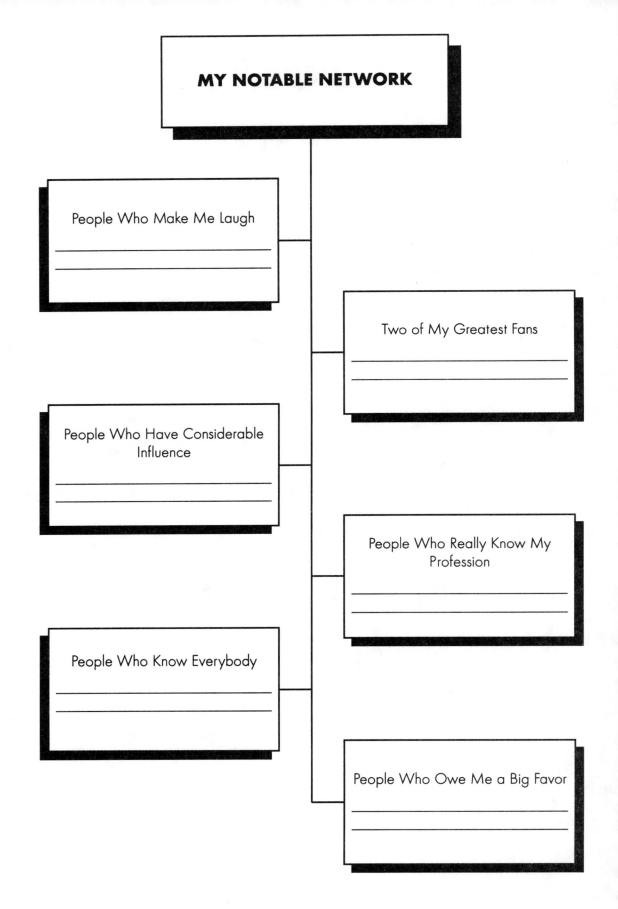

MY NOTABLE NETWORK

People Who Make Me Laugh

_____

_____

Two of My Greatest Fans

_____

_____

People Who Have Considerable Influence

_____

_____

People Who Really Know My Profession

_____

_____

People Who Know Everybody

_____

_____

People Who Owe Me a Big Favor

_____

_____

POLITICAL HORSE CENTS

TOPIC   Political Scripts

LEARNING OBJECTIVE   Participants will be able to describe behavior patterns that are characteristic of individuals following selected political scripts.

NUMBER OF PARTICIPANTS   Any number, divided into groups of 8 players each

PLAYING TIME   10-15 minutes

REFERENCE   Block, P. (1988). *The empowered manager: Positive political skills at work.* San Francisco: Jossey-Bass.

REQUIRED MATERIALS   Pencils, Racing Program, Race Track, deck of Racing Cards, Political Horse Cents Score Cards, and a supply of pennies.

TO PLAY

1. Introduce players to the concept of political scripts.
2. Go over the learning objective for the game.
3. Explain that they are going to play a game entitled "Political Horse Cents." The game is an imaginary horse race between eight horses with eight different political scripts.
4. Advise players that they are going to speculate on which horses will win, place, and show. Explain to players that, for the purposes of this game, *win* means to come in first, *place* means to come in second, and *show* means to come in third.
5. Pass out a pencil and one copy of the Racing Program to each player.
6. Ask players to read over the descriptions and win/loss records for each of the eight horses appearing on the program.
7. Have players write a *W* in the left-hand margin for the horse they think will win. Ask them to write a *P* for the horse they think will place and a *S* for the horse they think will show.
8. Ask players to divide themselves into groups of eight.
9. Pass out one copy of the Race Track, a deck of Racing Cards, and eight pennies (to be used as markers) for each group.
10. Have players place a penny on the Racing Board in each of the eight post positions 1-8.
11. Have players check their Racing Forms (column 4) to see which post positions their horses are in.
12. Inform players that the race is about to begin. The winner will be the first horse to reach cell H (the finish line). The next horse to read cell H is the horse that places. The

third horse across the finish line is the horse that shows. The race is over after the first three horses have crossed the finish line.

13. Ask the youngest member of the group to shuffle the deck of Racing Cards and place them face down beside the Racing Board.

14. Direct the person to the left of the shuffler to draw the top card and place it face up next to the draw pile.

15. Explain that the drawn card represents one of the horses in the race. If, for example, a seven is drawn from the top of the deck, horse number 7, Stiff Rump, advances from the post position cell to cell A.

16. Ask the drawer in each group to move the appropriate penny on her/his board one space.

17. Advise participants that play is to continue clockwise within each group, with each member drawing a card from the top of the draw pile and moving that horse's marker one space on the board.

18. Have groups continue with their horse races while you move around, answering any questions they may have.

19. When all the groups have finished their races, pass out a copy of the Political Horse Cents Score Card to each player.

20. Carefully go over the directions to the score card.

21. Have players tally the points they earned for their races.

22. Have the player(s) in each of the groups with the most points stand. Declare them to be the winner(s) and the ones with the most "political horse cents."

23. Debrief players. Have players identify the horse they picked to win. Ask them why they chose the horse. Discuss whether or not individuals with this political script usually win at their place of work.

POLITICAL SCRIPTS

Political scripts refer to the notions we have about influencing others. They can have a major impact on what individuals are able to accomplish in their respective organizations. According to Peter Block, there are eight scripts that individuals most often carry around in their heads. They include rescuer, looking good, being pleasing, withdrawing, rebelling, being aggressive, being formal, and being superrational. Following are the characteristic behaviors of individuals playing such scripts:[1]

Rescuer

- Highly sensitive to others' discomforts.
- Willing to postpone getting what they want.
- Believe that their rewards will come in the next life, the next job, the next performance review.

[1]Published with permission of Jossey-Bass, 350 Sansome Street, San Francisco, CA 94104.

- See others as being in need of their help.
- Helping others makes them feel good about themselves.

Looking Good

- Have high standards, which they freely voice.
- Like clear objectives for tasks.
- Don't expect anything more from others than what they expect from themselves.
- Keep themselves and their work areas clean and neat.
- Strive for perfection in their work.

Being Pleasing

- Make a conscious effort to nod their heads when listening to someone.
- Attempt to please everyone, make them happy.
- Avoid placing strong, explicit demands on others.
- Willing to take the blame for others' mistakes rather than embarrassing someone else.
- Being able to "fit in" with people around them is of utmost importance.

Withdrawing

- Worry that their supervisor will place demands on them that they will not be able to meet.
- Are generally silent in meetings, sharing only a minimal amount of information with others.
- Prefer to work alone.
- Don't make a habit of bothering co-workers, preferring to take care of their own business.
- Like to deal with difficult issues at a later time, preferably when they have more control over the situation.

Rebelling

- Consciously break the norms and rules of their employing organization.
- Like to wear clothes that are a little different, yet acceptable.
- Prefer to make up their own rules.
- Strongly espouse democratic values and the virtues of participative management.
- Enjoy conflict and disagreement.

Being Aggressive

- Make a habit of going after what they want.
- Let people know where they stand.
- Don't care for all that "touchy-feelie" stuff.
- Need to be constantly in control of the situation.
- Believe that only the strong survive.

Being Formal

- Place a high value on being polite to others.
- Like to put off or avoid conflicts.
- Hesitate to bring up difficult issues.
- Are comfortable with rules, policies, and procedures.
- Are happiest when life and work are very orderly.

Being Superrational

- When faced with confusion or disappointment, they try to cope by understanding it.
- They like to work with hard facts and data.
- Place little confidence in intuition.
- Frequently lose track of their own feelings.
- Being able to understand difficult issues or messy situations makes them feel good.

RACING CARDS

To prepare a deck of Racing Cards, take two regular decks of playing cards and remove the nines, tens, jacks, queens, and kings. Use the remaining cards (i.e., the aces and the dueces through the eights) as a Racing Deck (aces count as 1).

![horse head illustration] HORSES	Jockey	Record for Past 10 Races	Post
SAVING GRACE: This horse is a dutiful caretaker of her trainer, jockey, and owner. Doing her best by winning means more money, thus financial comfort for the humans in her life. SAVING feels depended on to make sure that her humans are comfortable and out of financial trouble. Rewards will be forthcoming for her when the needs of her people are met.	Ned Needful	5/10	1
MR. PRISSY: This horse is tireless in his efforts to win. He pushes himself to his limits while exhibiting perfect grace of movement. During the race, he keeps his eye on the finish line. PRISSY has been known to kick dirty straw out of his stall. He never spends time in the company of horses with lesser ideals.	Vera Proud	7/10	2
AMIABLE ANDY: This is a very loving animal. He nuzzles his humans, often seeming to understand their moods. ANDY is not in the least temperamental and strives to do exactly as his trainer directs. He is well liked by other horses in the stable. When he loses a race, he hangs his head in shame, so that his owner won't blame his jockey for the loss.	Smelly Jones	0/10	3
TOUCH ME NOT: A nervous horse, afraid of failing his trainer, he sometimes shuts down temporarily when he has difficulty doing what he's supposed to do, though he never makes a fuss. TOUCH keeps to himself and rarely associates with the other horses in the stable. He is very self-sufficient.	Snooty Prince	4/10	4
ROGER ROGUE: This independent horse manages to win by doing it his way. At an early age, ROGER took a liking to caps and now in each race wears one to match his jockey's. He asserts himself in sessions with his trainer, often ending in compromise. Although a "filly's man," ROGER enjoys taunting other male horses to gain a reaction. He's a free spirit who truly enjoys the race.	Dash Daring	2/10	5
LIBERATED LOLA: This horse wants to win the race and lets nothing stand in her way. Pats and caresses from her trainer are shunned. A no-nonsense filly, she controls her pace and chooses her position in the race. Her jockey is just along for the ride. LOLA never seems to notice other horses as she plunges ahead toward the finish line.	Willie Wimpy	4/10	6
STIFF RUMP: A regal beast, he carries his head high, but he always nods to other horses and never fails to let the fillies pass through the stable door ahead of him. STIFF goes through his paces with his trainer in an orderly fashion, never attempting to change any part of the routine. STIFF will do all he can to avoid having his trainer or jockey become upset with him and very rarely pits his will against theirs. An orderly existence is his greatest joy.	I. M. Uptight	5/10	7
LOTS 'O LOGIC: The real thinking human's horse, he has been known to stop dead in the middle of an unfamiliar track during the initial practice races, as if to get "the lay of the land." LOTS also listens to trainers and jockeys discuss track conditions in order to plan his race strategies. This horse seems to pout after losing a race, but in reality he's just trying to figure out what went wrong. LOTS doesn't intuitively warm up to his fellow creatures, usually sizing them up first.	Sen Sybowl	1/10	8

RACE TRACK

	1	2	3	4	5	6	7	8
H								
G								
F								
E								
D								
C								
B								
A								

Directions: Record in the far right-hand column the points you earned for the race. First record the points you earned on the horse you bet to win. If it won, placed, or showed, record the points specified in column 2 (0 points are given for horses that did not win, place, or show). Next record your points for the horse you bet to place and the horse you bet to show. Finally, tally your winnings at the bottom of column 4.

If You Bet the Horse to...	And the Horse Ended Up...	You Should Collect This Amount	Your Points
Win	Win	100	
Win	Place	75	
Win	Show	50	
Place	Win	75	
Place	Place	75	
Place	Show	50	
Show	Win	50	
Show	Place	50	
Show	Show	50	
		Total points +	

RESUMÉ RACE

TOPIC Resumé Preparation

LEARNING OBJECTIVE Participants will be able to give some of the basic rules for preparing effective resumés.

NUMBER OF PARTICIPANTS Any number of players divided into small groups of four members each

PLAYING TIME 25-30 minutes

REFERENCE Jackson, T. (1992). *The perfect job search.* New York: Doubleday.

REQUIRED MATERIALS Resumé Puzzle pieces, small brown paper lunch bags to hold puzzle pieces, and a deck of Resumé Question Cards

TO PLAY

1. Introduce players to the fundamentals of preparing a resumé.
2. Go over the learning objective for the game.
3. Explain to players that they are going to prepare a resumé in the form of a puzzle, place the pieces of their puzzles in small lunch bags, and race each other to be the first in their group to reassemble their resumés.
4. Pass out a complete Resumé Puzzle to each participant (seven separate pieces).
5. Ask participants to write the appropriate information on each piece of the puzzle.
6. Pass out a small brown paper lunch bag to each player. Ask participants to put all of the pieces of their Resumé Puzzle into their bag.
7. Divide the group into smaller groups of four players each.
8. Pass out a deck of Resumé Question Cards to each group.
9. Ask the youngest person in each group to shuffle the cards and place the questions face upward in the middle of the group.
10. Advise players that the game will begin with the person to the left of the dealer drawing and answering a Resumé Question Card first. Without looking at the answers on the back, the players are to read and answer each question aloud. The player who gives the correct answer gets to reach into the brown paper bag and remove one piece of her/his Resumé Puzzle.
11. Inform players that the first person to retrieve and assemble all of the pieces of her/his resumé wins the resumé race.
12. Tell players to begin racing in a clockwise direction around the group.
13. When all of the groups have a winner, ask the winners to stand. Declare them "resumé racing champions."
14. Debrief players. Discuss with participants whether the resumé style for the puzzle is the best style for them. Identify other styles which might be more appropriate for certain players.

Millions of resumés are circulated by job seekers each year. Unfortunately, most of these resumés are poorly written. Individuals who develop outstanding resumés gain a distinctive competitive edge over other job hunters.

In a matter of seconds, a resumé must attract favorable interest. It serves as a personal advertisement, and can mean the difference between success and failure in securing the much coveted interview. The resumé must appear alive and interesting to people at all levels. It should sell a person's abilities without the reader being offended by the selling effort. Furthermore, an effective resumé keeps on selling a person throughout the interview and salary negotiation process.

Resumés contain several types of information. These include:

Personal Data. Give job seeker's name, address, home and business phone numbers. Other information such as age, sex, marital status, physical data and health, should be included only if they support a person's job objective.

Work Experience. Truly outstanding accomplishments which are relevant to a person's job objective are highlighted. This information is the core of the resumé. It shows a potential employer what the job seeker is capable of doing for her/his company.

Education. All relevant formally accredited education is listed. Relevant education and training obtained through military schools, correspondence courses, seminars, company sponsored training, and adult continuing professional education courses may also be included.

Optional Information. Anything which adds to the influencing power of the resumé should be considered. Some of the more common types of optional information are:

- Awards and honors
- Professional memberships
- Civic and social organization memberships
- Foreign language skills
- Business travel experience
- Patents and licenses
- Military service information
- Security clearances

THREE STYLES OF RESUMÉS

Even though there are a number of very important and specific rules for writing a resumé, there is no one "right" resumé style or format. The style of resumé used should be suited to the job seeker's career objective and background. The final choice will depend on which assets a person has to emphasize and which liabilities an individual needs to downplay. The three most common resumé styles are the chronological, functional, and combination.

Chronological Style

This style presents a person's background in chronological order, beginning with the most recent position and working backwards in time. The page is arranged according to dates. Following each date is a job title and the employer's name. The most recent position typically occupies the most space. Approximately 60 percent of all resumés are written in the chronological style.

Advantages of the chronological resumé style are:

- Professional interviewers are more familiar with it.
- It is the easiest to prepare.
- A steady employment record is put into the best perspective.
- It provides the interviewer with a guide for discussing work experience.

Here are the disadvantages of the chronological resumé:

- It starkly reveals employment gaps.
- It may put undesired emphasis on job areas that an applicant wants to minimize.
- Skill areas are difficult to spotlight unless they are reflected in the most recent job.

Functional Style

This style organizes experiences by function, such as marketing or engineering, usually listing the strongest or most relevant ones first. It omits the employer's names and the dates worked.

Advantages of the functional resumé format are as follows:

- It stresses selected skill areas that are marketable.
- It helps camouflage a spotty employment record.
- It allows the applicant to emphasize professional growth.
- Jobs not related to current career goals can be played down.

The functional resumé has the following disadvantages:

- Many employers are suspicious of it, and will want to see additional work history information.
- It does not highlight companies and organizations for which a person has worked.
- Extra care must be taken to be clear and concise to overcome the employer's initial unfamiliarity.

Combination Style

This style capitalizes on the strengths of the functional format, but includes company names and dates in a separate section. It allows the job seeker to stress the preferred and most relevant skill areas, at the same time satisfying the employer's desire to know names and dates.

Advantages of the combination resumé are as follows:

- It provides an opportunity to emphasize the applicant's most relevant skills and abilities.
- Gaps in employment can be de-emphasized.
- It can be varied to emphasize chronology and de-emphasize functional descriptions, or vice versa.

Disadvantages of the combination resumé are as follows:

- It takes longer to read, and an employer can lose interest unless it is very succinctly written and attractively laid out.
- An applicant's most recent work experience is played down.

RESUMÉ QUESTION CARDS

To prepare a deck of Resumé Question Cards, photocopy the following items using card stock paper and cut them out. Write the answer to the question on the back of each card (see answers in App. A).

True or False In preparing a resumé, you should personalize your writing.	**True or False** In preparing a resumé, you should use first and second person pronouns.	**True or False** In preparing a resumé, you should set a natural and warm tone combined with a crisp, clear style.
True or False In preparing a resumé, you should use action or power words (i.e., use words that excite).	**True or False** In preparing a resumé, you should use brief and direct descriptions.	**True or False** In preparing a resumé, you should write dollar figures in number form.
True or False In preparing a resumé, you should use short, concise sentences.	**True or False** In preparing a resumé, you should write in the language of your potential employer.	**True or False** In preparing a resumé, you should make your selling pitch future-oriented.
True or False In preparing a resumé, you should reflect your uniqueness.	**True or False** In preparing a resumé, you should mention your employer's name, if possible.	**True or False** In preparing a resumé, you should quantify your achievements.

True or False

In preparing a resumé, you should make it accomplishment-oriented.

True or False

In preparing a resumé, you should sell your ability as well as your experience.

True or False

In preparing a resumé, you should place personal data at the top.

True or False

In preparing a resumé, you should include a summary of your main selling points at the top.

True or False

In preparing a resumé, you should spark the reader's interest early. (Give her/him a reason for reading on!)

True or False

In preparing a resumé, you should use a format that highlights your main selling points and minimizes your liabilities.

True or False

In preparing a resumé, you should use open space liberally. Keep it neat and easy to read.

True or False

For highlighting and creating favorable first impressions with your resumé, you use capital letters, underlining, italics, indentations, bold type, and bullets or dashes.

True or False

In preparing a resumé, you should separate division headings and subheadings with open space.

True or False

In preparing a resumé, you should emphasize each category of information.

True or False

In preparing a resumé, you should keep paragraphs short.

True or False

In preparing a resumé, you should break up long ideas into short sentences or phrases.

True or False

In preparing a resumé, you should use single spacing.

True or False

In preparing a resumé, you should emphasize only accomplishments that directly relate to your job objective.

True or False

If many of your jobs are irrelevant to your job objectives, you should write a brief summary giving highlights of each, as well as the total period of time covering these activities.

True or False

If any former job titles do not accurately reflect your real responsibilities in these positions, you should use functional titles when preparing a resumé.

True or False

If your situation permits, use exact dates when preparing a resumé.

True or False

In preparing a resumé, you should list your highest educational degree first.

True or False

If you feel you have the equivalent of an academic certificate in terms of training and experience, and can give data to support it, consider listing such in your resumé.

True or False

Prior to printing your resumé, you should write several drafts, have a professional proofread and critique the final copy of it.

True or False

In preparing a resumé, you should put your resumé on a computer or word processor that can print to a laser printer.

True or False

In preparing a resumé, you should leave wide margins (at least 1- to 1½-inches on the sides, and 1½ inches on top, and 1 inch on the bottom).

True or False

In preparing a resumé, you should use a color, size, and texture of paper that stands out among any number of resumés. You should also avoid extremes.

True or False

In preparing a resumé, you should have several copies printed on a laser printer or small press.

True or False

In preparing a resumé, you should use popular clichés.

True or False

In preparing a resumé, you should mention any disabilities you may have.

True or False

In preparing a resumé, you should include all interesting personal data.

True or False

In preparing a resumé, you should give the reasons for leaving your last job.

True or False

In preparing a resumé, you should list your references.

True or False

In preparing a resumé, you should give your salary requirements.

True or False

In preparing a resumé, you state your present salary.

True or False

In preparing a resumé, you should be very modest.

True or False

In preparing a resumé, you should give many supporting details.

True or False

In preparing a resumé, you should inflate your experience and skills a little.

True or False

In preparing a resumé, you should make effective use of charts, pictures, and any other materials that might illustrate your main selling points.

True or False

In preparing a resumé, you should use abbreviations generously.

True or False

In preparing a resumé, you should list several job objectives.

True or False

You should make your resumé three pages in length.

To prepare a Resumé Puzzle, photocopy the following items using card stock paper and cut them out.

PERSONAL DATA

_____
Name

_____
Address

_____
Phone Number

ACCOMPLISHMENTS

- _____
  Highlighted Accomplishment

- _____
  Highlighted Accomplishment

- _____
  Highlighted Accomplishment

JOB #1

19__-19__

_____
Position Held

_____
Employer

_____
Contributions

JOB #2

19__-19__

_____
Position Held

_____
Employer

_____
Contributions

JOB #3

19__-19__

_____
Position Held

_____
Employer

_____
Contributions

EDUCATION

19___

_____
Diploma, Certificate, or Degree Earned

_____
Name of Educational Institution

_____
Address of Educational Institution

EDUCATION

19___

_____
Diploma, Certificate, or Degree Earned

_____
Name of Educational Institution

_____
Address of Educational Institution

U.S. BOSS'S PAGEANT

TOPIC   Career Promotion Styles

LEARNING OBJECTIVE   Participants will be able to identify which of four career promotion styles they rely on most to get what they want careerwise.

NUMBER OF PARTICIPANTS   Any even number

PLAYING TIME   10-15 minutes depending on the number of players

REFERENCE   Carney, T. (1987). *Assessing styles of career management* (Instrumentation Kit). San Diego: University Associates Inc.

REQUIRED MATERIALS   Two sets of Pageant Questions and Answers Cards (one set for the facilitator and the other for contestants), name tags (see App. B), and straight pins

TO PLAY

1. Introduce players to the concept of career promotion styles.

2. Go over the learning objective for the game.

3. Ask four volunteers from the audience to come forward, and have each randomly draw a Pageant Questions and Answers Card.

4. Explain to players that these individuals represent finalists in the U.S. Boss's Pageant.

5. Pin on each finalist a name tag using the name that appears on the Pageant Questions and Answers Card they have just drawn.

6. Explain that for the next few minutes everyone is to pretend that they are at a U.S. Boss's Pageant and that the four individuals with the Pageant Questions and Answers Cards are the four finalists.

7. Advise players in the audience that, based on each boss's answer to the final pageant question, they will decide the next "Boss USA."

8. Tell the four finalists that, if they become the next "Boss USA," they will receive numerous gifts and a chance to compete in the "World Boss's Pageant."

9. Read aloud the final question (the question appearing on the Pageant Questions and Answers Cards) to the finalists. One by one, ask each boss to answer the question based on the information contained on her/his Pageant Questions and Answers Card.

10. After each of the finalists has had an opportunity to answer the final question, determine the winning boss. Ask players in the audience to vote for either Boss #1, Boss #2, Boss #3, or Boss #4 by raising their hands as you call out their names.

11. Declare the boss receiving the most votes "Boss USA."

12. Declare the boss receiving the next highest number of votes the "Runner-Up Boss USA." Remind the runner-up that, if for any reason "Boss USA" is unable to fulfill her/his responsibilities, she/he will become the new "Boss USA."

13. Debrief players. Ask participants to tell which boss they voted for and why. Ask them to tell to what degree their career promotion style resembles the style of the boss for whom they voted.

CARNEY'S FOUR CAREER PROMOTION STYLES

Tom Carney has developed an instrument that he purports to measure an individual's "career management style." The four styles include the Careerist, Entrepreneur, Loyalist, and Technician. According to Carney, *Careerists* make use of highly developed political skills to get into the good graces of the "powers that be." They use their contacts and extensive network to rapidly move up in the organization. *Entrepreneurs* make themselves indispensable by taking on and solving the organization's most difficult problems. In return they hope to gain a great deal of influence and visibility. *Loyalists* gain entrance into the "inner circle" of an organization by being loyal and trustworthy. They anticipate that this loyalty will be rewarded with lifelong employment. *Technicians* work to keep their career on track by being very competent at what they do. They want to be recognized for their contributions to the company and given assignments that afford them the opportunities to use their technical expertise.

To make a set of Pageant Questions and Answers Cards, photocopy the following on card stock paper and cut out the individual cards.

Careerist Katie

Question: If someone were to choose you as her/his boss, what could she/he expect to receive in return?

Answer: She/He can expect to ...
- Be introduced to all the important people in her/his business.
- Be taught all the tricks of office politics.
- Be promoted within the first month.

Entrepreneurial Eddie

Question: If someone were to choose you as her/his boss, what could she/he expect to receive in return?

Answer: She/He can expect to ...
- Be in charge of an important task force.
- Be afforded the opportunity to find solutions to major problems.
- Be permitted to make dramatic changes in the organization.

Loyal Lonnie

Question: If someone were to choose you as her/his boss, what could she/he expect to receive in return?

Answer: She/He can expect to ...
- Become a member of the "inner circle."
- Have her/his loyalty rewarded by systematic promotions over time.
- Be recognized for her/his insistence on "going by the book."

Technical Thomas

Question: If someone were to choose you as her/his boss, what could she/he expect to receive in return?

Answer: She/He can expect to ...
- Have her/his technical competence recognized.
- Be given opportunities to further develop her/his skills.
- Be paid on a par with managers in the organization.

Chapter Seven
CAREER MANAGEMENT GAMES

Career management refers to the art of keeping one's career on track—keeping it moving toward designated career goals. The process involves doing some of the right things as well as avoiding doing some of the wrong things. Two games in Chap. 7 approach the topic of career management from a broad perspective. *Career Success Test* identifies things individuals can do to make their careers more successful, and *Enhancement Scramble* offers ways companies can help employees better manage their careers. Other games in the chapter (such as *Corporate Dig, Mentor Mania,* and *Mystery Careers*) place emphasis on specific career management skills. They stress the importance of being able to read an organization's culture, select the right mentor, and transfer job skills from one occupation to another.

Chapter 7 also contains games focusing on the pitfalls that can derail a person's career. *Chinese Cookie Crumble* looks at some ethical and not so ethical means colleagues may use to promote themselves at work. *Ethical-Political* draws players' attention to how company politics can influence their perceptions of what constitutes ethical behavior. *Mind Your Table Manners* tests participants' knowledge of proper dining decorum in selected European countries.

CAREER SUCCESS TEST

TOPIC   Advice for Career Success

LEARNING OBJECTIVE   Participants will be able to recount pieces of advice often given for being successful in a career.

NUMBER OF PARTICIPANTS   Any number

PLAYING TIME   8-12 minutes

REFERENCE   None

REQUIRED MATERIALS   Pencil and a Career Success Test for each player

TO PLAY
1. Discuss people's willingness to offer unsolicited advice on any topic, ranging from what brand of toothpaste to use to the best place in the country to retire.
2. Go over the objective of the game.
3. Divide the group into pairs.
4. Pass out materials (pencils and the Career Success Tests).
5. Explain that each picture on the test represents a common piece of career advice. The participant's job is to decipher the messages and then write the pieces of advice on the appropriate lines below the pictures.
6. Tell players they have five minutes to complete the test.
7. Direct players to begin.
8. After five minutes call, "Stop."
9. Have players check their own tests as the correct answers are given.
10. Determine which pair has the most correct answers. Declare these pairs "Senior Career Coaches."
11. Debrief players. Discuss which pieces of advice members of the group have followed and/or have passed on to others. Ask participants to cite instances in which these pieces of advice have paid off for them.

Directions: Carefully examine the following pictures. Each image represents a common piece of career advice. See how many you can decode in the next five minutes. Record your answers on the appropriate lines at the bottom of the page.

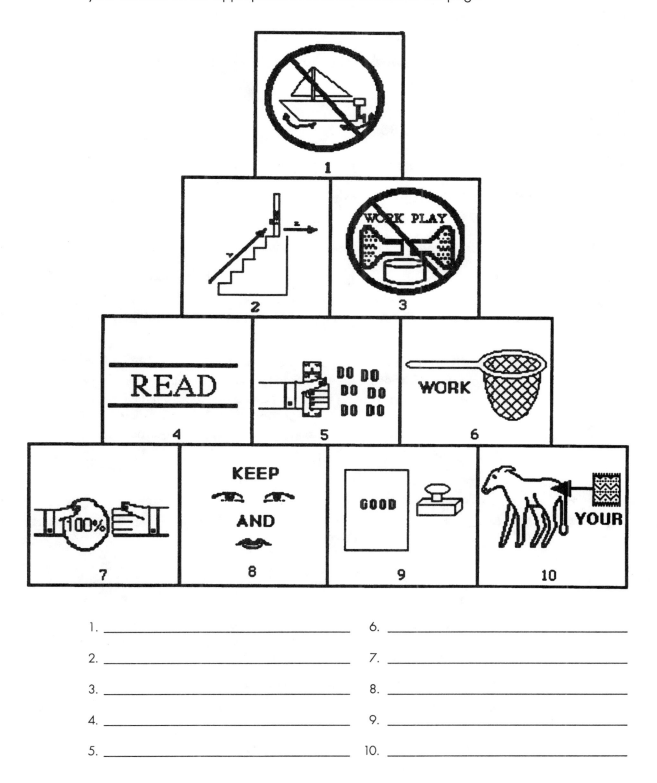

1. _____   6. _____

2. _____   7. _____

3. _____   8. _____

4. _____   9. _____

5. _____   10. _____

CHINESE COOKIE CRUMBLE

TOPIC   The Rewards and Stings of Office Politics

LEARNING OBJECTIVE   Participants will be able to identify ethical and highly unethical ways individuals attempt to promote themselves at work.

NUMBER OF PARTICIPANTS   Any number up to 30

PLAYING TIME   15-25 minutes depending on the number of players

REFERENCE   Dubrin, A. (1990). *Winning office politics*. Englewood Cliffs: Prentice Hall.

REQUIRED MATERIALS   Chinese Career Fortune Cookies and a small wicker basket

TO PLAY
1. Introduce players to the concept of good political strategies (strategies that are both effective and ethical) and questionable political strategies (strategies that are sometimes effective but often unethical) for getting ahead at the office.
2. Go over the learning objective for the game.
3. Explain to players that you will be passing around a basket from which they are to choose a Chinese Career Fortune Cookie. Some of the cookies will contain good career fortunes, indicating that they have benefited from their good political strategies. Other cookies will contain negative career fortunes indicating that they have been stung by a co-worker engaging in questionable career politics.
4. Advise players that they will be asked to read their fortunes aloud to the entire group.
5. Pass around a basket containing the Chinese Career Fortune Cookies. Ask each player to take out one cookie.
6. One by one, ask players to open their cookies, retrieve their fortunes, and read them aloud.
7. If the fortune is "good," ask participants to give their opinions of the strategy used. Have them tell whether they have used the strategy and how effective they found it to be.
8. If the message is "unfortunate," ask players to comment on whether or not a similar incident has ever happened to them. Have them tell how they dealt with the situation or how they should have dealt with it.
9. Declare those with good fortunes winners.
10. Declare those with misfortunes victims. Advise them that this is the way the career cookie sometimes crumbles.
11. Debrief players. Discuss ways workers can prevent themselves from being victims of dirty office politics.

To make a batch of Chinese Career Fortune Cookies, photocopy the following fortunes and misfortunes and cut them into little slips. Cut out small pieces of cream-colored construction paper. Place the slips of paper inside the construction paper and fold into the shape of Chinese Fortune Cookies. Tape the cookie closed with a small piece of tape.

Career Fortunes

You've been an asset to the company. Your work is excellent, and you're always on time. You get that big promotion.

Your expertise and charm has won a huge account for your company. You get a big salary increase without even having to ask.

Your certain and tasteful methods of dealing with an extremely difficult environmental group protesting your company's policies has earned you great recognition from the CEO. You get the Outstanding Employee of the Year Award.

You have conscientiously tried to do your best at your job. Your supervisor is extremely pleased with you and gives you a superb performance appraisal.

The boss finally fires his lazy brother-in-law, leaving a big plush office empty. The boss thinks you're executive material and gives you the office.

You've volunteered for difficult special assignments and gone on lots of out-of-town business trips. You get a brand new luxurious company car.

Your department has been extremely productive in spite of having more work than you can handle. You get permission to hire a new employee of your choice to get even more done.

Excessive amounts of waste material from one product line has been an ongoing problem. You discover a creative way to use this waste that will pay more than the local recycling plant. You get the $500 Employee Idea of the Month Award.

Your old computer system is on its last leg. Because of the high quality of your work and your taking classes to upgrade your computer skills, you are given a state-of-the-art computer and laser printer.

You've given your company 20 years of hard work and dedication. In recognition of this, you are given a one week all-expense-paid vacation in Hawaii for you and your family.

Career Misfortunes

You and a co-worker are having a friendly lunch and she/he asks you how you feel about the boss's spouse. You reply that you found her/him to be rather aloof, perhaps from shyness. Your co-worker tells the boss that you think her/his spouse a social snob.

You've worked on a project with another person, who did very little of the work and criticized all you did. In spite of this, the project turns out quite well and your co-worker takes all the credit.

Your rival for promotion subtly starts a rumor that, because your brother works for a competing business, you may leak information to him. The rumor snowballs and has you selling company secrets to the highest bidder.

A jealous co-worker has kept a record of all the blunders you've made since joining the company. She/He gives the record to the committee considering your promotion.

As a power play, you attempted to encourage ill feelings between two co-workers. Unknown to you, they have been best friends for years and discovered what you were up to. They go to your supervisor and complain.

Your rival for promotion hires an investigation firm to dig into your past. Though never found guilty of the charges, you were accused of embezzlement in a former company and asked to resign. Your rival can't wait to share it with higher-ups.

An employee whom you supervise has asked you for preferential treatment in working on a project that was already promised to someone else. Though you didn't see her/him, she/he saw you at that intimate little restaurant with your boss's spouse. The employee threatens to inform your boss.

Your new supervisor is an old college rival, and you've disliked each other since then. She/He uses the excuse of reorganizing the workload to eliminate your position and you.

The Board of Directors wanted you and the person who worked with you to present the special project you did for them at a meeting. Your co-worker tells you the meeting is at 3:00 P.M. when it's really at 10:00 A.M. You aren't there and she/he takes the credit for the work.

A co-worker engages you in a heated political debate, during which she/he says passingly that the boss wants all reports written on the new forms. You continue sending reports in as you always had done, causing the boss to send all your reports back. Your co-worker reminds you that she/he told you that day you were talking politics.

You asked your supervisor to proofread a report you were to present to the Board of Directors. The report contains some glaring errors, but, because she/he doesn't want you to look good, you are told that it looks great.

A valued customer placed an order with you three weeks ago and needs the order now. You call the plant manager, who tells you that there was a little trouble with the machine that makes that product, and you should be getting the order in a few days. She/He does not tell you that actually the plant workers have been on strike for five weeks.

You have a choice between taking the accounts of two different clients. You ask a co-worker for advice and she/he tells you that you should take client X because it is a larger account. However, this co-worker has inside information that company X is in serious financial trouble. She/He asks to take company Z, which is financially secure and promises to expand in the future.

As Director of Public Relations, you want all employees in the company to wear a tailored uniform to enhance the company's public image. The store managers told you it was a great idea. However, store employees complained that the uniforms were uncomfortable and did not allow for the freedom of movement required for their jobs. Rather than discussing the problem with you, the store managers just told the employees not to wear the uniform if they didn't want to.

Your rival for a building contract made a bid to do the work at a significantly lower price than what you know it would cost to do the work. She/He got the contract and later used the excuse of material cost increases to explain the cost overrides. The final cost of the project far exceeded your modest estimate.

A company improvement project, for which you headed the committee, received great lip service from management. You approach management every other week to check on the status of funds to be allocated for the project, and you are told that, "We're working on it." After a year, you learn that no effort at all has been made to locate the funds.

Your rival for promotion, a person very full of her/his importance, has constantly found fault with your efforts. Before an important meeting, he/she provokes you into a burst of temper as top management enters the room. Her/His stunned expression convinces management that she/he is the innocent victim of your outburst.

A highly skilled employee under you demands that you guarantee her/him a bonus at the end of a very important project. She/He demands the guarantee be put in writing or she/he will quit now at a critical point. You put it in writing, and at the end of the project you both get pink slips.

You are the nephew/niece of the CEO and are placed in different entry-level jobs for a period of time to learn the ropes. Your various immediate supervisors are afraid that you'll soon get her/his job and assign you to projects that are impossible to do. After failing in those jobs, you are put in an unchallenging job in shipping.

Your rival is the first to be interviewed for promotion by a top corporate executive. As she/he comes out of the interview, she/he whispers to you that the executive is extremely religious. In your interview you frequently quote remembered verses from the Bible, and the executive thinks you're a nut.

CORPORATE DIG

TOPIC Corporate Cultures

LEARNING OBJECTIVE Participants will be able to analyize aspects of a company's culture by examining various artifacts.

NUMBER OF PARTICIPANTS Any number in groups of four to five members each

PLAYING TIME 25–30 minutes

REFERENCES Moskowitz, M., Levering, R., and Katz, M. (1984) *The 100 best companies to work for in America*. Reading: Addison-Wesley.

Moskowitz, M., Levering, R., and Katz, M., eds. (1990). *Everybody's business: A field guide of the 400 leading companies in America*. New York: Doubleday Currency.

Derdak, Thomas, ed. (1988). *International directory of company histories* (Vol. 1, pp 217–219). Chicago: St. James Press.

REQUIRED MATERIALS Pencils, Corporate Time Capsules, and Observation Sheets

TO PLAY

1. Introduce players to the concept of corporate culture. Discuss from a career development/management perspective why it is important to be able to read the culture of an organization.
2. State the learning objective for the game.
3. Explain that they are going to be given a Time Capsule containing various artifacts (actually pictures of artifacts) of an actual company. Using only the artifacts, their job will be to extrapolate a list of characteristics they believe to be true about this company's culture and, if possible, to name the company. They will receive 5 points for coming up with with the name of the company and 1 point for each correct observation they record.
4. Divide the group into small groups of four to five players each.
5. Pass out pencils, a Time Capsule, and an Observation Sheet to each group.
6. Inform players that they have 10 minutes to complete their Observation Sheets.
7. Give groups 10 minutes to complete their Observation Sheets.
8. After 10 minutes, give players the company's name and brief description of its culture. Have participants score their Observation Sheets.
9. Declare the group or groups with the highest score the winners. Bestow on them the title of "Junior Corporate Anthropologists."
10. Debrief players. Brainstorm ways of deciphering a company's culture. Discuss what they might place in a time capsule if they were making one for their employing organization.

Figure 7.1. Analyzing a company's culture.

Culture refers to how a society goes about meeting its needs (providing food and shelter for its members, rearing its young, and settling disputes among its members). In recent years career development specialists have applied the term to organizations. When used in this context, "culture" refers to "how an organization does things" (e.g., where it looks for new talent, how good performance is rewarded, how key business decisions are made). To better understand an organization's culture, take a close look at the following:

- The product or services provided
- The legacy that founders have left
- Persons considered heroes
- Individuals looked on as deviants or outcasts
- Formal organization charter
- Informal networks wielding influence
- The professional group carrying the most clout
- The coalitions having the most power
- Persons who have sponsored the company stars
- Organizational slots reserved for heirs
- Various legends and/or myths

- Valued rituals and traditions
- Important symbols, including status symbols
- Cherished buzz words
- Dominant themes captured in a company's slogans and icons
- The norms with respect to job performance and promotions
- The norms with respect to dress, personal appearance, and social behavior
- The firm's taboos
- Favorite company sport
- Favorite chartable causes
- Favorite social "hideouts"

THE ANHEUSER-BUSCH CULTURE

In 1860 Eberhard Anheuser, a successful soapmaker, assumed ownership of a small brewery in St. Louis, Missouri. The early success of the brewery was due to the brewing talents of Anheuser's son-in-law, a German immigrant named Adolphus Busch, who is considered the founder of the company. Anheuser's aggressive business acumen and Busch's brewing expertise, which included using only the finest ingredients, became the foundation on which the success of Anheuser-Busch was built.

Busch used a formula similar to that of a beer brewed in the Bohemian town of Budweis, which produced a light beer quite different from the heavier beers being made in local breweries. As brewing innovations occurred, the formula of the beer was improved. Pasteurization, bottling, and refrigerated rail cars all contributed to Anheuser-Busch's ability to more widely distribute its beer. It wasn't until 1891 that the name Budweiser was purchased from the Bohemian town.

In the 1870s Anheuser gave over the reins of the daily brewery operations to Adolphus Busch. Adolphus continued an aggressive advertising campaign by creating a beautiful brewery, using only the finest horses to draw the colorful green and red beer wagons around the city, distributing replicas of a historical painting entitled "Custer's Last Fight" to bars across the country, and commissioning two songs in the early 1900s extolling the company name and Budweiser beer. At Adolphus' instigation, employees came to be seen as members of the family, taken care of and remaining loyal to the company for life. This would result in the best possible product and the greatest defense against the competition and other threats to the company's well-being. Under Adolphus' leadership, the premium beer, Michelob, was first brewed in 1896. Aggressive advertising of both beers achieved the desired result, as Anheuser-Busch became the top brewery in the country over the reigning Pabst in 1904.

Adolphus passed away in 1913 and his son August took over. Flexibility was the saving grace of the company as it first went through World War I and then prohibition. The first diesel engine, patented by Busch and used to increase production in the brewery, became a subsidiary business during the war. The diesel engines powered submarines. With the advent of prohibition, Anheuser-Busch diversified into such areas as refrigeration cabinets, truck and bus bodies, yeast, soft drinks, and corn and malt syrups for those who did a little home brewing. During prohibition, Anheuser-Busch lobbied for repeal and had beer trucks loaded and ready to roll when it ended in 1933. Though he survived the prohibition battle, August was in poor health and, sadly, committed suicide in 1934.

Adolphus Busch III took the reins after his father's death. In Adolphus III's tenure as head of the company, the manufacture of baker's yeast begun during prohibition increased greatly and eventually the company became the nation's largest producer of compressed baker's yeast. The yeast subsidiary was sold in 1988. Under Adolphus III, Anheuser-Busch would again show its partriotic colors during World War II. A new subsidiary produced ammunition hoists for military use, and freight cars formerly used to ship beer to the West Coast were instead supplied to the government for shipping war provisions. Once again Anheuser-Busch received national recognition and increased beer sales.

When Adolphus died childless in 1946, his younger brother, August Jr., succeeded him as chief officer of the company. August Jr., better known as "Gussie," continued the aggressive sales promotions of his predecessors. Gussie would whistle-stop all over the country entertaining customers and would-be customers in his 84-foot private car, and at home he entertained in royal style at his 34-room chateau outside St. Louis. Anheuser-Busch became the first beer producer to advertise on a radio station. Under Gussie's watchful eye, the company purchased the St. Louis Cardinals, thus roping in another group of potential customers, baseball fans. August Jr. was also responsible for diversification into real estate, can manufacturing, and in 1959 the entertainment industry with the opening of Busch Gardens in Tampa.

August Busch III, who had been groomed from birth for the position, became president of the company in 1975 upon his father's retirement. In 1977 he was elected chairman of the board, the position he holds today. With August III leading the way, the company not only opened or acquired four new breweries, added the country's second largest baking company and Seaworld to its holdings, and engaged in the largest brewery expansion project in the history of the company, but also diversified into such things as recycling, snack foods, and international marketing.

Anheuser-Busch has consolidated much of its media marketing into an in-house group. Different marketing strategies are planned and targeted at specific groups rather than trying to appeal to all the tastes of the public at large in one ad. This type of advertising is also used for foreign markets. The company purchases subsidiaries with an eye either to providing a source of products related to beer production or to increasing the company's name recognition and popularity, thus enhancing the company's public image.

Although Anheuser-Busch, under the leadership of August III retains the same tough image it had under the earlier generations' rule, he manages the company differently than his predecessors. He uses a management control system based on planning, teamwork, and communication that has greatly increased the efficiency of the company and made it into a more modern corporation. However, key people in the organization are handpicked by

August III, who reserves the right of making important decisions for himself. His board of directors has included two women, one Hispanic and one black. August III's son, August IV works in the company and will presumably be next in line for the top slot.

August III expects employees to go the extra mile to produce the best possible product, and the employees respond by doing so with a sense of strong company loyalty and pride. In return for their devotion, employees receive top wages and good job security, though the benefits package may be better elsewhere. Employees are entitled to two free cases of beer a month.

To keep up with other companies, Anheuser-Busch started a quality of worklife program in 1974 where employees meet with top management to discuss their concerns. Personal counseling is available for employees desiring help with problems, and an ombudsman is there to help with employees' disputes with their bosses. An employee suggestion program has met with some success.

Anheuser-Busch continues to rank as the number one brewery under August III while retaining the values of the company founder: hard work, top quality products, and aggressive marketing necessary for company survival. Tours of the historic buildings of Anheuser-Busch's beginnings in St. Louis are still offered to visitors. The fierce screaming eagle and the beautiful and powerful clydesdale horses remain company symbols. The toughness and flexibility demonstrated by Anheuser-Busch in its past will be great assets in maintaining its future success if the company is to remain number one in brewing.

TIME CAPSULES

So that people living 500 to 1000 years in the future might have a better understanding of present cultures, time capsules are sometimes created. Various objects, documents, and pictures of objects are placed into a secure environment. This vault or capsule is then buried in the ground or placed inside the floor of a new building under construction. The capsule then awaits the discovery of future generations. To assure their discovery, information about some time capsules is placed in libraries.

To construct the time capsule for *Corporate Dig*, place copies of the individual pictures found on the following three pages into a standard shoebox and write "Time Capsule" on the outside of the box.

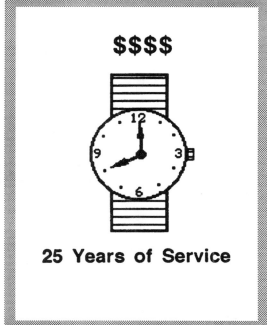

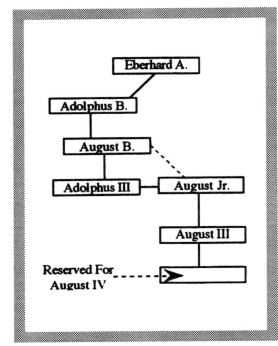

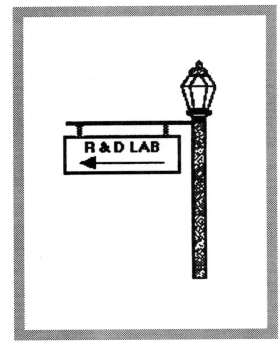

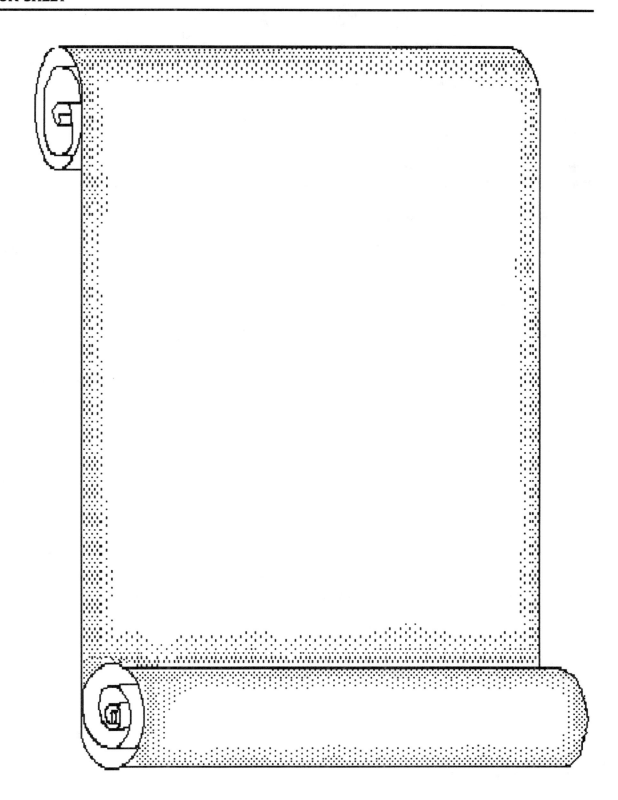

ENHANCEMENT SCRAMBLE

TOPIC Career Enhancement Interventions

LEARNING OBJECTIVE Players will be able to recognize various career enhancement interventions.

NUMBER OF PARTICIPANTS Any number

PLAYING TIME 10-20 minutes

REFERENCE Derr, C. B. (1988). *Managing the new careerists*. San Francisco: Jossey-Bass.

REQUIRED MATERIALS Pencil and Career Enhancement Scramble Puzzle

TO PLAY

1. Introduce players to the concept of organization career enhancement interventions.
2. Go over the learning objective for the game.
3. Divide the group into dyads.
4. Pass out Career Enhancement Scramble Puzzle to players face down.
5. Explain that the dyads are going to engage in a little competition. The goal of the competition is to unscramble the names of more career enhancement interventions than any of the other groups.
6. Inform players they have only eight minutes to unscramble the interventions.
7. Call, "Scramble!" Eight minutes later call, "Stop!"
8. Give players the answers as they check their worksheets for accuracy.
9. Determine which dyad unscrambled the most interventions. Declare them winners.
10. Debrief players. Have players identify some of the interventions available at their places of employment. Discuss some of the interventions they would like available to them.

Figure 7.2. Career enhancement interventions.

Assessment Centers	Simulated activities and analogous work situations that give participants feedback on performance and managerial potential.
Career Coaching	Encouraging and training managers to act as career guides and developers of subordinates.
Career Counseling	Counseling by career development specialists.
Career Pathing	Structuring of clusters of job assignments and movement options eventually leading to increased pay and status.
Career Workshops	Workshops designed to assist individuals in career development and transitions.
Education Development	Menu of benefits offered to assist in an individual's personal career growth
Fall Back Transfers	Lateral moves with the option of returning to a former position if the move is not successful.
Flexible Scheduling	Allowing options such as flextime, leaves of absence, part-time work, and sabbaticals.
High Potential	Systematic efforts to identify promising young employees.
Individual Growth Plans	Comprehensive career plans made by employees subject to management approval.
Information Centers	Banks of information about career opportunities within a company.
Information Systems	Accessing computer information relevant to individuals' career planning.
Job Enlargement	Expanding the responsibilities associated with a job.
Job Enrichment	Encouraging innovation in employees and rewarding them for it.
Job Matching	Matching vacant internal positions with individual development plans of employees.
Job Posting	Announcement of vacant positions to employees before external recruitment.
Job Rotation	Use of cross-functional or lateral transfers to introduce variety and growth into an employee's career.
Lifelong Employment	Psychological contract of lifelong employment with steady progress and benefits dependent on meeting minimum standards.
Mentoring	Use of sponsors to help young/new employees develop their careers.
Succession Planning	Identification and training certain individuals for key positions.

SOURCE: Published with permission of Jossey-Bass, 350 Sansome Street, San Francisco, CA 94104.

Directions: Following are examples of the many ways organizations meet the career development needs of their employees and at the same time meet some of their own human resource needs. Career enhancement interventions focus on helping individual workers grow and develop professionally. They benefit the organization by having the most qualified people in the "right places" at the "right times." Unscramble the letters to find out what the interventions are.

ACEDUNOTI DVTMENOPEEL   _____

BOJ INPGOTS   _____

BOJ TTAOOINR   _____

CRRAEE PGANTHI   _____

DDIIINULVA HORGWT   _____

EMORNTGNI   _____

ERAECR COHCAGNI   _____

FMARIINTOON CSREETN   _____

IGHH LPTONEIAT   _____

JBO TIACMHGN   _____

LAFL KBCA SFARSTRNE   _____

LLGIFENO PMLYOENTME   _____

MASSENSSET CTERNSE   _____

MFINRAINOOT MSYTSES   _____

OBJ MTLRGEEEENNA   _____

OBJ RCHIMNENET   _____

RCAERE SSKROOPWH   _____

RRCEEA NGOCNLSUEI   _____

SCSCSNOIEU GNPILNAN   _____

XLEBFLIE HDCULGINSE   _____

ETHICAL-POLITICAL

TOPIC Ethical Dilemmas

LEARNING OBJECTIVE Participants will be able to discuss the role politics plays in their perceptions of what is and isn't ethical.

NUMBER OF PARTICIPANTS Any number divided into groups of 4-5 players each

PLAYING TIME 15-25 minutes depending on the number of rounds played

REFERENCE None

REQUIRED MATERIALS Pencils and Ethical-Political worksheets

TO PLAY

1. Introduce players to the concepts of ethics and company politics.

2. Go over the learning objective for the game.

3. Explain that the game Ethical-Political is a friendly competition between groups of participants. The group(s) with the highest score(s) at the end of the game will be declared the winner(s).

4. Have the large group divide itself into smaller groups of four to five players each. It is best if members in the groups know each other.

5. Pass out a pencil and a copy of the Ethical-Political Worksheet Round #1 to each player.

6. Go over the directions to the worksheet very carefully. Give players five minutes to record their answers in column 1 on their worksheets.

7. Give players three minutes to poll themselves and record the group's majority opinion in column 2 on their worksheets.

8. Inform players that the group will receive 5 points for every incident in which all of the individual member's judgments (column 1) agree with those of the majority (column 2). In other words, 5 points will be awarded for each incident when every person's column 1 answer in the group agrees with the group's majority opinion.

9. Give players two minutes to change any answers they desire to change in column 1.

10. Ask groups to compute their scores. This is done by (a) recording a +5 in column 3 each time all of the group members' column 1 answers agree with the entire group's majority opinion recorded in column 2; (b) recording a −5 in column 3 each time any member's column 1 answer disagrees with the majority opinion recorded in column 2; and (c) tallying the scores for the six incidents and recording the total at the bottom of column 3.

11. Determine which group(s) ended with the highest score(s). Declare them the winner(s).

12. To play a second round, pass a copy of Ethical-Political Worksheet Round #2 and repeat steps 6–12.

13. Debrief players. Ask players if they changed any of their judgments to conform to the group's. Have them discuss their reasons for doing so. Have players discuss incidents in real life when what they believed was the ethical thing to do differed from what was considered among their colleagues to be the politically expedient thing to do.

Directions: Read each critical incident carefully. Do not discuss any incident with other group members at this time. Decide whether you believe the behavior in each incident is ethical. Check (✔) "Yes" in column 1 if you think the behavior is ethical. Check (✔) "No" in column 1 if you think it is unethical.

After all the members in your group have completed column 1, have someone in the group poll the members to see how the majority voted for each item. Record the majority opinion in column 2. If the majority of the group thought the behavior was ethical, check (✔) "Yes" in column 2. If the majority of the group thought the behavior was unethical, check (✔) "No" in column 2.

Critical Incident	1	2	3
1. A client tells John confidentially of a strategy she/he will use to win concessions from John's superiors. Would it be unethical for John to tell all if his boss asks him directly about the client's intentions?	☐ Yes ☐ No	☐ Yes ☐ No	
2. The boss has passed a dress code at the Stuffed Shirt Company because a number of older workers have complained about some of the younger workers choice of clothing. Has the boss acted in an ethically responsible manner?	☐ Yes ☐ No	☐ Yes ☐ No	
3. Catherine's company has purchased an expensive video tape to be used in orientation classes for new employees. She has made copies for each division. Is this an ethical action on her part?	☐ Yes ☐ No	☐ Yes ☐ No	
4. Fred is applying at the Ball Bearing Company for a maintenance position, which requires significant experience repairing Johnson machinery. Fred has occasionally assisted his former supervisor in working on these machines; so he claims competence. Is this ethical?	☐ Yes ☐ No	☐ Yes ☐ No	
5. Production at the Morgan Iron Works usually is going at top speed. Management refuses to hire more help and insists that all orders be filled on time. Workers must frequently work overtime and on such short notice as to cause child care and other family problems. Is management acting ethically?	☐ Yes ☐ No	☐ Yes ☐ No	
6. Janice wants her boss, the owner of the LaBelle Dress Shop, to carry a new line of clothing that she finds personally attractive. Her boss wants feedback from the customers. Janice polls several customers who can afford the new line and tells her boss that a majority of their customers would be interested. Is Janice being honest?	☐ Yes ☐ No	☐ Yes ☐ No	
Total Score ➡ ➡ ➡	➡	➡	

Directions: Read each critical incident carefully. Do not discuss any incident with other group members at this time. Decide whether you believe the behavior in each incident is ethical. Check (✓) "Yes" in column 1 if you think the behavior is ethical. Check (✓) "No" in column 1 if you think it is unethical.

After all the members in your group have completed column 1, have someone in the group poll the members to see how the majority filled in column 2. Record the majority opinion of the group in column 2. If the majority of the group thought the behavior was ethical, check (✓) "Yes" in column 2. If the majority of the group thought the behavior was unethical, check (✓) "No" in column 2.

Critical Incident	1	2	3
1. Don is a manager at an apartment complex suffering storm damage. He calls three contractors to get estimates for repairs. One is his brother-in-law who needs the work. The brother-in-law bids lowest with the assistance of Don and gets the job. Is this ethical?	☐ Yes ☐ No	☐ Yes ☐ No	
2. Marilyn is in charge of hiring a new maid for the hotel where she works. She turns down a male applicant because she feels men do not fit this occupation. She tells him that the reason he is not being hired is insufficient experience. Is this a matter of questionable ethics?	☐ Yes ☐ No	☐ Yes ☐ No	
3. As a bonus, Ralph gives all his male salespeople tickets to the local ice hockey tournament. Not to be unfair to the women, he gives them tickets to a popular theater performance. He made fun of Bob for requesting to trade his hockey tickets for theater tickets. Is Ralph being ethical?	☐ Yes ☐ No	☐ Yes ☐ No	
4. Dr. Wilson has a patient who insists on a prescription for cough syrup that costs much more but isn't any more effective than the over-the-counter remedy. To make the patient happy, he writes the prescription. Is this evidence of poor medical ethics?	☐ Yes ☐ No	☐ Yes ☐ No	
5. The directors of the city water department decide to build a much needed water treatment plant. When it is started up, the new plant emits an offensive odor for several hours a day. The directors insist that the odor comes with the plant and the neighbors will get used to the odor after a while. Are the directors acting in an ethical manner?	☐ Yes ☐ No	☐ Yes ☐ No	
6. A national businesspersons' organization is coming to the city for their annual convention. The Windsor Arms has tripled its room rates for the event. The companies of the participants will be paying and rooms will be scarce, but is this kind of increase an ethical practice?	☐ Yes ☐ No	☐ Yes ☐ No	
Total Score ➡ ➡ ➡	➡	➡	

MENTOR MANIA

TOPIC Mentoring Roles

LEARNING OBJECTIVE Participants will be able to match themselves with compatible mentoring partners.

NUMBER OF PARTICIPANTS 14–22 players

PLAYING TIME 20–30 minutes

REFERENCE Murray, M., and Owen, M. A. (1991). *Beyond the myths and magic of mentoring: How to facilitate an effective mentoring program.* San Francisco: Jossey-Bass.

REQUIRED MATERIALS Mentoring Roles Inventory (Mentor), Mentoring Roles Inventory (Mentee), Mentor Tags (green), Mentee Tags (white), straight pins, pencils, and felt-tip markers

TO PLAY

1. Discuss the concepts of mentor, mentee, and roles.

2. Go over the learning objective for the game.

3. Randomly pass out Mentor Name Tags to one-half of the players. Supply Mentee Name Tags to the other half of the participants.

4. Pass out markers and ask players to neatly print their names on their tags.

5. Pass out straight pins to all players. Ask them to pin their tags to their shirts or blouses.

6. Pass out pencils and copies of the Mentoring Roles Inventory (Mentor) and the Mentoring Roles Inventory (Mentee) to the appropriate parties.

7. Go over the directions to the inventories and allow players 10 minutes to complete them.

8. Have players compute their mentoring codes (see instructions following) and record them at the bottom of their inventories.

9. Discuss the meaning of the mentoring codes with participants. Explain that the codes represent their preferences for playing certain mentoring roles or their preferences for having a mentor play certain roles to them. Another way of putting it is that the codes represent the types of help mentors would like to give and the types of assistance mentees would like to receive.

10. Ask participants not to share their codes with any other player at this time.

11. Inform participants that the object of the game, Mentor Mania, is to locate a compatable mentoring partner (i.e., another player with the same or similar mentoring code). Mentors will seek out mentees as partners, and mentees will look for compatible mentors.

12. Advise players that they will have 10 minutes to interview prospective mentors or mentees. However, they can ask a single individual only three questions. Furthermore,

the three questions must be yes- or no-type questions (i.e., interviewees can only answer the questions with a yes or a no).

13. Provide participants two minutes to look over their inventories. Explain that they will not be permitted to take their inventories with them as they move about the room conducting their interviews with prospective mentors or mentees.

14. Ask players to place their inventories face down on their tables or chairs.

15. Give mentors and mentees 10 minutes to interview one another.

16. At the end of 10 minutes, direct participants to select a mentoring partner. Mentors are allowed only one mentee.

17. Give players one minute to get their chosen partners' mentoring codes and record it at the bottom of their inventories.

18. Help participants compute their "mentoring congruence" scores (see the following instructions).

19. Declare players with the highest congruence scores winners.

20. Debrief players. Discuss the types of help mentors were most interested in giving and mentees were most interested in receiving. Have players identify other things that should be taken into consideration when selecting a mentor/mentee.

MENTORING CONCEPTS

A more experienced worker (mentor) may help a less experienced colleague (mentee) become more skilled at her/his craft, become more knowledgeable about the organization for which they both work, and/or become more effective in setting appropriate career goals. Sometimes such assistance is formally planned, organized, and supported by the employing company. More often it takes place on an informal basis. Regardless of the degree of formality, mentoring almost always involves a more experienced employee (mentor) helping a less experienced worker (mentee) to develop. The relationship between the two workers is a helping relationship and involves the playing of various roles identified in the Mentoring Roles Inventory.

Mentoring Codes

Mentoring codes represent the two mentoring roles a mentor most prefers to perform or the two mentoring roles a mentee most prefers their mentor to perform. A player may determine her/his code by:

1. Completing the Mentoring Roles Inventory.

2. Tallying the totals for each of the six mentoring roles.

3. Recording the letter (A, C, E, P, S, or V) of the mentoring role with the highest score at the bottom of the Mentoring Roles Inventory.

4. Recording the letter of the mentoring role with the second highest score to the right of the first code letter.

Computing Mentoring Congruence Scores

Using the mentoring codes, a mentoring congruence score can be calculated to represent the degree of similarity between the roles a mentor would like to perform and the roles a prospective mentee might want her/him to perform. A congruence score between 0 and 5 is obtained based on the similarities between the first two letters of a mentor's and a mentee's codes. To compute a congruence score for a particular mentor and mentee, assign a score of:

5 in the cases of *identical matches* (i.e., instances in which a mentor's two code letters are the same and appear in the identical order as a mentee's code letters):
Example: Mentor's code letters = AC
Mentee's code letters = AC

4 when the *first two letters* of the mentor's and mentee's codes *are the same* but *not* in the *same sequence*:
Example: Mentor's code letters = AC
Mentee's code letters = CA

3 when the *first letters* of the mentor's and mentee's code are *the same* but the second letters are different:
Example: Mentor's code letters = AC
Mentee's code letters = AE

2 when the *first letter* of one of the mentor's or mentee's codes *match* the *second letter* of the other code:
Example: Mentor's code letters = AC
Mentee's code letters = CE

1 when the *second letters* of the mentor's and mentee's codes *match*:
Example: Mentor's code letters = AC
Mentee's code letters = EC

0 if *none* of the letters in the mentor's and mentee's codes *match*:
Example: Mentor's code letters = AC
Mentee's code letters = SV

Directions: If you were going to be a mentor, what mentoring roles would you most prefer to play? On a scale from 1 to 5, rate your desire to perform the following mentoring tasks.

5	4	3	2	1
Very Strongly Desire	Strongly Desire	Desire	Partially Desire	Do Not Desire

ADVISOR (Help mentee set and achieve career goals.)

_____ Help mentee clarify career interests, competencies, and values.

_____ Assist the mentee in setting specific career goals.

_____ Jointly develop strategies for achieving career objectives.

_____ **Total**

COACH (Help mentee meet job performance norms.)

_____ Model exemplary work outputs.

_____ Share effective and efficient performance practices.

_____ Provide feedback regarding the mentee's job performance.

_____ **Total**

EXPLAINER (Provide mentee information on policies and procedures.)

_____ Inform mentee on the nature of the organization's culture.

_____ Tutor mentee on how to get things done in the organization.

_____ Assist mentee with routine paper work and procedures.

_____ **Total**

PROTECTOR (Help mentee avoid costly career mistakes.)

_____ Point out things that might reflect negatively on mentee.

_____ Maintain good relationship between mentee and her/his immediate superior.

_____ Agree to no-fault conclusion of mentoring relationship.

_____ **Total**

SPONSOR (Help the mentee secure positions and assignments.)

_____ Make introductions to influential people in the organization.

_____ Make recommendations for assignments and advancement.

_____ Publicly praise the mentee's accomplishments and abilities.

_____ **Total**

VALIDATOR (Provide mentee psychological support during transition.)

_____ Make the mentee feel welcome and a part of the organization.

_____ Serve as a confidant, offering reassurances and encouragement.

_____ Assist the mentee in resolving crisis situations.

_____ **Total**

Your mentoring code _____   Prospective mentee's code _____   Congruence score _____

Directions: If you were going to have a mentor, what mentoring roles would you most prefer she/he play? On a scale from 1 to 5, rate your desire to have a mentor perform the following mentoring tasks.

5	4	3	2	1
Very Strongly Desire	Strongly Desire	Desire	Partially Desire	Do Not Desire

Advisor (Help mentee set and achieve career goals.)

_____ Help mentee clarify career interests, competencies, and values.

_____ Assist the mentee in setting specific career goals.

_____ Jointly develop strategies for achieving career objectives.

_____ **Total**

Coach (Help mentee meet job performance norms.)

_____ Model exemplary work outputs.

_____ Share effective and efficient performance practices.

_____ Provide feedback regarding the mentee's job performance.

_____ **Total**

Explainer (Provide mentee information on policies and procedures.)

_____ Inform mentee on the nature of the organization's culture.

_____ Tutor mentee on how to get things done in the organization.

_____ Assist mentee with routine paper work and procedures.

_____ **Total**

Protector (Help mentee avoid costly career mistakes.)

_____ Point out things that might reflect negatively on mentee.

_____ Maintain good relationship between mentee and her/his immediate superior.

_____ Agree to no-fault conclusion of mentoring relationship.

_____ **Total**

Sponsor (Help the mentee secure positions and assignments.)

_____ Make introductions to influential people in the organization.

_____ Make recommendations for assignments and advancement.

_____ Publicly praise the mentee's accomplishments and abilities.

_____ **Total**

Validator (Provide mentee psychological support during transition.)

_____ Make the mentee feel welcome and a part of the organization.

_____ Serve as a confidant, offering reassurances and encouragement.

_____ Assist the mentee in resolving crisis situations.

_____ **Total**

Your mentoring code _____   Prospective mentee's code _____   Congruence score _____

MIND YOUR TABLE MANNERS

TOPIC   Cultural Diversity

LEARNING
OBJECTIVE   Participants will be able to explain what is considered to be "proper dining decorum" in France, Germany, Italy, and the United Kingdom.

NUMBER OF
PARTICIPANTS 20-24 players divided into four groups

PLAYING TIME 20-25 minutes

REFERENCE   Braganti, N. L., and Devine, E. (1992). *European customs and manners: How to make friends and do business in Europe.* New York: Meadowbrook.

REQUIRED
MATERIALS   Table markers, Mealtime Questions, and Mealtime Courses

TO PLAY
1. Prior to the game, set up four tables with at least six chairs at each. Mark each table for a different country (i.e., a large banner-shaped sign with the name of the country on it).

2. Introduce players to the concept of cultural diversity.

3. Go over the learning objective for the game.

4. Ask group members to go to one of four tables marked France, Germany, Italy, and the United Kingdom. See to it that the four groups are fairly equal in the number of players.

5. Inform players that they are going to be in competition to see which group knows the most about appropriate eating habits in their country. Each time a group gives a correct answer, each member will receive one course of a seven-course meal for that country.

6. Advise players that the first group to receive all seven courses of their meal will be considered the winning group.

7. Have each group select one of its members to act as the spokesperson for their table. Explain that this person will be giving their table's official answers to all questions. However, the group is allowed to discuss its answer before it is given aloud by its spokesperson.

8. Think of a number between 1 and 50, and write it down on a piece of scrap paper. Have each spokesperson guess the number you have written down. The group that comes the closest plays first.

9. Read a Mealtime Question for the first group's country. Give them 10 seconds to answer. Questions may be repeated once.

10. If the answer is correct, give each member of the group the first course for their country's meal (see Mealtime Course Preparations). If the answer is incorrect, proceed to the next group in a clockwise direction.

11. Continue the reading of questions and serving of mealtime courses until one group has accumulated all seven courses.

12. Declare the first group to receive all seven courses winners.

13. Debrief players. Have participants tell some of the ways their co-workers have become more culturally diverse. Discuss how being more culturally literate can benefit one careerwise.

France

1. In France, it is polite to accept a drink you are offered before dinner. (T)
2. Keep one hand off the table while dining at a French table. (F)
3. It is okay to add salt and pepper to food served at a meal in a French home. (F)
4. At a French table, a spoon and fork placed above the plate are for dessert. (T)
5. While dining family style in France, it's perfectly acceptable to use your bread to sop up gravy. (T)
6. In France, the big meal of the day (*dejeuner*) is served from noon to 2:30 P.M. (T)
7. Leaving a bit of food on your plate at a French dinner table is an expression of appreciation for the meal. (F)
8. In France, it is proper to smoke between the main course and dessert. (F)
9. Restaurants in France add a 10–15 percent tip to your bill, but you may leave 10–20 francs more if the service was exceptional. (T)
10. In France, business dinners are more common than business lunches. (F)
11. Turning down a second helping is an insult to your French hostess. (F)
12. Adding sparkling water to your wine is an insult to your French host. (T)
13. In France, it is okay to be late to cocktail parties, but you must be on time to dinner parties. (T)
14. Only polite, quiet conversation is acceptable at the French dinner table. (F)
15. At a French meal, bread is broken with the fingers, never cut. (T)

Germany

1. In Germany, women should always wear a dress or skirt to an elegant restaurant. (T)
2. You may be late when invited to dinner at a German home because cocktail hours are always long. (F)
3. At an informal German dinner, you may receive a plate with food already on it. (T)
4. It is proper in Germany to eat your sandwich with a knife and fork. (T)
5. When passing food to another at a German table it is customary to say *bitte* (bit-teh) (T)
6. When you finish your German meal, always lay your knife and fork beside your plate. (F)
7. It is acceptable to drink at a German dinner party after the host has toasted you. (F)
8. In Germany, traditionally a man toasts a woman, but she may do so first if she wishes. (F)
9. After dinner in a German home, if the host doesn't refill your glass, it is a signal that it is time to leave. (T)
10. A German man holds the door for a woman to enter a restaurant, but she should follow him to the table. (T)
11. In Germany, it is not proper to ask for coffee with a meal. (T)
12. You may bring a gift of a bottle of any type of wine to your host at a German dinner party. (F)
13. If you can't eat all of the food on your plate at a German meal, it's best to think of a good excuse. (T)
14. At a German table, the spoons are generally placed above the plate. (T)
15. Appetizers are rarely served with drinks at a German dinner party. (T)

Italy
1. When cheese is served in Italy, pick it up with your knife and put it on your bread or cracker. (T)
2. Italians are never offended if a guest drinks a bit too much wine at their dinner parties. (F)
3. Punctuality to a meal depends on which region of Italy you are in. (T)
4. When eating spagetti at an Italian table, cut it or twirl it around your fork with the aid of a spoon. (F)
5. When offered seconds at an Italian dinner, decline at first until your host or hostess insists, at which time it is polite to accept. (T)
6. It is acceptable to smoke between each course of an Italian dinner. (F)
7. At an Italian table, expect to find a roll or bread next to your plate rather than on a bread plate. (T)
8. When you finish an Italian meal, place your knife and fork on the plate with the fork tines up. (T)
9. Italian hostesses may cut pizza, chicken, or even steak with a pair of scissors. (T)
10. It is proper for your host or hostess to pour the wine in Italy. (F)
11. You may begin eating at an Italian table as soon as the wine is poured. (F)
12. If you are dining in an Italian home, do not expect all the food to be piping hot. (T)
13. If you are invited to a dinner or another Italian social event, it is expected that you will bring a date. (F)
14. The place settings at an Italian table may consist of a stack of three plates. (T)
15. At an Italian table, the guest of honor is given the seat at the head of the table. (F)

United Kingdom
1. When dining in British restaurants, both men and women should dress up. (T)
2. High tea is a full meal in Great Britain. (T)
3. Tea is usually served after a British lunch or dinner. (F)
4. At a formal meal in Great Britain, you may not smoke until after a toast is made to the Queen at the end of the meal. (T)
5. A single woman eating alone in a British restaurant may indicate that she would like company by bringing a book with her. (F)
6. British waiters and waitresses say, "You're welcome" every time they bring something to your table. (F)
7. Be prompt when invited to dinner in a British home. (T)
8. At British upper-class dinners, women usually leave the table and go to another room to talk while men remain to enjoy port and cigars after the meal. (T)
9. Having garlic on your breath is socially acceptable in Great Britain. (F)
10. It is best to accept if your British host invites you to an event that required getting tickets, but you may decline an invitation to dinner. (T)
11. In Great Britain, spouses are included in an invitation to an evening function or large party. (T)
12. Home entertaining for business is frowned upon in Scotland. (F)
13. When invited to dinner in a British home, it is proper to bring flowers or have them sent beforehand. (T)
14. At a dinner party in a British home, the meal will probably end around 11:00 P.M.; so plan to leave between 11:30 and midnight. (T)
15. When eating out in Britain, expect to get a smaller breakfast than in the United States but other meals will be larger. (F)

To prepare mealtime courses for each country, photocopy the following items. Cut the items out and glue them to the inside of paper snack plates.

French Courses

Pate de foie gras at
Chez de Presidente
Paris

Escargots a la bourguignone at
Chez de Presidente
Paris

Confit d'oie and ratatouille at
Chez de Presidente
Paris

Bottle of Bourdeaux and champagne at
Chez de Presidente
Paris

Salad a la Francoise at
Chez de Presidente
Paris

Cheese and fruit at
Chez de Presidente
Paris

Dessert crepe and un expre's at
Chez de Presidente
Paris

German Courses

Stein of beer or glass of Rhine wine at
Gasthaus der Hasenpfeffer
Dusseldorf

Dumpling soup at
Gasthaus der Hasenpfeffer
Dusseldorf

Wienerschnitzel at
Gasthaus der Hasenpfeffer
Dusseldorf

Kartoffelpuffer at
Gasthaus der Hasenpfeffer
Dusseldorf

Spatzle and/or rye bread at
Gasthaus der Hasenpfeffer
Dusseldorf

Green salad or hot potato salad at
Gasthaus der Hasenpfeffer
Dusseldorf

Bienenstich or Kirchtorte and coffee at
Gasthaus der Hasenpfeffer
Dusseldorf

Italian Courses

Prosciutto and melon with Verdicchio wine at
The Gondola Ristorante
Venice

Tortellini at
The Gondola Ristorante
Venice

Bisetecca alla Florentina with Chianti at
The Gondola Ristorante
Venice

Caponata and bread at
The Gondola Ristorante
Venice

Florentine salad at
The Gondola Ristorante
Venice

Cassata alla Siciliana at
The Gondola Ristorante
Venice

Cheese, fruit, and coffee at
The Gondola Ristorante
Venice

British Courses

Sherry, nuts, and crisps at
The House on the Commons
London

A prawn cocktail or chicken and leek soup at
The House on the Commons
London

Roast beef and Yorkshire pudding at
The House on the Commons
London

Baked trout at
The House on the Commons
London

Tossed greens at
The House on the Commons
London

Assorted vegetables at
The House on the Commons
London

Trifle and coffee at
The House on the Commons
London

MYSTERY CAREERS

TOPIC Transferable Skills

LEARNING OBJECTIVE Participants will be able to identify the occupations that selected public figures prepared to enter.

NUMBER OF PARTICIPANTS Any number

PLAYING TIME 3-5 minutes

REFERENCES Kiernan T. (1976). *Arafat—The man and the myth.* New York: W. W. Norton & Co.

Philip C. (1985). *Robert Fulton, A biography.* New York: Franklin Watts.

Young, H. (1989). *The iron lady.* New York: Farras Straus Giroux.

Stambler, I. and Landon, G. (1969). *Encyclopedia of folk, country, & western music.* New York: St. Martins Press.

REQUIRED MATERIALS Pencil and Mystery Jobs playing sheet

TO PLAY

1. Introduce the concept of transferable skills.
2. Go over the learning objective for the game.
3. Explain to participants that they will be given a playing sheet, Mystery Jobs, containing the pictures and names of four well-known individuals. From a short list of job choices, they are to select the fields for which each public figure originally prepared.
4. Pass out a pencil and one Mystery Jobs playing sheet, face down, to each player.
5. Tell participants they have one minute to make their selections.
6. When everyone is ready, say, "Go."
7. One minute later call, "Stop."
8. As you supply the correct answers, have players check their own answers.
9. Ask players who got all four answers correct to raise their hands. Declare them winners.
10. Debrief players. Have participants give personal examples of individuals who have taken jobs in fields different from the ones they formally prepared to enter. Discuss how skills developed in one field may be transferred to other occupations.

Directions: Select the job for which each person prepared. Circle choice A, B, or C.

Robert Fulton

A   Fisherman

B   Teacher

C   Silversmith

Margaret Thatcher

A   Political scientist

B   Chemist

C   Economist

Yassir Arafat

A   Religious leader

B   Soldier

C   Civil engineer

Willie Nelson

A   Farmer

B   Songwriter

C   Accountant

ANSWERS TO GAMES

Career Success Test

1. Don't rock the boat.
2. Move up, then out.
3. Don't mix pleasure and business.
4. Read between the lines.
5. Pay your dues.
6. Network.
7. Give 100 percent.
8. Keep your eyes open and your mouth closed.
9. Make a good impression.
10. Cover your ass.

Company Capers (Manufacturing)

Company Capers #1: The Big Wheels		
GM	Ford	Chrysler
Toyota	Honda	Mitsubishi
Volkswagen	Nissan	Daimler

Company Capers #2: Computers		
National Cash Register	IBM	Apple
Microsoft	Hewlitt Packard	Wang
Compaq	Digital	Control Data Corp.

Company Capers #3: Health and Beauty		
Unilever	Bayer	Noxell Corp.
Gillette	Squibb	Upjohn
Colgate Palmolive	Abbott Labs	Estee Lauder

Company Capers #4: Petroleum Companies		
Exxon	British Petroleum	Pennzoil
Texaco	Shell	Mobil
Chevron	Amoco	Phillips 66

Company Capers #5: Sins and Other Pleasures		
RJR Nabisco	Anheuser Busch	Gallo
Phillip Morris Co.	Seagrams	Bally
Coors	American Brands	G. Heileman

Company Capers #6: Conglomerates		
GE	3M	Greyhound Dial
ITT	Tenneco	Jacuzzi
Litton Industries	TRW	United Technologies

Company Capers #7: On the Grocer's Shelves		
Coca Cola	Gerber	Tyson
Hershey	General Mills	Quaker Oats
Land O' Lakes	Sara Lee	Campbell's

Company Capers #8: Hotels and Restaurants		
Marriott	Holiday Inn	Best Western
Hilton	Sheraton	Pizza Hut
McDonald's	Kentucky Fried Chicken	Wendy's

Company Capers #9: Read All About It		
The Tribune Company	Hearst	Random House
Reader's Digest	NY Times	Simon & Schuster
Dow Jones	McGraw-Hill	The Washington Post

Company Capers #10: Travel and Transport		
Union Pacific	American Airlines	UPS
Amtrak	Roadway	U.S. Air
Federal Express	United Airlines	Burlington Northern

CORPORATE DIG

Company: Anheuser Busch

Sample Observations (Answers will vary)

Has a strong head of company.

Top management controls all important decisions.

Is a major maker of food products.

Is environmentally conscious.

Provides employee assistant programs, including employing counseling.

Actively courts suggestions from employees.

Individuals in key positions are hand-picked by top management.

There is little turnover in the company. Employees stay at the company for life.

Strongly supports the sport of baseball. Owns the St. Louis Cardinals.

Workers earn highly competitive wages for the work they do.

There is pride in company traditions.

It is a public company that encourages employee ownership.

Is aggressive in its advertising practices.

The major emphasis is on quality.

Top management positions are reserved and held by Busch family members.

Active research and development programs are conducted.

The company applies the latest technology.

Products are diversified.

Accept other observations that appear to be characteristic of the Anheuser Busch company.

Empowerment Puzzle

The following items may be accepted in any order:

1. Providing the Necessary Skills
2. Granting Sufficient Authority
3. Articulating a Vision
4. Explaining How a Project Fits into the Big Picture
5. Stating Relative Importance of Projects
6. Supplying Adequate Information
7. Allocating Ample Resources
8. Building Employees' Self-Confidence
9. Extending Permission to Take Acceptable Risks
10. Giving Feedback

Enhancement Scramble

1. Education development
2. Job posting
3. Job rotation
4. Career pathing
5. Individual growth
6. Mentoring
7. Career coaching
8. Information centers
9. High potential
10. Job matching
11. Fall back transfers
12. Lifelong employment
13. Assessment centers
14. Information systems
15. Job enlargement
16. Job enrichment
17. Career workshops
18. Career counseling
19. Succession planning
20. Flexible scheduling

Getting No Respect

See High Status Occupations and Low Status Occupations lists with game materials.

Heads Up 2000   p. 163

1. Heads
2. Heads
3. Tales (Correct answer is 15 percent.)
4. Tales (Correct answer is 1 out of 3.)
5. Tales (Correct answer is 17 percent.)
6. ~~Tales~~ Tails (Correct answer is 20-40 percent.)
7. Heads
8. Tales (Correct answer is 1,500,000.)
9. Heads
10. Heads

Hocus Focus

1. T	**6.** F
2. F	**7.** T
3. T	**8.** T
4. T	**9.** T
5. F	**10.** F

Honey, They've Shrunk the Company

See Downsizing Chart with game materials.

HRD Crossout

Across	Down
1. Vocational	1. Trainer
2. Specialist	2. Careers
3. Coordinate	3. Develop
4. Technology	4. Educate
5. Management	5. Writing
6. Instructor	6. Designs
7. Evaluation	7. Analyst
	8. Planner
	9. Promote
	10. Mentors

Saying: The Human Resource Development field attracts people with a wide variety of skills.

Innies and Outies

~~**1.** ADVERTISING~~	~~**25.** HOME FURNISHING~~
~~**2.** AGRICULTURE~~	**26.** HOME REMODELING
~~**3.** AIR TRANSPORTATION~~	~~**27.** INSURANCE~~
~~**4.** AUTOMOBILES~~	~~**28.** JEWELRY~~
~~**5.** BANKING~~	~~**29.** LAW~~
6. BIOTECHNOLOGY	~~**30.** MANUFACTURING~~
~~**7.** BUSINESS SYSTEM~~	~~**31.** MEDICINE~~
8. CABLE TV	~~**32.** MILITARY SERVICES~~
9. CAREER COUNSELING	**33.** MORTGAGE REFINANCING
~~**10.** CATERING~~	~~**34.** PERSONAL COMPUTER~~
~~**11.** COAL MINING~~	**35.** PHARMACEUTICALS
12. COMPUTER NETWORKING	~~**36.** REAL ESTATE~~
13. CONSUMER PRODUCTS	**37.** RESTAURANTS
~~**14.** DEFENSE INDUSTRY~~	~~**38.** SAVINGS AND LOAN~~
~~**15.** DEPARTMENT STORES~~	~~**39.** SECURITIES~~

16. DISCOUNT MERCHANDISING		**40.** SECURITY	
17. ENVIRONMENTAL SERVICES		**41.** SOFTWARE	
18. FEDERAL GOVERNMENT		**42.** SPORTS MARKETING	
19. FOOD CHAINS		**43.** ~~STATE AND LOCAL GOVERNMENTS~~	
20. HEALTH BENEFITS		**44.** ~~STEEL~~	
21. HEALTH CARE		**45.** ~~TEACHING~~	
22. HEALTH MAINTENANCE ORGANIZATIONS		**46.** ~~TELEPHONE COMPANIES~~	
23. HEALTH SERVICES		**47.** ~~TIMBER~~	
24. ~~HOME CONSTRUCTION~~		**48.** WASTE MANAGEMENT	

Interviews ala Internationale

Denmark	France	Germany	Great Britain
1. True	1. False. The letter may be passed on to others who do not speak English.	1. True	1. True
2. False. Weekends are reserved for family.	2. False. These companies are usually more flexible.	2. False. Address it to the company in case the person is away.	2. False. You will need to leave time for questions.
3. False. Foreign businesswomen are readily accepted.	3. False. Women are flirted with, but not looked down upon.	3. False. The Germans look for minimal risks and long-term deals.	3. True
4. True	4. True	4. True	4. False. The demands of your company's attorney may be used to get the deal in writing.
5. True	5. False. Refreshments are not usually offered.	5. True	5. True
6. False. Denmark's industrial vacation runs from June 20 to August 15.	6. True	6. False. Germans seldom do business at home, and you should apologize if you have to call.	6. False. "Pretty soon" can mean a week or two.
7. False. Business has become extremely fast-paced.	7. False. They dislike confrontations and hate to lose.	7. False. Germans have a strong sense of privacy and are uncomfortable with this type of behavior.	7. False. They know that Americans are fascinated by their pubs and are being kind.
8. False. Though their English is good, they are not adept in the subtleties of the language.	8. True	8. True	8. True
9. True	9. True	9. True	9. False. They feel that gifts are personal and that business and personal life are separate.
10. True	10. True	10. False. Such a short meeting probably indicates that they are not interested.	10. True

Greece	Italy	The Netherlands	Poland
1. True	1. True	1. False. Coffee in the A.M., tea in the P.M., and cold drinks in hot weather are all proper.	1. True
2. True	2. False. Little work is done at home or on weekends.	2. True	2. False. Copiers are usually slow and of poor quality.
3. False. Foreigners are expected to be punctual.	3. False. Any urgency shown could weaken your position.	3. False. The Dutch are very reliable.	3. True
4. False. The Greeks love to bargain and if you don't, you won't be taken seriously.	4. True	4. True	4. False. Poles are not used to high technology; so such things are not necessary.
5. True	5. False. Business is not done at social gatherings.	5. False. Even small occasions are celebrated.	5. False. Using feminine wiles may possibly get you more concessions than even the men in your group.
6. False. Greeks love to complain; so you may need to check some place else to get the real picture.	6. True	6. False. It may be seen as higher costs of your goods.	6. True
7. True	7. False. The phone system is poor in Italy; so a fax would be better.	7. True	7. False. Final decisions will be made by a few people at the top.
8. True	8. True	8. True	8. False. Only if you wish, since the company usually provides one.
9. True	9. False. It is because you are a foreign woman.	9. False. The Dutch deal rapidly; so choose the price you want and stick to it.	9. True
10. False. Greek men like women in business, but feel that having families should be a woman's most important role.	10. True	10. True	10. True

Spain	Sweden	Switzerland	Turkey
1. True	1. True	1. False. English is the language of business in Switzerland.	1. True
2. False. The Spanish are highly class-conscious and may respect you less.	2. False. Materials should be given only to decision makers.	2. False. Swiss women are not usually found in top management.	2. False. You will have no problem being accepted.
3. False. He will take you seriously.	3. True	3. True	3. True
4. False. They are attempting to see you as a person before doing business with you.	4. False. Several will likely be needed.	4. True	4. False. Be sure to accept.

	Spain	Sweden	Switzerland	Turkey
	5. True	5. False. For social events, spouses should be invited.	5. False. You also give your card to the receptionist.	5. False. Do not drink alcoholic beverages unless your Turkish guests do.
	6. True	6. True	6. False. Your presentation should be brief and to the point.	6. True
	7. False. Even trivial family matters take precedence over business.	7. False. These are not necessary.	7. True	7. True
	8. False. They will be insulted by the direct approach.	8. True	8. False. They will likely quiz you about the competition.	8. False. A top hotel will make an impression.
	9. True	9. True	9. True	9. False. The receptionist and everyone else you are introduced to should receive one.
	10. True	10. False. You only invite those you are negotiating with.	10. True	10. True

Jobs Analyst

	People	Data	Things	Ideas
J	Jailer	Jacket preparer	Janitor	Job analysts
	Judge	Jewel inspector	Jockey	Joke writer
	Juggler	Jet wiper	Joiner	Journalist
O	Occupational therapist	Office clerk	Oceanographer	Operations research analysts
	Office manager	Olive brine tester	Offset printer	Optometrist
	Optician Dispenser	Order caller	Ornament maker	Orthodontist
B	Bailiff	Battery tester	Bandsaw operator	Ballistics expert
	Barber	Billing clerk	Baker	Biochemist
	Battalion chief	Bookkeeper	Butcher	Bursar
S	Salesperson	Secretary	Sewing machine operator	Sanitary engineer
	Social Worker	Surveillance system monitor	Still operator	Scientist
	Supervisor	Survey worker	Street Cleaner	Seismologists

Accept other appropriate answers.

Jobpardy

Answers are with the game materials.

Percentage of Women
in 10 Occupations

Dental hygenists	9	9.0%
Editors and reporters	9	9.0%
Firefighters	9	8.6%
Household child care workers	9	7.3%
Painters, sculptors, craft artists, and artist printmakers	9	7.1%
Prekindergarten and kindergarten teachers	5	0.4%
Real estate sales	5	0.3%
Receptionists	4	9.7%
Secretaries	0	7.0%
United States Senators	0	2.4%

Weekly Wages as Percentage of *Men's* Earnings

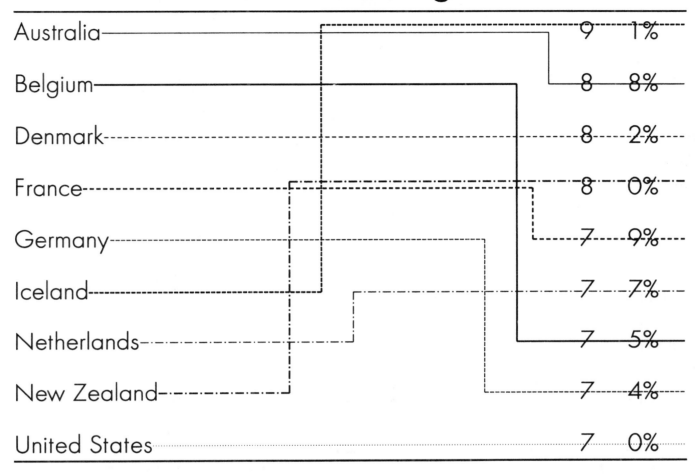

Australia	9 1%
Belgium	8 8%
Denmark	8 2%
France	8 0%
Germany	7 9%
Iceland	7 7%
Netherlands	7 5%
New Zealand	7 4%
United States	7 0%

Percentage of Employed Women Working Part-Time

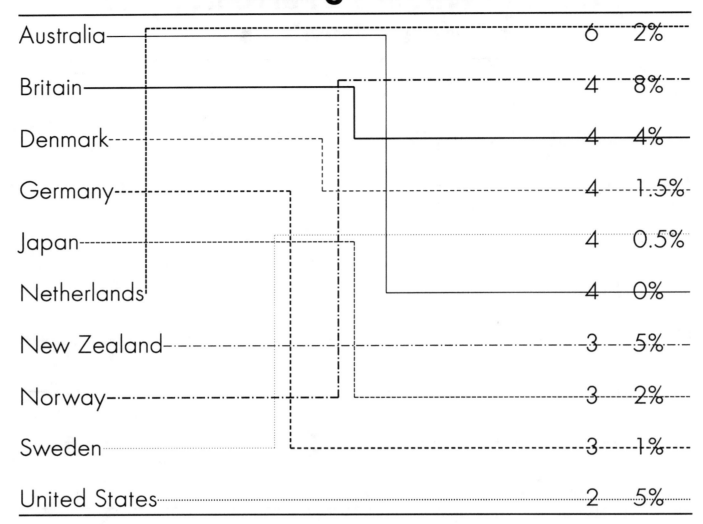

Australia	6 2%
Britain	4 8%
Denmark	4 4%
Germany	4 1.5%
Japan	4 0.5%
Netherlands	4 0%
New Zealand	3 5%
Norway	3 2%
Sweden	3 1%
United States	2 5%

Occupational Ignoramus Cards

Successful careers just happen.

FALSE: While luck or circumstance plays a role in the development of a career, truly successful careers usually require careful planning.

Most of the job offerings today require a four-year college degree.

FALSE: Many of the new openings are technical in nature and require some technical training but not four-year college degrees.

Individuals learn much about how to manage their career from the mistakes they make.

FALSE: They often learn what not to do from mistakes but seldom what to do.

If you are frustrated at work, you should quit your job immediately.

FALSE: A person should first attempt to resolve some of matters causing the frustration. It is best to find another job before quitting the old one.

The earlier a person selects a career the better.

FALSE: Most people don't know enough about themselves and the work world to make an informed career choice until they are well into their late twenties.

The only way to find a job is to find a job vacancy.

FALSE: People often create their own jobs by going into business for themselves or convincing others that they can make or save them money.

The job market dictates what career a person should choose.

FALSE: Individual interests, skills, and values determine the occupations at which a person will be successful and find personally satisfying.

You must have good contacts to get a really good job.

FALSE: While contacts are important, people find out about jobs in other ways.

Tests are able to tell you what career you should enter.

FALSE: Tests can only provide a person information about themselves. While this information is helpful in deciding on a career, it does not specify a single career.

A person is hired because she/he is the best candidate.

FALSE: A candidate's powers of persuasion, personal appearance, and political clout often result in them rather than the most qualified getting a job.

Women are better in careers traditionally held by women.

FALSE: Women are better off in careers for which they have the interests and abilities. They have been successful in almost every type of career.

If you are over 40 years of age it is much more difficult to get a job.

FALSE: It depends more on the job being sought and the person's skills than on her/his age. Furthermore, 40 is not considered such an advanced age today.

To get ahead in a career, you should learn to be very aggressive.

FALSE: A person needs to have and work a plan, be willing to take some risks, and take the initiative as opportunities come along.

Changing careers is costly and very risky.

TRUE: While some risk and expenses are involved in changing careers, staying with an old career also carries with it many risks and potential expenses.

A good resumé is written in the chronological style listing all past positions and employers.

FALSE: This style works for people with long, prestigious work histories but does little for less experienced workers.

By virtue of their abilities, most individuals are suited for a variety of jobs.

TRUE: Specific abilities are required in a variety of jobs.

Employment agencies work for job seekers.

FALSE: They are usually paid by the employing organizations and focus most directly on meeting their needs.

In addition to the income it provides, a job affects a person's life in many other ways.

TRUE: Jobs also affect where a person lives, their associates, their recreation, and the time available to spend with family.

Personnel departments do most of the hiring.

FALSE: They are often involved in the recruiting and screening of applicants. The actual hiring is typically left up to managers and supervisors.

During her/his lifetime, a person is likely to work at several different occupations.

TRUE: It is estimated that most individuals will work at three to five occupations during their working lives.

The sole purpose of an interview is to get a job offer.

FALSE: Interviews have several other purposes (such as to collect information about the company or to be invited back for another interview).

Apprentices are paid as they learn a trade.

TRUE: Individuals working as apprentices are usually paid a partial wage.

When asked to do so, you should present a salary to a prospective employer.
FALSE: This gives an employer an advantage when negotiating salary. Based on their current skills a new hire might suggest an acceptable salary range.

Besides taking a job in a field, there are many ways of finding out if a person might enjoy working in an occupation.

TRUE: Job shadowing, reading, volunteer work, and interviewing those in the field are some other ways.

The unemployment rate for individuals holding college degrees is typically lower than that for high school dropouts.

TRUE: The unemployment rate typically goes down in proportion to the amount of education a person has received.

The best way to begin planning for a career is to find out more about your career interests (i.e., what types of tasks you most enjoy doing).

TRUE: A good career is one that a person enjoys doing over time.

Most people find job openings through word of mouth.

TRUE: Forty-eight percent of currently employed workers found out about their jobs through family and friends.

If a person is highly interested in several occupations, she/he should research each of the options before making a choice.

TRUE: Only after a closer look at each of the options will a person be able to rule them in or out as viable choices.

Approximately 5 percent of current workers find out about their jobs through newspaper ads.

TRUE

If a person chooses an occupation with which she/he is unhappy, she/he can switch to another career if she/he so desires.

TRUE: While doing so is not always convenient, there is always the option to change careers.

Approximately the same percentage of workers find out about jobs through college placement offices as those who find out about jobs through employment agencies.

TRUE: 6 percent and 4 percent, respectively.

In choosing an occupation to enter, one should always take into consideration the number of projected openings for that field (i.e., its outlook).

TRUE: However, this should not be the only or prime factor to be considered.

Nearly one-fourth of all workers find out about jobs through direct contact with employers.

TRUE: Approximately 24 percent.

In most occupational fields, women earn less than men doing the same work.

TRUE: Women on average earn approximately 30 percent less.

Sending a large number of unsolicited resumés to prospective employers is a poor way to get a job interview.

TRUE: Direct contact in person or over the phone is much more likely to result in getting an interview.

After a job interview, it is advisable to mail the interviewer a thank-you note.

TRUE: This keeps the person's name in front of the interviewer, shows interest in the job, and provides the opportunity to highlight past accomplishments.

Logo Roundup

1. Chrysler Corporation
Third in U. S. automaking
Eleventh in world automaking
Founded: 1925
Headquarters: Detroit, Mich.

2. Sterling Winthrop, Inc.
First in aspirin
Founded: 1901
Headquarters: New York

3. Hilton Hotels Corporation
Third in hotels
Founded: 1919
Headquarters: Beverly Hills, Cal.

4. Black & Decker
First in power tools
Founded: 1910
Headquarters: Towson, Md.

5. Ralston Purina Company
First in pet foods, bread, batteries
Second in baby food
Third in cereals
Founded: 1894
Headquarters: St. Louis, Mo.

6. Amtrak
First in passenger rail service
Founded: 1971
Headquarters: Washington, D.C.

7. Bell South
1155 Peachtree St. N.E.
Atlanta, GA 30309-3610

8. Burlington Industries
First in fabrics for clothing
Founded: 1923
Headquarters: Greensboro, N.C.

9. Alcoa
First in aluminum
Founded: 1888
Headquarters: Pittsburgh, Penn.

10. Chase
Second in banking
Founded: 1799
Headquarters: New York

Matching Orientations

1. Getting Ahead
2. Getting Ahead
3. Getting Ahead
4. Getting Secure
5. Getting Secure
6. Getting Secure
7. Getting Free
8. Getting Free

9. Getting Free
10. Getting High
11. Getting High
12. Getting High
13. Getting Balanced
14. Getting Balanced
15. Getting Balanced

Mega Mergers

See the Merger Chart with the game materials.

Mind Your Table Manners

See the Mealtime Questions with the game materials for answers.

Mystery Careers

1=C,   2=B,   3=C,   4=A

Notes and Quotes

1=B, 2=C, 3=C, 4=A, 5=B, 6=A, 7=C, 8=C, 9=C, 10=A, 11=B, 12=A

Pathways Puzzle

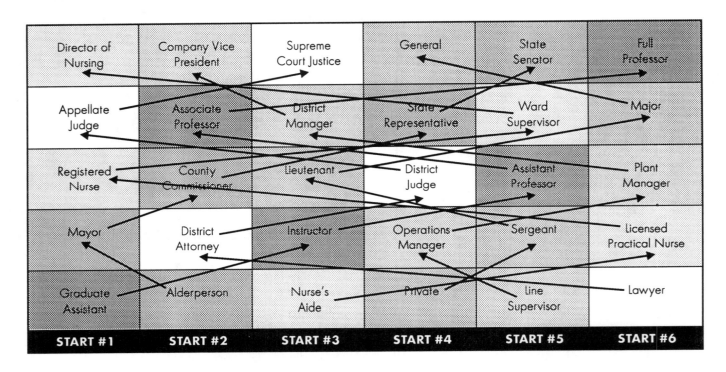

Playing the Odds

1. 93 percent of employers have less than 100 workers.
2. 68 percent of all workers are satisfied with their jobs.
3. 59 percent of U.S. workers are paid by the hour.
4. 50 percent of employees say their boss is generally fair.
5. 29 percent of American workers want their boss's job.
6. 39 percent of employees fired because of incompetence.

7. 24 percent of small business owners hold a degree.

8. 7.9 percent of American clergy are women.

9. 6.2 percent of all American workers moonlight.

10. 6 percent of the nation's workers walk to work.

Resumé Race

1.	Personalize your writing.	True
2.	Use first and second person pronouns.	True
3.	Set a natural and warm tone combined with a crisp, clear style.	True
4.	Use action or power words. Use words that excite.	True
5.	Use brief and direct descriptions.	True
6.	Write dollar figures in number form.	True
7.	Use short, concise sentences.	True
8.	Write in the language of your potential employer.	True
9.	Make your selling pitch future-oriented.	True
10.	Reflect your uniqueness.	True
11.	Mention your employer's name, if possible.	True
12.	Quantify your achievements.	True
13.	Make it accomplishment-oriented.	True
14.	Sell your ability as well as your experience.	True
15.	Place personal data at the top.	True
16.	Include a summary of your main selling points at the top.	True
17.	Spark the reader's interest early. (Give her/him a reason for reading on!)	True
18.	Use a format that highlights your main selling points and minimizes your liabilities.	True
19.	Use open space liberally. Keep it neat and easy to read.	True
20.	For highlighting and creating favorable first impressions, use capital letters, underlining, italics, indentations, bold type, and bullets or dashes.	True
21.	Separate division headings and subheadings with open space.	True
22.	Emphasize each category of information.	True
23.	Keep paragraphs short.	True
24.	Break up long ideas into short sentences or phrases.	True
25.	Single space.	True
26.	Emphasize only accomplishments that directly relate to your job objective.	True
27.	If many of your jobs are irrelevant to your job objectives, write a brief summary giving highlights of each, as well as the total period of time covering these activities.	True

28. If any former job titles do not accurately reflect your real responsibilities in these positions, use functional titles.   True

29. If your situation permits, use exact dates.   True

30. List your highest educational degree first.   True

31. If you feel you have the equivalent of an academic certificate in terms of training and experience, and can give data for it, consider listing such in your resumé.   True

32. Prior to printing, write several drafts, and have a professional proofread and critique the final copy of your resumé.   True

33. Prepare your resumé on a computer or word processor that can print to a laser printer.   True

34. Leave wide margins (at least 1 to 1 ½ inches on the sides, and 1 ½ inches on top, and 1 inch on the bottom).   True

35. Use a color, size, and texture of paper that stands out among any number of resumés. Avoid extremes.   True

36. Have several laser or typeset copies printed.   True

37. Use popular clichés.   False

38. Mention any disabilities you may have.   False

39. Include all interesting personal data.   False

40. Give reasons for leaving your last job.   False

41. List your references.   False

42. Give your salary requirements.   False

43. Give statement of present salary.   False

44. Be very modest.   False

45. Give many supporting details.   False

46. Inflate your experience and skills a little.   False

47. Make effective use of charts, pictures, and any other materials that might illustrate your main selling points.   False

48. Use abbreviations generously.   False

49. List several job objectives.   False

50. Make your resumé three pages long.   False

The Happy Hierarchy (Correct Order)

1. Survival

2. Safety

3. Belongingness

4. Self-esteem

5. Self-actualization

Top Five (Novice Class)

Most Stressful	Highest Income	Best Job Security
Firefighter (1)	Basketball player (NBA) (1)	Hospital administrator (1)
Race car driver (Indy class) (2)	Baseball player (major league) (2)	Civil engineer (2)
Astronaut (3)	Race car driver (Indy class) (3)	Industrial engineer (3)
Surgeon (4)	Football player (NFL) (4)	Bank officer (4)
Football player (5)	Surgeon (5)	Technical/copy writer (5)

Top Five (Pro Class)

Requiring Greatest Strength	Has the Most Perks	Best Environment to Work in
Firefighter (1)	Attorney (1)	Mathematician (1)
Dairy farmer (2)	Hotel manager (2)	Actuary (2)
Undertaker (3)	Clergyman (3)	Statistician (3)
Roustabout (4)	Basketball coach (4)	Computer systems analyst (4)
Seaman (5)	Senator/Congressperson (5)	Historian (5)

Titans of Turnover

See the Occupational Longevity Chart with the game materials.

Translation, Please

1. All work and no play makes Jack a dull boy.
2. A woman's work is never done.
3. Hard work never killed anybody.
4. Last hired, first fired.
5. You have to pay your dues.
6. People tend to rise to their own level of incompetence.
7. It's close enough for government work.
8. No bees, no honey; no work, no money.
9. A job well done is its own reward.
10. He works like a dog.

Unemployment Line

See the Unemployment Rate Sheets with the game materials.

Where in the USA Is Jo(e) Trainer?

Case	City	Company	HRD Job
1	San Francisco	Levi Straus	Instructor
2	New York City	Time, Incorporated	Evaluator
3	St. Louis	Anheuser Busch	Instructional designer
4	Nashville	Hospital Corporation of America	Manager
5	Fort Worth	Tandy Corporation	Career development specialist

This Certifies That

_____

has been bestowed
the title of

and is therefore entitled to all the privileges and
considerations due the bearer of said title.

_____
Awarded by

_____
Date

Certificate of Achievement

It is hereby acknowledged that

_____

has demonstrated outstanding ability
with respect to

_____

and is therefore entitled to special
considerations of all types throughout
the remainder of her/his natural life.

_____
Awarded by

_____
Date

These ribbons can be given to participants in recognition of their achievements.

Large, brightly colored poster boards with styrofoam backing are perfect for gameboards.

Lego blocks, lifesavers, and pieces of old games make good individual markers for board games.

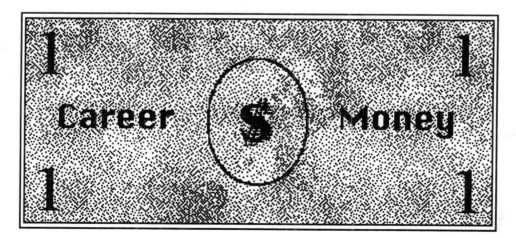

Lego Person   Lifesaver   Monopoly Piece

The following items can be photocopied onto green paper for use as play money.

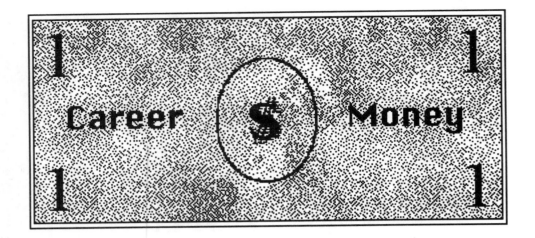

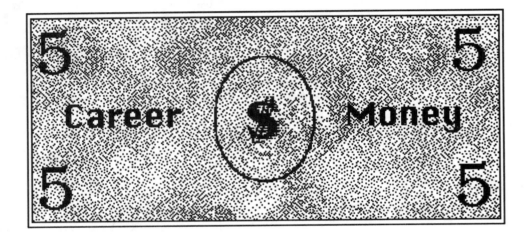

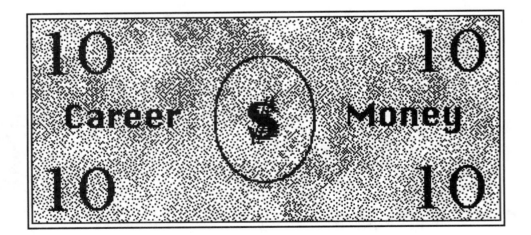

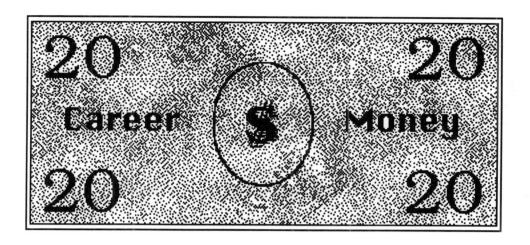

These items can be photocopied and used as name cards.